# Whispers In the Rain

## 48 Lessons on the Roadmap to Love and Enlightenment

### HAL S. EISENBERG

Lucky Book Publishing

# MY GIFT TO YOU

I am so glad you're here!

As my Gift to you, get FREE Access to a journal :
**A Journey of Reflection** by scanning
the QR Code below or visiting

https://subscribepage.io/freegifts

---

---

# Praise for Whispers In the Rain : 48 Lessons on the Roadmap to Love and Enlightenment

---

**This work is not just a collection of words, but an echo of healing energy**

"I had the great honor of witnessing my beloved friend Hal's spiritual and physical healing process up close in the magical surroundings of Palenque and its waterfalls. Sharing those transcendental moments amidst the grandeur of the ancient Mayan civilization and the purity of nature allowed me to deeply understand the strength and wisdom he now captures in his book, "Whispers in the Rain." This work is not just a collection of words, but an echo of the healing energy we experienced together, an inspiring guide that invites you to connect with your own essence and find your path to well-being. If you are on a path of physical, emotional (mental), and spiritual healing, this book will resonate even more deeply with you."

**- Leydi Morales Gómez, Peptide Treatment Facilitator**

## A beautiful journey of reconnection with ourselves.

"In this book, Hal eloquently takes us through a journey to reconnect with ourselves and what truly matters to us. Chapter by chapter, through his beautiful story, he helps us to move away from the distractions and the unnecessary noises and brings us back to our core. This book will speak to you in different ways as you progress in life. It is the kind of book that you can read multiple times and draw something new from it every time."

**-Danielle C Baker, RECE, Author of Bringing Up The World, podcast & TV host**

## What a beautiful and empowering book!

"Hal's book " Whispers In the Rain" is a breath of fresh air. A beautiful written journey that leaves you in a state of peace and deep presence with every lesson ( chapters). Meeting different aspects of ourselves through a magical healing path is such an empowering concept for recognizing how deeply loved we are by divine intelligence. Hal did a remarkable job at capturing the reader's heart and giving a space of deep reconnection and healing with our being throughout the entire book. I highly recommend it!"

**- Ellie Laliberté, Award Winning International Author of Letters From You To You**

**Simply Inspiring!**
"Hal's "Whispers in the Rain" beautifully merges spiritual wisdom and storytelling, inspiring growth, awakening, and connection. A powerful, emotional journey of purpose and divine insight."

**- Shelley A. Murdock, Author, IN SEARCH OF LONGEVITY and HEALTH & FIT FOR LIFE**

**This book is one of my favorites in a long time!**
"Whispers in the Rain is a beautifully crafted novel that invites readers to pause, reflect, and appreciate the whispers of life around them. Hal S. Eisenberg has created a timeless gem that will linger in the hearts of its readers, making it a must-read for anyone seeking a captivating and emotionally resonant journey. This book is one

of my favorites in a long time, and it deserves a place on everyone's bookshelf as a guide to living. It offers profound insights on accepting both the light and shadow, as well as the delicious reasons for life."

**- Lilly White, creator of Power up your life events, Archetype Consultant, Soul Coach, Author, Breakfast with Soul, Bali Spiritual Guide**

**Take back your power!**
"This book is a great opportunity to start making your commitment to yourself in your healing journey."

**- Heather Coleman MBA, Author of Our Money Narrative**

**I feel changed and lit on fire!**
"Starting with the title, this powerful story grabbed my heart, and has still not let go. Hal starts this story as if he were painting a picture. And then it goes deeper. In his confrontation with Cancer, then his meeting with Forgiveness, my own heart broke, opened up, I felt hot tears flow down my cheeks and I understood his inner

journey so profoundly. Those who dare to take 48 lessons, these whispers in the rain to heart, will come out changed, lit on fire. Thank you Hal for your wisdom and the greatest gift, giving us access to YOUR awakening."

**- Ashlee Cramer, Co-founder Michael and Mom Talk Cancer**

**It will capture your heart!**
"In the opening pages of Whispers in the Rain, Hal S. Eisenberg tells us "My deepest aspiration is to ignite the flame of possibility in others". His 48 Lessons on the Roadmap to Love and Enlightenment does exactly that, one gorgeous lesson at a time. Each lesson is an invitation to sink into a different world soaked in imagery, analogy, poetry, wisdom and love.
When you reach the last page, your heart will be full and your mind overflowing with the potential of all that love brings. I am grateful for every word in this beautiful book."

**- Teri Kingston, TEDxCoach, Speaker and Author of Get Ready for TED when TED is Ready for You.**

## A must read!

Whispers in the Rain brings the reader to heavenly realms of clarity, glory, inspiration; and a wondrous knowledge that the journey of life is worth its price.

**- Johnny Regan, Founder of The Global Vision Conference**

## This book takes us on a profound journey.

As Hal's friend, LMSW & a life coach for over 27 years, his book is a must-read life-changing, heart and soul, profound journey revealing the true essence of our core: Love. Through his evocative writing, we are not mere readers; we become fellow travelers on his transformative path, witnessing profound lessons gleaned from a life touched by love. This is more than just a book; it is an invitation that Hal's words inspire us to "see yourself as you truly are: a being of light and love, capable of infinite compassion and understanding." His narrative gently reminds us that "to embrace love's entirety, you must first love yourself." Experience deep understanding and interconnectedness, vital for how we connect and see each other. Ultimately, Hal's book illuminates the simple yet eternal message that the great spiritual teachers were, at their core, messengers of love itself. This powerful reminder that "you are not separate from the universe. You are the universe experiencing itself in human form" is why we can share these vital lessons, generation to generation, enriching our shared human experience.

**- Regina Rossi-Lamothe, LMSW, Life Coach, Dance Fitness Instructor**


**A beautiful book for the soul!**

"Whispers in The Rain" is thoughtful, spiritual and deeply healing for the soul. If you are ready to meet the parts of yourself that are wanting to guide you into your wholeness, you will want to read this amazing book. Grab a cup of coffee and sit in nature, let yourself be as present as you can be, you won't want to put it down!

**- Dionne Nicholls-Germain, Bestselling Author,** *The 90-Day Conquering Unforgiveness Journal: For High-Performing High Achievers*


**A beautifully written, transformative work!**

Whispers in the Rain is one man's soul journey that speaks to our deepest longing for connection, guidance, and transformation. The author's encounters with his guides are profoundly moving, reminding us that such support is not only real, but attainable if we open our hearts. This book gently reveals the interconnectedness of all things and invites readers to step into their own journey with courage and hope. A beautifully written, transformative work that lingers in the heart and soul long after the last page.

**- Chrissy Leppla, Educator, Littleton School District 65**

**A beautiful guide for seekers and dreamers!** Whispers in the Rain is a transformative experience aimed at guiding individuals toward self-love and enlightenment. This beautifully crafted guide offers 48 heartfelt lessons on the roadmap to love and enlightenment, each serving as a gentle invitation to pause, reflect, heal, and realign with love: life's true compass of a fulfilled life. Designed to help readers navigate their own spiritual paths, it emphasizes the importance of love, protection, faith, and companionship while fostering deeper meaning and spiritual growth. A must-read for seekers, dreamers, and anyone ready to rediscover the divine within and around them.

**- Marina Varona**

**A powerful journey of healing and forgiveness!**

This book shares one man's journey but speaks to anyone who's loved or lost. It's about healing, connection, and forgiveness - starting within. It reminds us that loving others begins with loving ourselves, that our past shapes us but doesn't define us, and that true peace comes through forgiveness. It's a guide to seeing with your heart, trusting your path, and finding strength in your story. A powerful read for anyone ready to grow and let go.

**- Chealsie Beedle**

# Acknowledgements:
## *A Symphony of Souls*

In the language of the heart, gratitude flows not as mere thanks, but as recognition of the divine orchestration that weaves souls together across time and space. This book exists because the universe conspired to place extraordinary beings along my path, each one a note in the divine symphony of transformation.

To the visionary souls at Lucky Book Publishing, who materialized in Toronto like answered prayers: your energy called to mine across a crowded conference room, defying my trepidation about that mystical city where the universe seems to speak directly to seekers. Toronto conferences have become portals of destiny in my life: places where a single conversation can alter the trajectory of eternity. Thank you for believing in whispers that others might dismiss as mere dreams.

To that sacred soul I encountered at a previous Toronto gathering... though you may never truly know the depth of your impact, your essence continues to illuminate my healing journey. I read your words like sacred texts, watch your videos like meditation, and carry your inspiration as a constant companion. In the soul affirming moments we shared, you planted seeds of transformation that have bloomed into this very book. Some souls touch us for an instant yet change us for a lifetime. You are living proof that angels walk among us. Not a moment goes by where you aren't loved with every cell in my body.

To Cha and Leydi, my guides through the mystical landscapes of Mexico: you move through villages like modern-day disciples, carrying healing in your hands and wisdom in your hearts. In the sacred shadows of Palenque, you helped me remember that the body knows how to heal when we listen to its ancient language. Your alternative approaches to wellness opened doorways I never knew existed. You are walking testimonies to the power of holistic healing... though I direct readers to our reluctant disclaimer for the legal dance we must perform in this cautious world.

To the constellation of souls who support my wildest dreams and most audacious visions: you stand by me whether I'm venturing to Mexico for peptide treatments that others call impossible, journeying to Canada for sacred ceremonies, or processing thousands of pages about transforming education globally. Your faith in the impossible makes miracles possible.

To the young souls in my classrooms and leadership programs who remind me daily why this work matters: you are tomorrow's change-makers... and knowing I might witness your world-transforming impact gives me reason to fight for every sunrise. You inspire me to stay alive, stay awake, and stay committed to humanity's highest potential.

To my son and his beloved wife, whose years-long vigil for a kidney transplant became a testament to perseverance and hope: your journey taught me that waiting can be its own form of prayer.

To Regina, my "ex-wife" who shattered every negative connotation of that term permanently when she became a living kidney donor to my son's wife (though she had no biological connection to either of them) years after the divorce: you proved that love transcends labels, that divorce can save lives rather than destroy them. Your selfless act redefined what it means to be "chosen family." Our future collaboration on this story will, I believe, change hearts and minds about what's possible after endings. Thank you for your consistent friendship.

To my sister Pamela and Calysta, and my beloved niece and nephew, Marybeth and Jeremy: you have redefined what family means by choosing love over obligation, presence over distance. Through every surgery, every adventurous journey, every holiday gathering, you've woven a sanctuary of belonging that reminds me home isn't a place... it's the people who show up. Marybeth, your decision to attend college closer to my heart than to convenience speaks volumes about the soul you are. Jeremy, your quiet strength anchors our family constellation. You four don't just remind me what family is; you are living proof that the most beautiful families are often the ones we consciously choose to nurture and celebrate.

To Vittoria, my soul companion and the ultimate example of what it means to be a Beautiful Soul: you are the silent force behind every dream made manifest, the tireless co-creator who sacrifices endlessly for others' success. In hockey terms, you're the assist that makes every score possible. Every soul deserves a Vittoria... someone who believes in their impossible dreams and works tirelessly to make them reality. May all your dreams find their wings. I love you dearly!

To Brian Ackley, my marketing director, creative collaborator, and co-pilot in transformation: your behind-the-scenes magic breathes life into every project, from our podcasts *Transforming Education* and *Conversations with Beautiful Souls* to the aesthetic flow of our shared vision. As co-writer of our upcoming book *The Faces of Social Emotional Learning*, you prove that some souls are meant to create worlds together. Your talents as film writer and producer are merely glimpses of your infinite creative potential.

To the unnamed angels who cross our paths with perfect smiles, unexpected text messages, and reminders of our worth: you may never know how your brief presence lights entire lifetimes. This is not about need; it's about recognition. Some souls teach through presence alone, simply by choosing to exist and breathe on this planet with us.

To the illuminated circle of spirits and angelic presences that surround me daily, working through this vessel in ways that transcend earthly understanding: I feel your presence in every moment of inspired flow, every synchronicity that defies logic, every door that opens when I need it most. Gratitude feels insufficient to capture the profound blessing of being chosen as a conduit for wisdom beyond my own comprehension. Though I don't always understand the mysteries of how divine energy moves through me, I am deeply aware of your constant guidance and eternally humbled by your trust in this imperfect vessel. You remind me that I am never truly alone, that every word written flows from a source far greater than myself.

And finally, to you, dear reader, who picked up this book at precisely the moment your soul was ready to receive these whispers: you are not accident but appointment, not coincidence but divine orchestration. Your journey through these pages completes the circle of why this book needed to exist.

In the end, we are all walking each other home. These acknowledgments are not endings but invitations: to recognize the sacred in the everyday, to honor the Divine that moves through ordinary souls, and to remember that gratitude is the language by which heaven and earth converse.

*May our soulship transcend the boundaries of time, ever enduring and ever shining.*

**Please consult the Author's Note: A Reluctant Disclaimer regarding any health and wellness approaches mentioned herein.**

# My Why

---

In a world increasingly divided by noise and distraction, I believe the path to healing begins with reconnection: to ourselves, to each other, and to the divine wisdom that pulses through all existence. "Whispers in the Rain" emerged not from mere thought, but from a profound spiritual experience... a sacred journey that called me to share the awakening I've witnessed in my own life.

During an extended period of healing when silence became my teacher, these lessons crystallized within me. What began as personal revelation transformed into a sacred responsibility: to be a bridge between worlds, to translate the whispers of universal wisdom into a language that speaks directly to the heart.

I wrote this book because I believe we stand at a pivotal moment in human consciousness. The challenges we face, both individually and collectively, cannot be solved through the same thinking that created them. We need a fundamental shift in perspective, a return to the timeless wisdom that reminds us we are all connected threads in the cosmic dance of creation.

My deepest aspiration is to ignite the flame of possibility in others. To help you recognize that enlightenment is not some distant, unattainable peak, but a journey we embark on with each conscious breath. When Maslow proposed his hierarchy of needs, many considered self-actualization the unreachable summit. I believe it is not only attainable but our birthright... and the world desperately needs each of us to claim it.

Through my work with The Passion Centre in Toronto, I discovered my soul's purpose as a visionary in action, creating inspired connections that elevate consciousness. This book represents that vision made manifest, an invitation to join the conversation about what becomes possible when we dare to dream beyond the boundaries of conventional thinking.

Being a visionary in action means carrying these teachings beyond the page and into the world. If you feel called to bring these messages to your community through speaking engagements, podcasts, events, or transformative workshops, I welcome the opportunity to continue this sacred conversation. The journey of awakening flourishes when shared, and I'm committed to creating spaces where wisdom can take root and grow. Feel free to contact me at https://www.haleisenberg.com or eisenbergleadership@gmail.com.

My why is simple yet profound: I believe in you. In your potential to transform, to awaken, to become a living embodiment of love in action. Every person who embraces this journey creates ripples that touch countless others. This is how we change the world: not through grand gestures, but through the quiet revolution of awakened hearts.

This book is my offering to that revolution.
May these whispers guide you home to yourself.

Dedicated to the beautiful souls
who have illuminated my journey,
teaching me the deep-seated
essence of love, companionship,
protection, faith, and more.
May our soulship transcend the
boundaries of time, ever enduring
and ever shining.

"I know how the story ends... at least part of it...
I don't know the how or the when,
but I do know I will leave this world loving you."

- JM Storm

# TABLE OF CONTENTS

# Author's Note:
# A Reluctant Disclaimer

---

Dear Reader,

In an ideal world, this book would stand alone as a testament to spiritual truth and an invitation to deep introspection, unburdened by the constraints of legal caution. However, we find ourselves in a reality where wisdom must sometimes don the garb of warning, and deep insights must be chaperoned by judicious advisories.

Because wisdom sometimes must wear the mask of warning, I present this disclaimer:

The contents of this book are born from personal experience, spiritual exploration, and the whispers of the universe. They are not intended to replace the guidance of medical professionals, the counsel of licensed therapists, or the diagnoses of trained physicians. Rather, they are meant to complement your journey towards holistic well-being, offering perspectives that dance at the edges of conventional wisdom.

While I believe in the transformative power of spiritual truth and the heartfelt impact of self-discovery, I acknowledge that our physical vessels sometimes require interventions beyond the realm of metaphysical exploration. Therefore, should you feel inspired to embark on any significant changes to your health regimen or lifestyle based on the insights shared herein, I implore you to consult with appropriate healthcare providers.

This disclaimer, though necessary in our litigious age, should not be seen as a diminishment of the truths explored in these pages. Instead, consider it a bridge between the mystical and the mundane, a reminder that our journey encompasses both the ethereal heights of spiritual awakening and the grounded reality of physical existence.

As you traverse the landscapes of consciousness laid out in this book, carry with you both the wonder of a spiritual seeker and the discernment of a pragmatic explorer. Let the words herein ignite your inner wisdom, but allow that flame to be tended also by the knowledge of those trained in the sciences of the body.

In essence, dear reader, take from these pages what resonates with your soul, but do so with the mindful awareness that your journey is uniquely yours, to be navigated with both intuition and informed guidance.

May your path be illuminated by inner truth and supported by outer wisdom.

With reverence for your journey,

*Hal*

# Prologue

---

I had a dream.

Not any dream, but a vision so vivid, so all-encompassing, that it shook the very foundations of my being. This dream, dear reader, was a journey through the entire spectrum of human experience... from the mundane to the extraordinary, from the comforting to the unsettling. It peeled back the layers of my consciousness, revealing truths I had long overlooked, truths that now demand to be shared.

Imagine, if you will, standing at the edge of a vast, unexplored wilderness. The air crackles with potential, and every breath fills you with a sense of anticipation. This is where my dream began... a threshold between worlds, where reality blurs with fantasy, and the impossible becomes possible.

In this mystical landscape, I found myself confronted with deep insights and even deeper questions. The dream spoke to me in a language beyond words, weaving together strands of meaning that echoed in the deepest chambers of my heart. It was a symphony of emotions, a mosaic of memories, each piece vital to the greater whole.

But what are dreams, really? Where do they come from, and what do they mean?

Dreams are portals to another realm, where our minds paint vivid scenes while we slumber. They can be as real as our waking life or as fantastical as our wildest imagination. Influenced by our memories, emotions, and deepest desires, dreams offer us glimpses into our innermost thoughts and fears. They are guides on a journey of self-discovery, lighting the path to understanding. As an educator, I've witnessed how dreams and visions can transform young minds. This particular dream showed me how spiritual awakening and educational transformation are deeply interconnected.

The dream I'm about to share with you transcended the boundaries of the ordinary. It was an odyssey that traveled the realms of reality and imagination, intertwining threads of truth and introspection. At times it was hyper-realistic, at others bizarrely abstract. It brought moments of blissful pleasure and episodes of heart-pounding terror. It could be mundane one instant and deeply meaningful the next.

But why share it with the world, you might wonder? This dream revealed the power of transformation... not personal change, but the ripple effect one awakened soul can have on countless others, especially in the realm of education and youth development.

Dreams have a way of touching us in ways we can't always explain. They speak to our souls, offering insights, healing, and revelations that transcend the confines of our waking lives. This particular dream urged me—no, compelled me—to share this journey with the world. The reason still eludes me, but I know that something extraordinary happened, something that demands to be put to paper and shared with you.

Perhaps within the pages of this extraordinary tale, you, dear reader, will find a glimmer of hope, a moment of clarity, or a pathway to healing. After all, dreams have a way of touching us in unexpected ways. So, let's embark on this journey together, and who knows? We might discover something remarkable along the way.

Why lessons, you might ask, rather than simple chapters? The answer lies in the very nature of this journey. Each segment of this dream revealed itself not as mere narrative, but as profound spiritual instruction, delivered with purpose and divine timing. These weren't just experiences to be recounted; they were teachings meant to be shared, each one building upon the last like steps on a sacred spiral staircase ascending toward greater understanding.

Through these lessons, I invite you to experience what I discovered: that spiritual awakening isn't a linear path but a series of revelations, each one opening doors to deeper wisdom. From the first stirrings of revelation at Palenque's ancient stones, through encounters with divine love, purification, and enlightened companions, to moments of pure illumination and harmony: each lesson carries its own gift, its own transformation.

What awaits you in these pages? First, you'll walk with me through the revelation of our deeper spiritual nature, discovering how ancient wisdom speaks to modern hearts. You'll explore the transformative power of divine love and experience the cleansing journey of purification. You'll meet enlightened companions who challenge our understanding of wisdom and witness the illuminating power of connection. Through harmony, you'll discover how all aspects of spirit dance together in perfect symphony, preparing us for even deeper mysteries.

This dream was an epic journey that took me to many places and shook me to my core. Mysterious guides would emerge, though I didn't yet know how they would transform my understanding of love, protection, faith, and the power of true companionship.

Months later, it still sits with me daily, and life doesn't feel quite the same. The memories of that night linger, haunting yet enlightening, like whispers from another realm. Each detail, each revelation, is etched into my consciousness, urging me to make sense of it all.

And so these lessons emerged, not chosen but revealed, each one a stepping stone across the waters of consciousness. They came not from my mind but through it, channeled from a source beyond my understanding. While I explore this phenomenon more deeply in the epilogue, I feel it is important to share now that these lessons chose their own form, their own timing, their own way of unfolding. They insisted on being called lessons rather than chapters because they are, at their core, teachings from the divine, filtered through my human experience.

I don't share this lightly. This book is a combination of what feels like a calling to share with whoever stumbles upon it, along with my soul's need to sort through this dream. It's quite the journey, with many ups and downs, moments of clarity intermingled with confusion, flashes of insight amidst moments of uncertainty. It's a rollercoaster of emotions, a whirlwind of thoughts and feelings that have left me both shaken and stirred.

But amidst the chaos, there is a sense of purpose, a guiding light that beckons me forward. And so, dear reader, I invite you to join me on this expedition into the depths of the subconscious, to unravel the mysteries of the mind and explore the vast expanse of human experience.

Before we dive in, let's talk about spirituality for a moment. Don't let that word scare you away! Spirituality is more than following religious doctrines or rituals. It's about delving into the depths of your soul and uncovering the essence of your existence. It's about seeking your own personal truth and embracing it wholeheartedly.

Through spirituality, we find meaning and purpose in our lives. We connect with something greater than ourselves... a universal energy, a divine presence, or a sacred purpose. It's a journey of self-discovery, a quest to understand our place in the universe and our connection to all living beings. Spirituality encourages us to explore our innermost thoughts and feelings, to tap into our intuition, and to trust our heart's knowing.

It's about finding your own personal meaning and values in life and expressing them through your thoughts, words, and actions. Spirituality invites us to transcend the limitations of our physical existence and awaken to the infinite possibilities that lie within us. It's a journey of growth, transformation, and enlightenment... a journey we're all called to embark on in our own unique way.

So, feel free to grab a cup of tea or coffee, settle into a comfortable spot, and join me on this extraordinary ride. Together, we'll navigate the winding roads of Southern Mexico, where the vibrant colors of "Viva La Mexico!" paint a stark contrast against the shadows that lurk beneath the surface. We'll travel rugged terrains and steep mountain passes, encounter obstacles and revelations, and witness the resilience of the human spirit in the face of adversity.

As we embark on this journey, remember: in the heart of darkness, amidst the shadows of doubt and fear, there glows an eternal flame of hope, illuminating the path that leads to our true essence, our true purpose. With each step forward, with each lesson learned, we inch closer to the radiant dawn of a new beginning, a new chapter in the story of our lives.

"Yes, let us journey on," a voice whispers, a gentle reminder of the boundless potential that lies within us, waiting to be awakened, waiting to be embraced. And so, hand in hand with the spirit of the dream, we embark upon this sacred quest, guided by the light of eternal wisdom, fueled by the flame of hope that burns within our souls.

Yes, let us journey on...

Before we step into the first lesson, let me share how I found myself at the ancient stones of Palenque that fateful night. I had traveled to Mexico seeking something I couldn't quite name... perhaps understanding, perhaps healing, perhaps simply adventure. The journey led me to this sacred site, where I secured a small room near the ruins, planning to spend several days exploring their mysteries.

That evening, as the sun painted the sky in vibrant hues of orange and purple, I sat in meditation at the base of the Temple of Inscriptions. The air hung heavy with humidity, thick with the whispers of centuries past. Something about this place called to my soul, though I didn't yet understand why. As twilight deepened into night, I returned to my room, my mind still swimming with images of ancient ceremonies and timeless wisdom.

Sleep came easily that night, but what followed wasn't ordinary slumber. In this dream state, consciousness expanded rather than dimmed. Colors became more vivid, sensations more acute. Time moved differently... sometimes flowing like honey, other times rushing like a mountain stream. Most remarkably, I maintained awareness that I was dreaming, yet this awareness didn't wake me. Instead, it allowed me to move between levels of reality, to interact with beings both physical and spiritual, to receive teachings that transcended ordinary understanding.

In this dream realm, physical laws bent like light through crystal. Manifestations of divine consciousness took form as guides and companions.

Thoughts became tangible, emotions painted the air with color, and ancient wisdom spoke directly to the heart. Yet despite its otherworldly nature, this dream space felt more real than my waking life, as if I had finally awakened to a deeper truth that had always existed beneath the surface of ordinary reality.

And so begins the first lesson, as the stones of Palenque whispered their secrets and the veil between worlds grew thin...

# Lesson #1: Revelation

*"When the heart opens, the universe speaks."*

---

The stones of Palenque held their secrets close in the dream-dark. Moonlight filtered through the dense canopy, casting mysterious shadows that danced across carved reliefs worn smooth by time. The Temple of Inscriptions loomed before me, its nine levels rising like a stairway to heaven, each tier whispering stories of ancient wisdom. The air hung thick with the sweet decay of jungle vegetation and the earthy scent of stone warmed by the day's sun.

As my dream-consciousness expanded, memories surfaced like bubbles in still water. Faces of those I'd loved and lost shimmered in the periphery of awareness, especially Stacy, my childhood friend whose life had been cut tragically short at sixteen. Even now, years later, her absence echoed through my heart, a reminder of life's precious fragility and the questions that haunt us about destiny and divine timing.

The jungle's nocturnal chorus grew louder, more intentional, as if nature itself was preparing for revelation. The very air began to change, becoming charged with ethereal presence that made my skin tingle. Colors deepened and shifted, the green of the vegetation taking on an almost luminous quality, the shadows between the stones revealing depths that hadn't existed moments before.

My fingers traced the intricate carvings, and a jolt of power surged through me... electric, familiar, yet utterly foreign. The sensation reminded me of that rare soul connection I'd once felt with a twin flame, but this... this was different. This was ancient, primal, a connection that transcended human bonds and reached into the very fabric of existence.

The air shimmered with possibility as I found myself drawn deeper into the heart of the ruins. Each step resonated with purpose, as if guided by an unseen hand. The jungle's cacophony faded, replaced by an almost tangible silence that spoke volumes. In that profound stillness, the boundary between physical and spiritual began to blur.

I surrendered to the essence of this spirit-touched realm, letting go of my everyday mind's need to analyze and understand. In that moment of release, they emerged in my awareness... the spirits of the ancient Maya, their presence both comforting and overwhelming. They whispered of balance, of harmony, of the delicate interplay between the physical and spiritual realms.

In the silence between worlds, their voices merged into one profound truth: "The greatest revelations come not from seeking, but from surrendering. When the heart opens, the universe speaks."

When I opened my eyes again, the world had transformed completely. Colors blazed with impossible vibrancy; shadows held depths that seemed to reach into other dimensions. At my feet lay a small, intricately carved stone, radiating an inner light that pulsed in rhythm with my heartbeat. As I cradled it in my palm, its warmth spread through me like liquid sunlight, a physical manifestation of the wisdom beginning to crystallize within.

But with understanding came unease. The oppressive heat of the jungle took on a sinister edge, mirroring the turmoil in my soul. Reality blurred further, past and present intertwining in a dizzying dance. The ancient Maya had faced their own apocalypse: drought, war, societal collapse. Their struggles echoed our modern crises:

pandemics, climate change, political upheaval. In this dreamscape, I stood at the crossroads of time, acutely aware of the parallels.

The stone in my hand vibrated with increasing warmth, its engravings seeming to writhe beneath my fingers. Its energy intensified, and with it came a flood of memories... not of ancient Maya, but of faces closer to home. Those who had shaped my own journey of transformation. Those who had left too soon.

And then, in a flash of golden light that pierced the jungle's shadows, there she stood: Stacy, forever sixteen, her presence both healing and heartbreaking. The stone in my hand grew warmer still, as if acknowledging the connection between past and present, between loss and revelation. Her appearance wasn't random; she had always been part of this journey, her brief life teaching me profound lessons about love, time, and the power of living with intention.

The true nature of my dream journey crystallized in that moment. Beyond uncovering ancient wisdom or confronting modern challenges, this quest beckoned me toward personal truth, a bridge between past reconciliation and future hope.

The pyramid loomed above me, no longer just a relic but a bridge between worlds. The jungle thrived with life, each leaf and stone holding a piece of the celestial puzzle. And I, standing amidst it all, was both student and teacher, seeker and guide.

The dream realm shimmered and dissolved; Stacy's smile lingered, a radiant source of love and encouragement. The carved stone in my hand hummed with potential, a physical link to the revelations that awaited.

I drew in, filling my lungs with the rich, ancient air of Palenque. Whatever awaited—challenges, wonders, or both—readiness coursed through me. For in this place where reality split and spirits roamed, I had found the first key to unlocking the secrets of the universe.

My heart raced as I stepped through the veil between worlds, every cell in my being alive to the revelations unfolding before me. The journey of the soul had begun.

# Lesson #2: Love

*"For love is the foundation of all spiritual truth, the force that binds together all teachings, all understanding."*

As Stacy's radiant presence began to fade from the dreamscape, her parting smile carried a profound message: love transcends all boundaries... even death. The stones of Palenque stirred with renewed essence, as if her brief visit had prepared the sacred space for what was to come. Here, where personal loss had cracked open my heart, letting grief pour out and wisdom pour in, I felt the stirring of something vast and ancient.

The grief of losing Stacy had taught me that love doesn't end... it transforms. Now, in this liminal space between worlds, that understanding deepened. The very air began to shimmer with golden light, and I sensed another presence emerging: not a memory this time, but something more primordial, more fundamental to the very fabric of existence.

A being manifested before me, her essence permeating the humid air like morning sunlight breaking through jungle mist. Unlike Stacy's familiar presence, this entity was both ancient and eternal, radiating a light that transformed the ruins' shadows into gentle veils. Her eyes held the depths of millennia yet sparkled with the same warmth I'd seen in my friend's final smile.

"Who are you?" I whispered, though, somehow, in the depths of my soul, I already knew.

She smiled, and in that smile, I felt every moment of love I'd ever experienced, from my mother's first embrace to Stacy's lasting friendship, from passionate romance to divine connection. "I am *Love*," she replied, her voice carrying the harmony of countless hearts beating as one. "Not just the love you've known, but all love that ever was or will be. I am the force that binds the universe together, that heals all wounds, that transforms loss into wisdom. Though you will meet many guides on your journey, I will remain your constant companion, weaving through your experiences like a golden thread."

In her gaze, she saw me with unprecedented clarity... not just who I was, but who I could become. She was a paradox made manifest: powerful yet gentle, ancient yet eternally new, transcendent yet deeply personal. I realized she would be more than just another guide; she would be the thread weaving together all the lessons to come.

"I will walk beside you," *Love* said, her words ringing with divine purpose. "Through me, you will meet other guides, each bringing their own wisdom. For love is the foundation of all spiritual truth, the force that binds together all teachings, all understanding. Through me, you will discover connections that transcend ordinary understanding, preparing you for guides who will help you bridge physical and spiritual realms."

She extended her hand, a smile playing on her lips. "Let us embark on this journey. For in the depths of love, there is infinite wisdom waiting to be discovered."

Taking her hand, a deep sense of both familiarity and wonder washed over me. It embodied coming home and stepping into the unknown all at once.

*Love* led me through the ruins, each step revealing new wonders. The jungle seemed to come alive around us, vibrant and thrumming with vitality. Leaves whispered ancient secrets, and hidden streams sang melodies of devotion.

"What do you want to show me?" I asked, my voice a soft breath in the sacred space.

In response, *Love* waved her hand, conjuring a shimmering image before us. It was a memory, long buried, of a past relationship. Watching, I felt a bittersweet ache tugging at my heart.

"This," *Love* whispered, "is the last time you experienced a love that was pure and real."

Tears welled, blurring the vision before me as the scenes unfolded, each moment filled with raw emotion and vulnerability. When the images faded, I turned to *Love*, my heart heavy.

"That was a glimpse into the depths of your own heart," she explained, her voice flowing with compassion. "A reminder of the love that still resides within you, waiting to be rediscovered."

We paused before a pristine pool, its surface a perfect mirror of the sky above. *Love* knelt beside the water and gestured for me to do the same. Gazing into the pond, I saw my reflection, but it was not the face I was accustomed to seeing. This reflection radiated peace and acceptance, a quiet strength emanating from within.

"See yourself as you truly are," *Love* whispered.

"A being of light and love, capable of infinite compassion and understanding. The journey ahead will not always be easy, but it will be worth it."

As the dream-light shifted, painting the ruins in hues of gold and amber, *Love* turned to me once more. "Remember," she said, her voice mixing with the evening breeze, "love is not just an emotion. It's a state of being, a force that connects all things."

The jungle around us swayed in agreement, leaves rustling and birds calling out in a symphony of life.

"To embrace love's entirety," *Love* continued, "you must first love yourself. Accept all parts of yourself, even those you find difficult to face. Forgive yourself for past mistakes and embrace the lessons they've taught you."

Her words sank deep into my soul, awakening something long dormant. The truth crystallized: this journey of love led not to external completion, but to the wholeness already pulsing within my soul.

Twilight descending upon Palenque, *Love*'s form began to shimmer, becoming one with the fading light. "You are never alone on this journey," she said, her voice echoing through the ruins. "The universe is always with you, guiding you, supporting you, and loving you. Trust in the process."

With a heart full of gratitude and a renewed sense of purpose, I watched as *Love* merged with the gathering darkness. The lessons of love were not just teachings to be learned, but truths to be lived and experienced in every moment.

Making my way back through the jungle, the night alive with the sounds of unseen creatures, love's transformative power shaped my path. Each step was a promise, each breath a reminder of the infinite potential that lay within.

The journey had only just begun, but already, I was reborn at my core. In the heart of ancient Palenque, I had rediscovered the most fundamental truth of all: the boundless, illuminating power of love.

# Lesson #3: Purification

*"Love reveals everything within us: not just the light, but also the shadows we carry."*

---

*Love*'s revelations had opened floodgates within my soul, bringing to the surface every emotion I'd ever felt: joy and sorrow, passion and pain, devotion and doubt. These feelings swirled through me like turbulent waters, beautiful yet overwhelming. *Love* reappeared. Her gentle eyes met mine, understanding flowing between us.

"When the heart opens fully to love," she said, her voice carrying ancient wisdom, "it must also be cleansed. For love reveals everything within us: not just the light, but also the shadows we carry. Are you ready to be purified?"

The night's revelations still resonating within me, I watched as dawn broke over Palenque. The first rays of sunlight pierced the jungle canopy, mixing with the morning mist to create a celestial light show. *Love* stood beside me, her presence both comforting and expectant.

"To continue your journey," she explained, "you must be prepared to receive deeper truths. Like a vessel being readied for sacred water, your spirit must be cleansed." Her form began to shimmer, and I sensed another presence drawing near. "Someone approaches who can help you with this next step."

From the shadows of the jungle, a figure emerged... radiant and serene, her eyes as deep and clear as a mountain spring. "This is *Purification*," *Love* introduced, her voice carrying reverence. "She will help you release what no longer serves you, making space for the wisdom yet to come."

*Love* and *Purification* exchanged a knowing glance, their energies harmonizing in a way that suggested there were countless souls they had guided together through this sacred process.

*Purification*'s presence was like a cool breeze on a humid day, refreshing yet powerful. "The path of spiritual awakening," she said, her voice flowing like a gentle stream, "requires us to release old patterns, fears, and limitations. Through water's blessing, we are made new."

*Love* nodded in agreement. "Just as water shapes stone over time, purification shapes the soul. This cleansing will prepare you for the companions you have yet to meet, the illumination that awaits, and the harmony that will bring all lessons together."

*Purification* led us to a small, crystal-clear stream that wound its way through the jungle. The water sparkled in the dappled sunlight, inviting and pure.

"This water," she explained, "can cleanse your soul. Step into it and let it wash away the heaviness that clings to you."

I paused at the water's edge, then stepped into its sacred waters embracing my feet. Energy surged through my body, the ancient current penetrating to my core.

"Close your eyes," *Purification* instructed, "and let the water take away your pain, your doubts, and your fears. Trust in the process and allow yourself to be renewed."

I closed my eyes and centered myself with a steady breath, surrendering to the moment. Memories of past hurts and regrets surfaced, but instead of clinging to them, I let them flow away with the current.

In the silence of my mind, I heard *Purification*'s voice, guiding me through the shadows of memory. "Forgive yourself for the mistakes you've made. Forgive others for the pain they've caused you. Let go of the anger and resentment that bind you. Embrace the purity of your soul, the light within you that is untouched by the shadows of the past."

Standing there, bathed in the cleansing waters, a deep sense of release washed through me. The burden that I had carried for so long simply lifted, replaced by a lightness that filled me with hope and possibility.

With renewed purpose, we made our way to the great pyramid of Palenque. Its towering presence loomed before us, showcasing the ingenuity and spiritual depth of the Mayan civilization.

"The pyramid holds a powerful positive vibration at its summit," *Purification* explained. "It's a beacon of light in the midst of the jungle, where people gather to perform rituals and spiritual cleanses."

Each step along the sacred stones dissolved layers of doubt and fear into dream-mist. The ethereal air shimmered with increasing power, invigorating my spirit. The stones beneath my feet thrummed with ancient resonance, drawing me toward the summit.

At the summit, an overwhelming surge of divine force greeted us. The air hummed with an otherworldly resonance, enveloping me in a cocoon of light and warmth. I surrendered to the sensations as they washed over me.

*Let go of the fear,* Purification's voice echoed in my mind. *Embrace the love that surrounds you and lives within you. This is your true essence.*

Images flashed before my eyes: moments of joy and sorrow, triumph and regret. Each one a fragment of my journey, a piece of the puzzle that made up my life. I understood now that purification wasn't about erasing these memories, but embracing them, integrating them into the intricate fabric of my soul.

With a final wave of transformative power, something fundamental shifted within me. The burdens of doubt, fear, and regret melted away, replaced by a sense of peace and empowerment.

Opening my eyes, I saw the world anew, vibrant and alive with possibility. *Love* stood beside me, her eyes filled with pride and joy.

"You have done well," her voice rippled like water over stones. "Remember, this journey is ongoing.

Each step you take is a step towards greater understanding, healing, and love."

As the dream-light transformed, painting the jungle in hues of gold and crimson, I felt ready to face whatever came next. In the heart of Palenque, amidst the whispers of the past and the promise of the future, I had embraced the journey of purification.

Atop the pyramid, cleansed and renewed in this sacred dreamscape, I faced the transforming light. My spirit, unburdened now, resonated with the ancient wisdom still waiting to be unveiled. Through this purification, I had discovered that becoming whole wasn't about erasing the past; it was about embracing every fragment of my soul's journey.

# Lesson #4: Enlightened Companions

*"Sometimes the deepest wisdom comes from the most unexpected sources."*

---

The sacred energies of purification still coursed through me, my spirit lighter yet somehow deeper, as if the cleansing had carved new channels for wisdom to flow. *Love* and I continued our journey through Palenque's dreamscape, where the jungle air shimmered with renewed possibility. The morning light filtered through the canopy differently now, each beam seeming to illuminate not just space, but truth itself.

*"Purification* has prepared you for what comes next," *Love* said, her eyes gleaming with anticipation. "Sometimes the deepest wisdom comes from the most unexpected sources. Are you ready to see with new eyes?"

Before I could respond, the air thickened with expectancy. A figure emerged from the shadows, radiating an aura of timeless knowledge. Her presence was both comforting and challenging, as if she held secrets that could only be understood by letting go of everything I thought I knew.

"This is *Wisdom*," *Love* introduced, her voice carrying reverence. "She brings companions who will show you how truth often hides in plain sight." Unlike *Love*'s warm radiance, *Wisdom* carried an essence that was cool and clear, like mountain air at dawn. Yet when their presences merged, they created a perfect balance of heart and mind.

*Wisdom*'s eyes gleamed with otherworldly light. "Greetings," she said, her voice echoing deep within my soul. "Through purification, you have created space for new understanding. Now you are ready to learn from those who embody wisdom in its purest form."

I felt ancient memories stir, recognition echoing across lifetimes. "What do you mean?" I asked, my voice wavering with anticipation.

*Wisdom*'s gaze softened. "In your world, you often seek wisdom from those with many years or impressive credentials. But true wisdom knows no such bounds. Sometimes, it speaks most clearly through those whose hearts remain pure and unclouded by the world's complications."

As if summoned by her words, two children materialized from the dream-shadows, their eyes alight with both innocence and ancient knowing. "This is *Insight* and *Understanding*," *Wisdom* introduced, her voice filled with pride. "They represent wisdom in its most essential form: unfiltered by prejudice, unburdened by expectation."

*Love* stepped forward, placing a gentle hand on my shoulder. "These children appear now because you have been cleansed of preconceptions about where wisdom can be found. Through purification, you have become like a child yourself... open, receptive, ready to learn from all sources."

*Insight* approached first, her youthful vitality illuminating the shadows of uncertainty. Yet despite her youth, resilience radiated from her, drawing me into her world with a smile that spoke of untold stories. In her presence, I felt the truth of *Love*'s words; wisdom could indeed come through unexpected vessels.

*Wisdom* shared *Insight*'s tale, revealing her life in Southern Mexico, where poverty and hardship coexisted with resilience and joy. *Insight*'s confidence and determination filled the air, casting a spell of awe and admiration. She embodied the essence of soul wealth, a richness that transcended material possessions.

In a moment that took my breath away, *Insight* revealed that today was her ninth birthday. The gravity of this revelation struck me deeply. Here was a child, so young yet so wise, celebrating a milestone amidst our spiritual journey.

"Happy birthday, *Insight*." The words carried my heart's gratitude, humbled by her presence.

*Insight*'s eyes sparkled with joy. "Thank you," she breathed. "Every day is a new opportunity to learn and grow, to see the world with fresh eyes and an open heart."

*Insight*'s story unfolded, and I found myself grappling with the harsh realities she faced. She spoke of selling trinkets under the scorching sun, her small hands clutching tightly to the hopes and dreams of her family.

"How can you be happy doing this?" I burst forth, unable to conceal my disbelief. "You're only nine years old. This isn't how a child should spend their birthday!"

*Insight* looked at me with eyes that held a wisdom far beyond her years. "It's not about being happy in the way you might think," she explained gently. "It's about love. Love for my family, love for my community. Every trinket I sell puts food on the table and sends my siblings to school. It's a small sacrifice for a greater purpose."

Her words painted a vivid picture of a community bound by love and friendship, where laughter echoed through the streets and shared experiences brought solace in the face of adversity.

"Isn't it hard?" I asked, my voice tinged with sorrow. "To carry so much on your shoulders?"

"It is," she admitted, her gaze steady. "But it's also beautiful. Every sacrifice I make is an act of love, a gift to those I care about. In their smiles, I find my joy."

*Wisdom* nodded in agreement, her presence a silent affirmation of *Insight*'s heartfelt words. "Indeed," she murmured. "In the face of adversity, it is often the simplest acts of love and sacrifice that illuminate the path forward."

As *Insight* stood beside us, her spirit unyielding despite the challenges she faced, *Understanding* approached. His steps were light and buoyant, like a child dancing in the sunlight. A joy and innocence radiated from his presence, a reminder of simpler times when the world was filled with wonder.

"Hello," he chirped, radiating warmth and enthusiasm. "I'm *Understanding*." Together with *Insight*, he guided me into the depths of wisdom's essence, their intertwined voices revealing life's sacred patterns. "Life is a journey," *Insight* began, ancient wisdom flowing through her young voice. "It blooms in moments of understanding and compassion, flourishing in the connections we forge and the empathy we share."

*Understanding* chimed in, his perspective simple yet profound. "It's about seeing with your heart as much as your eyes. Every perspective holds its own truth."

Their teachings challenged my preconceived notions about wisdom. Could it be that understanding and compassion were the true cornerstones of enlightenment?

"I never thought about it like that before," I admitted, feeling a shift in my perspective. "I always thought wisdom was just about what you know."

*Understanding* shook his head, a playful grin on his face. "Understanding flows from how we touch each other's hearts." His eyes sparkled with innocent wisdom. "That's where true knowledge lives."

Guided by *Love*, *Wisdom*, *Insight*, and *Understanding* through the mystical dreamscape, gratitude surged through my being. Their teachings unveiled the true richness of human experience: a wealth measured not in possessions but in connections. The realm around us shimmered with newfound brilliance, our collective experiences weaving a transcendent mosaic, our souls dancing between light and shadow as we walked the path of enlightenment.

"Remember," *Wisdom* breathed, her voice a soothing caress to my spirit, "the journey is just as important as the destination. Embrace each moment with an open heart, and you will find the answers you seek."

The landscape shifted and changed as we walked. I sensed that another lesson awaited, another piece of the puzzle that would bring me closer to the truth.

"What's next?" I asked, my voice filled with anticipation.

*Wisdom* smiled, her eyes twinkling with a knowing light. "There is something I want to show you," she murmured. "A truth that lies at the heart of your journey."

Though these young guides illuminated the path with their pure wisdom, I sensed that darker trials awaited... challenges that would test not just my understanding, but my resilience.

The dreamscape shifted around us, reality morphing into new possibilities. Each step resonated with purpose, drawing me deeper into truths that would reshape my understanding of existence itself.

# Lesson #5: Illumination

*"True healing can only come
when the heart is open, the spirit is pure,
and wisdom lights the way."*

---

The wisdom of the children still echoed in my heart, their simple truths illuminating corners of understanding I hadn't known existed. Through *Love*'s guidance and *Wisdom*'s presence, each lesson had built upon the last... from the initial revelation at Palenque's stones, through purification's cleansing waters, to the unexpected wisdom of young souls. Now the dreamscape continued to transform, golden light filling the clearing as if in response to these accumulated insights.

*Wisdom* turned to me; her eyes gleaming with that ancient knowing I'd come to recognize. "Your journey thus far has prepared you for something profound," she said. "Through love, you opened your heart. Through purification, you cleared away obstacles. Through our young companions, you learned to see with new eyes. Now you are ready for illumination, and for the one who can help you embody these teachings."

*Love* stepped forward, her presence radiating warmth. "There is another guide you must meet," she said, her voice blending comfort with determined purpose. "One who can help you integrate all you have learned, transforming understanding into healing."

The air crackled with anticipation, humming with a presence that vibrated through my very being. We arrived at dream-touched waters, shimmering with mesmerizing hues of cerulean and turquoise. At the water's edge stood a figure radiating an aura of tranquility and astuteness; his presence commanded attention while offering comfort, his eyes holding an understanding that seemed to transcend time itself.

"This is *Healing*," *Wisdom* introduced, her voice carrying reverence. "He has long watched your journey, waiting for the moment when you would be ready to receive his gifts. For true healing can only come when the heart is open, the spirit is pure, and wisdom lights the way."

*Healing* regarded me with gentle eyes, filled with compassion and understanding. "Welcome," he said, his voice a soothing melody. "I am here to help you transform these lessons into living truth. For knowledge without healing is incomplete, just as healing without wisdom cannot last."

At the threshold of this sacred dream-realm, a new companion emerged. His aura of tranquility cast a radiant glow upon our gathering, completing the circle of healing that had begun to form around me.

"This is *Connection*," *Healing* introduced, his voice warm with affection. "A guide who will help you understand the deeper bonds that link us all." His compassionate smile and welcoming demeanor exuded a warmth that enveloped us like an embrace.

Despite the serene surroundings, the heat of the dream weighed heavily upon me, beads of sweat trickling down my brow. The oppressive warmth contrasted sharply with the cool, refreshing waters, mirroring my internal struggle.

*Wisdom* and *Healing* exchanged knowing glances before encouraging me to cool down in the water. Hesitantly, I submerged myself in the lagoon. The cool waters provided immediate respite, soothing my weary body and mind. This act of surrender symbolized a release of the tensions and burdens that had clung to me for so long.

Vulnerable and open, I listened; *Connection* began to speak. His words flowed in Spanish, a language I understood only in fragments, yet his voice carried divine power beyond language itself.

*"Que la luz divina brille sobre ti y te guíe en tu camino hacia la sanación,"* he prayed, his voice carrying a tender authority vibrating through the very molecules of the water around us.

*Wisdom* translated softly, "May the divine light shine upon you and guide you on your journey to healing."

I absorbed the essence of *Connection*'s prayer. Though I couldn't understand the specifics of his words, their power reverberated deep within my soul. Each syllable carried a sacred resonance, penetrating the barriers of language to touch the core of my being.

As *Connection* continued to pray, his voice rising and falling like a sacred chant, I felt a sense of peace enveloping me. My burdens lifted, replaced by a comforting warmth that spread through every fiber of my being. The lagoon's waters felt like an extension of this divine essence, cradling me in their embrace as *Connection*'s prayer wove a web of healing around me.

We formed a circle, our hands clasped together in a bond of shared faith and hope. The unity of our spirits was palpable, proof of what we could achieve together. *Connection*'s voice lifted in prayer, invoking the name of God with fervent devotion. Each word he spoke seemed to align with the fundamental nature of the universe, with the divine energies that permeated the air.

In that sacred moment, I surrendered myself to the healing energies that flowed through me. I felt surrounded by a powerful force of healing and protection. The warmth reminded me of *Love's* first embrace, now deepened by *Connection*'s sacred touch. Like when Stacy had appeared in the temple, I felt the transcendent power of divine love working through mortal vessels, each guide adding their unique light to illuminate my path.

The prayer, though foreign to my ears, resonated in the language of my soul. It was as if each syllable carried a sacred vibration that penetrated the barriers of language, touching the core of my being. *Connection*'s voice became a vessel for the divine, his words a conduit for the transformative power of faith.

As *Connection* released me from his grasp, a wave of peace washed over me, dissolving the remnants of fear and doubt. I felt lighter, as if the burdens I had carried were lifted, replaced by a sense of serenity and trust. In that moment, I knew that I had been touched by the hand of divine healing, a spiritual blessing that reaffirmed my faith in the unseen forces that guide us.

As his final words hung in the air, I opened my eyes to find myself surrounded by a shimmering aura of healing light. The radiant glow was a tangible reminder of *Connection's* sacred prayer, revealing divine intervention. It was as if pure divine presence had imprinted itself upon my soul, leaving an indelible mark of love and grace.

With a heart full of reverence, I thanked *Connection* for his blessings and turned to *Wisdom*, whose serene smile offered reassurance and comfort. Together, we stood in silent communion, united by the profound experience we had shared. The divine presence that enveloped us illustrated the interconnectedness of all beings, a reminder that we are never truly alone on our journey.

Preparing to part, *Wisdom*'s voice broke the silence, her words a peaceful caress to my soul. "Remember, true healing comes not only from within, but from the connections we share with the divine and with each other."

Her words resonated through my entire being, echoing the lessons I had learned from *Connection* and *Healing*. The bonds we form, the love we share, and the faith we hold are all integral to our journey of healing and self-discovery. With a renewed sense of purpose, I embraced the knowledge that my individual existence was but one note in the divine symphony of universal consciousness..

During our final blessings, I marveled at the deep connection we had shared. Deep within this dreamscape, amidst the swirling waters of faith and healing, I had felt the presence of God with startling clarity. Yet even as I basked in this divine communion, something shifted in the dream's atmosphere. A shadow flickered at the edges of awareness, hinting at trials yet to come. But for now, cradled in this sacred moment, I remained held in the embrace of something far greater than myself.

# Lesson #6: Harmony

*"When we align all aspects of our being... body, mind, and spirit... we create a symphony that resonates with the universe itself."*

---

*Connection*'s prayer lingered in the dreamscape like incense, its sacred essence weaving through the fabric of consciousness. Each lesson until now had been a note in a growing symphony: *Love* opening my heart to divine connection, *Purification* washing away old barriers, *Wisdom* and her young companions revealing truth in unexpected places, and *Healing* integrating it all into transformative power.

*Wisdom* and *Healing* materialized beside me, their presence grounding yet elevating. *Love*'s temporary absence was felt, but her influence remained, threading through every insight, every revelation that had brought me to this moment.

"*Síguenos*," *Wisdom* breathed, her voice carrying ancient knowledge. "All you have learned must now come into harmony."

*Healing* nodded, his eyes filled with compassion. "Each lesson has been a separate instrument," he explained. "Now it's time for them to play together in perfect symphony."

The dream-realm shimmered around us as *Healing*'s fingers began weaving invisible rhythms through the air. "Music," he said, "is more than sound. It is the language of the soul, the voice of harmony. Through it, we can understand how seemingly separate elements create something greater than themselves."

As if in response to his words, vibrant Latin rhythms filled the air. The infectious beat of Gloria Estefan and The Miami Sound Machine's "Conga" echoed through the dreamscape, its familiar vitality carrying deeper significance now. This wasn't just music; it was an invitation to embody all I had learned, to let every lesson flow together in dance.

*"Everybody gather 'round now*
*Let your body feel the heat.*
*Don't you worry if you can't dance.*
*Let the music move your feet.*

*It's the rhythm of the island,*
*And like sugarcane, so sweet.*
*If you want to do the conga,*
*You've got to listen to the beat."*

My initial hesitation melted as I recognized the symbolism of this moment. The rhythm was *Love*'s heartbeat, the movement was *Purification*'s flow, the joy was the children's wisdom, and the healing power of music itself brought everything into alignment. The landscape around us transformed, responding to this harmonious integration, shifting from uncertainty into a vibrant, pulsating world of possibility.

"Do you feel it?" *Wisdom* asked, her eyes shining. "This is how harmony works. When we align all aspects of our being... body, mind, and spirit... we create a symphony that resonates with the universe itself."

The dance became a living prayer, each movement echoing *Purification*'s cleansing flow, now transformed into joyous celebration. The rhythm carried me back to the crystal waters where I'd first learned to let go, but now that release had evolved into dynamic expression. Even in *Love*'s physical absence, her essence moved through every step, every beat, every breath. Yet even as we moved in celebration, I sensed something more profound approaching. This harmony wasn't just an end; it was a preparation.

The dance's joy shimmered with an edge of emptiness... *Love*'s absence. Her missing presence carved a hollow in the dreamscape, casting shadow-thoughts across our revelry.

Sensing my melancholy, *Wisdom*'s form shimmered closer, her touch ethereal, her dream-eyes holding ancient understanding. "Do not mourn her absence," she breathed, her words floating on dream-currents. "*Love* will return to you in due time. Trust in the ebb and flow of the universe."

Though her words brought comfort, the ache in my heart remained, evidence of my deep-rooted longing. Yet I could still feel *Love* surrounding me, guiding me through the intricacies of my subconscious with an invisible hand.

I had discovered a truth that resonated through the dreamscape: love, in all its forms, is the melody that binds us together, transcending time and space.

"The ceremony awaits," *Healing* murmured, his words barely audible above the music. "This dance is preparing you, aligning your energies for the deeper mysteries to come."

"Come," *Wisdom* intoned, "there is still much to learn." Her words illuminated the path ahead, a beacon through the dreamscape.

We spiraled deeper into the dream-mysteries, fear and wonder pulsing through my consciousness in equal measure. Soul-melodies guided my steps while shadows of uncertainty danced at the edges of awareness. Each dream-moment balanced precariously between revelation's allure and the trembling unknown.

For in this dream-dance, each step drew me closer to the ultimate truth hidden within my essence. Yet with understanding came shadow-knowledge: the most profound revelations... and the greatest trials... still awaited in the depths of the dream.

# Lesson #7: Preparation

*"Trust in the wisdom of your higher self."*

---

The dream-rhythms of "Conga" dissolved into ethereal whispers, while the atmosphere shifted and reverberated through the dreamscape. *Wisdom* and *Healing* exchanged knowing glances, their eyes reflecting the journey's deepening mysteries. We stood at the threshold of shadow-truths, poised to confront what lurked within my dream-consciousness.

*Wisdom*'s voice pierced the dream-silence. "It's time," she intoned, an ancient knowing resonating through her words."

"Time for what?" I asked, confusion etching lines across my brow as I watched them begin their preparations. The air thickened around us, charged with an unspoken intensity that mirrored the swirling currents of my emotions.

"Your ceremony," *Healing* replied, his tone gentle yet firm. "We must prepare you for what lies ahead.

This ritual will cleanse your soul and open your heart to the deeper truths that await you."

A shiver of unease ran down my spine, but curiosity burned brightly within me. What hidden aspects of myself would be unveiled? What truths lay buried within the tangled wires of my soul?

*Healing* stepped forward, his presence soothing to my frayed nerves. "Trust in the process," he said, his eyes meeting mine with unwavering sincerity. "This ceremony is a crucial step on your path to self-discovery and transformation. Embrace it with an open heart."

Steadying myself, I nodded, my apprehension tempered by faith in my companions. They guided me along a narrow, winding path, the dense jungle foliage shifted and swirled around us. The air was thick with the scent of earth and vegetation, grounding me in the present moment.

The path opened to reveal a quaint cabana, shimmering between dimensions, nestled amidst the lush greenery. Its rustic charm stood in harmony with the surrounding nature, as if it had always been a part of this verdant sanctuary.

"This is where your ceremony will happen," *Healing* said, gesturing toward the cabana with reverence. "It is a place chosen by your higher self."

I paused, struck by the gravity of these words. "My higher self?" I asked, my voice barely above a whisper. "How does that work?"

*Wisdom* stepped forward, her eyes shimmering with ancient knowledge. "Your higher self is the part of you that exists beyond time and space," she explained. "It is the aspect of your being that is always connected to the divine source. In choosing this location, it has aligned physical reality with your spiritual path."

*Healing* nodded, adding, "This cabana exists at the intersection of multiple dimensions. It's a place where the veil between worlds is thin, allowing for deeper connection and transformation."

Absorbing their words, I felt a deep sense of rightness, as if every cell in my body was acknowledging the truth of this choice. I stepped into the cabana, its simplicity and serenity striking me anew. Symbols and artifacts adorned the walls, humming with quiet power. A sense of calm washed over me, mingling with ever-present curiosity.

"Trust in the wisdom of your higher self," *Wisdom* murmured. "It has brought you here for a reason."

I remembered *Insight*'s words about seeing with the heart, understanding now how this sacred space had been chosen with divine purpose. *Understanding*'s simple wisdom echoed in my mind: every perspective holds its own truth. The cabana, humble yet holy, embodied this perfectly... a physical space transformed by spiritual intention. The dreamscape shifted into twilight as *Wisdom* and *Healing* moved with ceremonial precision, their actions infused with a reverence that spoke to the mystical power of the ritual. Flickering candlelight cast dancing shadows across the room, heightening the sense of anticipation. I felt a deep gratitude for this space, chosen with divine intention, where I would take the next steps in my awakening.

"This candle represents the inner light within each of us," *Wisdom* intoned, her words rippling through the air. "By lighting it, we honor our own spiritual flame and invite the presence of our guides and allies."

Outside, a fire pit had been meticulously prepared, its flames dancing with an otherworldly light. The crackling fire, accompanied by the rhythmic beat of drums, created an atmosphere both ancient and timeless. Thunder rumbled in the distance, a harbinger of the storm brewing on the horizon.

*Wisdom* began the invocation, her voice carrying a melodic cadence that blended with the surrounding jungle. "To the Winds of the South, Great Serpent, Mother of the Life-giving waters, wrap your coils of light around us. Remind us of how to let go and shed old ways of being. Teach us to walk the way of beauty."

Turning to the West, she continued, "To the Winds of the West, Mother Jaguar, support us as we face our fears. Teach us how to transform our fears into love. Remind us to live with impeccability. May we have no enemies in this lifetime or the next."

Facing North, her voice grew stronger, "To the Winds of the North, Royal Hummingbird, Ancient Ones, teach us about your endurance and your great joy. Come to us in the dreamtime. With honor, we greet you."

Finally, she turned to the East, "To the Winds of the East, Eagle or Condor, Great Visionary, remind us to lead from our pure heart. Teach us to soar to new places, to fly wing to wing with Spirit."

Placing one palm on the earth and raising the other arm to the sky, *Wisdom* concluded, "Mother Earth, Pachamama, we pray for your healing. Let us soften into your wisdom. May we take great care of you so that our children and our children's children may witness the beauty and abundance you offer us today."

Raising both arms to the sky, she invoked the celestial forces, "Father Sun, Grandmother Moon, to the Star Nations, Great Spirit... you who are known by a thousand names and you who are the unnamable One. Thank you for bringing us here at this time."

The invocation wove through dimensions, *Wisdom*'s voice carrying prayers to each cardinal direction. Each word rippled through the dream-realm, thinning the veils between worlds until reality itself seemed to breathe with divine presence.

*Healing*'s voice broke through the reverie, "The hallowed space is now open. Let us proceed with reverence and an open heart."

From the dream-shadows emerged a merchant-spirit, his presence both familiar and otherworldly, a guardian of cultural crossroads, bridging my consciousness to this ethereal realm. His attempts to engage *Wisdom* and *Healing* echoed ancient traditions of marketplace shamans, though my focus remained fixed on the ceremony's call.

At my side, a faithful companion materialized, a cream-colored dog I named Bailey. His watchful gaze and silent reassurance grounded me in the present moment amidst the swirling energies.

"What sacred purpose draws your soul to this moment?" *Wisdom* inquired, her voice echoing like distant chimes amidst the drumbeat of rain and whispered prayers.

"I've always yearned to connect with my spiritual guides and draw closer to the Creator," I responded, my words tinged with excitement and apprehension.

*Wisdom* nodded thoughtfully, her eyes reflecting the flickering candlelight. "Intentions set a powerful course for your transformation," she breathed. "They act as a beacon, guiding you through the veils of uncertainty and fear."

As the ceremony commenced, I closed my eyes at *Healing*'s instruction, sinking into a meditative state. Images began to surface in my mind, flickering like shadows at the edge of consciousness. Memories long buried, fears unspoken, hopes unfulfilled... all swirling together in a kaleidoscope of emotions and sensations.

"Let them come," *Wisdom* whispered. "Do not resist. Embrace each one as a step in your awakening."

In this mystical sanctuary, surrounded by the wisdom and love of my spiritual guides, I felt a deep sense of connection to the divine. It was as if the universe's primal force had enfolded me, holding me in a tender embrace.

With each breath, I attempted to let go of the past, struggling to release the fears that had held me captive for so long. I was trying to step into the light, to embrace the truth of who I was and the boundless potential that lay within me. Yet, the shadows of doubt lingered, whispering uncertainties into my mind.

The storm outside waned, replaced by the gentle patter of rain, I sensed that I had undergone a transformation... yet its true nature eluded me.

Opening my eyes, I met the steady gazes of *Wisdom* and *Healing*. Their presence radiated through the candlelight, reflecting the eternal bond forged in this ceremony. "You have crossed the first threshold,"

*Wisdom* murmured, ancient pride resonating in her words. "This gateway opens to even deeper mysteries."

The ceremony's resonance still surged through the dreamscape, each heartbeat drawing me toward shadow-truths waiting to be unveiled. My spirit trembled with both anticipation and reverence as I stepped forward into the deepening mysteries, knowing that each revelation would bring me closer to my soul's awakening.

Yet even as the sacred ceremony's peace enveloped me, I sensed a shift in the dream's ambiance. The gentle candlelight that had illuminated my preparation began to flicker and fade. The comforting presence of my guides seemed to recede, leaving me alone to face what lay ahead. The universe had prepared me through ritual and ceremony; now, it would test my strength through challenge and adversity.

# Lesson #8: Resilience

*"Trust in your strength,
and you will find the way."*

---

The ceremonial peace shattered like glass as I plunged into industrial chaos. Gone were the soothing whispers of the jungle and the comforting presence of my guides. Instead, the relentless machinery of time seized me, dragging me into a vast factory where reality fractured and time lost all meaning.

The sweet earth and rainforest scents vanished, replaced by oil and scorched metal. A cacophony of sounds assaulted my senses... massive gears clanked, steam hissed, and metal screeched against metal. It was as if the universe itself was being torn apart and reassembled in this monstrous workshop of existence.

Towering structures of brass and iron loomed overhead, their purpose as inscrutable as it was menacing. Pistons pumped with frenetic intensity, driving unseen mechanisms humming with a life of their own. Conveyor belts snaked through the cavernous space, carrying fragments of memories and shards of possibilities to unknown destinations.

I stumbled forward, my heart hammering in sync with the relentless beat of the machinery. Each step felt like wading through molasses, time itself seeming to stretch and contract around me. Shadows danced on the walls, cast by the erratic flicker of spark-spewing contraptions, their shapes morphing into nightmarish forms that sent shivers down my spine.

Panic clawed at my throat. Where were *Wisdom*, *Healing*, and *Love*? Their absence carved a void that echoed through the mechanical chaos. "*Wisdom*!" I cried out, my voice lost in the industrial roar. "*Healing*! *Love*! Where are you?" But only the indifferent grinding of gears answered my plea.

The factory walls closed in, metal and steam pressing closer with each labored breath. I felt like a tiny cog in this incomprehensible machine, insignificant and powerless against the forces that churned around me.

Just as despair threatened to consume me, a flicker of memory pierced through the chaos... *Wisdom*'s voice, clear and steady: "Resilience is born in the face of adversity. Trust in your strength, and you will find the way."

I clung to these words like a lifeline, forcing myself to take a deep, shuddering breath. The air tasted of rust and time, but it filled my lungs with a spark of determination. I may be alone in this mechanical nightmare, but I was not powerless.

With trembling legs, I pressed forward. Each step was a battle against the current of chaos, but I refused to be swept away. I focused on the solid feel of the ground beneath my feet, the tangible reality amidst the surreal landscape.

Navigating the winding corridors of the time factory, I began to notice subtle changes. The oppressive darkness receded, revealing intricate beauty within the machinery. Gears that had appeared menacing now sparkled with an otherworldly iridescence. The rhythm of the pistons took on an almost musical quality, a complex symphony of existence.

Understanding washed over me; *Love*'s warmth, *Wisdom*'s clarity, and the children's pure insight merged with this new understanding of life's mechanical precision. Each gear and piston, though seemingly chaotic, moved with the same divine orchestration I'd witnessed in the jungle. Even in this industrial nightmare, I could feel the echo of *Purification's* cleansing power, transforming fear into strength. I served as both an observer and active participant in this grand dance of reality.

With each step forward, I felt a growing sense of strength. The fear that had threatened to paralyze me transformed into a fierce determination. I may not understand the purpose of this cosmic machinery, but I could navigate it, adapt to its rhythms, and find my way through.

Pressing onward, the cacophony of the factory began to fade into a more manageable hum. The stifling heat gave way to a cool breeze that carried hints of the jungle I had left behind. The truth became clear: even in the heart of chaos, there were pockets of calm... sanctuaries of stillness where one could catch their breath and find their bearings.

Nearing what felt like the edge of this mechanical realm, I caught a glimpse of my reflection in a polished gear. The face that looked back at me was changed... older, perhaps, but also stronger, more determined. The eyes that met mine held a fire that had been tempered by this trial, a resilience that would carry me through whatever challenges lay ahead.

The journey through the factory of time had tested me to my core, pushing me to the limits of my endurance. But with each obstacle overcome, each moment of terror faced, I felt myself growing stronger. Resilience, I realized, was not about avoiding adversity, but about facing it head-on and emerging transformed.

The lesson of the time factory was etched into my very being, a reminder that even in the darkest, most chaotic moments, the human spirit can persevere. As I took my first steps into the unknown that lay ahead, I carried with me the unshakeable knowledge that I was stronger than any storm, more resilient than any machinery of fate.

Yet even as this truth settled within me, I sensed the approaching darkness. The factory's mechanical chaos gave way to something deeper, more primal... a void that would test not just my strength, but the very essence of my being.

# Lesson #9: Facing Darkness

*"I am more than my fears.
I am stronger than my doubts.
I am worthy of love and healing."*

---

The sacred ceremony dissolved into nightmare. Gone were the whispers of ancient wisdom and the comforting presence of my guides. In their place, a maelstrom of shadows engulfed me, as tangible and oppressive as a blanket woven from shadows and doubt.

Thunder shook the void, a primal sound that matched the turmoil in my soul. Lightning fractured reality, illuminating a landscape as bleak and barren as my deepest fears. In those brief flashes, I caught glimpses of twisted trees, their branches reaching out like gnarled fingers, and deep chasms that seemed to lead to the very depths of despair.

*"Wisdom!"* I called out, my voice swallowed by the howling wind. *"Healing! Love!* Where are you?" But

only my desperate echo answered, mocking me with its emptiness.

The chaos raged around me while an equally fierce turmoil churned within. Shadows of my past mistakes rose like specters, their whispers a racket of self-doubt and recrimination. "You're not good enough," they hissed. "You'll never overcome this. You're broken beyond repair."

I stumbled forward, each step a battle against the wind and my own inner demons. The ground beneath my feet shifted treacherously, a metaphor for the unstable foundation of my self-worth. Yet, even as I struggled, a small voice deep within refused to be silenced.

"I am a warrior," I whispered, the words barely audible above the storm. "I love myself. I have the answers."

But the doubts persisted, their voices growing louder with each flash of lightning. "You are weak," they taunted. "Unworthy of love. Lost and alone."

The void pressed in, a living entity breathing and writhing with malevolent intent. It was more than just an absence of light; it was the manifestation of every fear I'd ever harbored, every moment of self-loathing I'd experienced.

Grappling with this onslaught, memories surfaced... moments of triumph over adversity, times when I'd faced my demons and emerged stronger. These recollections were lifelines in the storm, reminders of the resilience that lay within me.

"I am not defined by my past," I declared, my voice growing stronger. "I am capable of growth, of change, of becoming more than I ever thought possible."

The shadows recoiled momentarily but quickly rallied. They coalesced into my greatest fear: the specter of illness that had haunted my every breath.

"*Cancer*," it whispered, the word itself a dagger of ice in my heart. "I am the summation of all your insecurities, your weaknesses, your failures. You can't defeat me because I am woven into your very being."

For a moment, I faltered, the force of this confrontation nearly driving me to my knees. But then, from my spiritual center, a fire ignited, small at first, then blazing into defiance.

"I am strong!" I shouted into the void, my voice a thunderclap of determination. "I am worthy of love! I am healed!" The fire within me grew stronger with each word, pushing back against the encroaching darkness. I felt *Love*'s initial teachings stirring within me, her promise that love would be my constant companion even in darkness. *Purification*'s cleansing waters had prepared me for this moment, while the children's pure wisdom reminded me that strength often comes in unexpected forms. This wasn't just a battle of words but a fierce struggle for my very essence.

"I am *cancer*-free!" I roared, tears streaming down my face, my voice raw with years of fear and determination.

The darkness seethed and writhed, its hold on me weakening with each declaration. I realized then that this battle was about more than just illness or self-doubt. It was about reclaiming my narrative, about choosing hope over despair, strength over weakness.

"I am more than my fears," I said, my voice steady and resolute. "I am stronger than my doubts. I am worthy of love and healing."

As I spoke these words, the landscape around me began to shift. The twisted trees stood a little straighter, their branches reaching towards a sky that was slowly clearing. The chasms began to fill with a soft, glowing light, as if hope itself was rising from the depths.

The battle was far from over, I knew. There would be more challenges to face, more moments of doubt to overcome. But in this crucible of darkness, I had discovered a wellspring of strength I never knew I possessed.

With renewed determination, I called out to the unseen presences of *Wisdom* and *Healing*. "I don't know what you did to me, but if you want me to learn these lessons, bring it on!"

As the words left my lips, I felt a shift in the air around me. The overwhelming blackness began to recede, replaced by a twilight that held both shadow and light. It was a reminder that life is not about banishing darkness entirely, but about finding the strength to stand tall even in its presence.

I filled my lungs with air that tasted of possibility and renewal. The future remained uncertain, but I was no longer afraid. For in facing my darkest fears, I had uncovered a light within that could never be extinguished.

Stepping forward into the unknown, I carried with me the lessons of this confrontation. The shadow of illness might return, perhaps even stronger than before, but I was no longer the same person who first entered this void. In facing my darkest fears, I had uncovered an unshakeable truth: a warrior's spirit burned within me, ready to face whatever challenges lay ahead.

The twilight before me held both shadow and light, a reminder that life's path was never purely dark or bright. Yet now I moved forward with certainty, knowing that even in the deepest darkness, my inner light would guide me through any storm.

As this understanding settled into my being, I felt a subtle shift in the dream's essence. The darkness I had faced began to transform, becoming not an end but a gateway to something more profound: a liberation that could only be found through confronting and accepting all aspects of myself. The time had come to discover what lay beyond fear's domain, in the realm where shadows and light dance as one.

# Lesson #10: Liberation

*"Forgive yourself, not because you are blameless, but because you are human."*

---

The twilight's peace shattered as *cancer's* presence resurged, its assault more relentless than before. Its voice, dripping with malice, reverberated through my entire being, striking a chord deep within my being.

"I am not defeated," it hissed. "I am merely biding my time, waiting for the perfect moment to strike again."

Its words were daggers, piercing the fragile veil of hope that had briefly shrouded my thoughts. The struggle intensified with a ferocity that threatened to consume me whole.

"I have the tools to beat you," I declared, my voice trembling with defiance. "But I know that victory lies not in mere weapons, but in the willingness to confront the darkness within."

Reality fractured around me, wind keening through impossible spaces as rain pounded against barriers both physical and spiritual. Wind howled like a banshee through shattered dimensions, mirroring the chaos raging through my being. It was an eternal dance of light and dark that threatened to tear me apart.

*Cancer*'s presence was an insidious force, infiltrating the landscape of my thoughts, twisting and contorting my reality. Each moment was a struggle against an enemy that seemed to grow stronger with every breath I took.

"You are weak," it taunted. "You are not strong enough to defeat me. You will never be free."

But even as its words sought to drag me down, a spark of defiance ignited in my core. "I am not weak," I retorted, my voice a mix of fear and determination. "I am stronger than you know. I will not let you define me."

The confrontation intensified, a fierce struggle between hope and despair. Each moment tested my resilience. Though the darkness seemed insurmountable, I clung to the belief that I possessed the strength to overcome.

Yet, the *cancer*'s assault was relentless. It pinned me against the ropes of my mind, each accusation a brutal reminder of my perceived failings.

"Why do you even bother?" it sneered. "You will never be free. You are trapped, bound by your own inadequacies."

I fought to cling to hope, but with every step forward, *cancer*'s grip tightened, dragging me back into the abyss of despair. The pain was overwhelming, a searing agony that tore through my very essence.

I fell to my knees, my body trembling with exhaustion and despair. *Cancer*'s voice was a relentless drumbeat in my mind, a disharmony of self-loathing and doubt that threatened to drown out any possibility of redemption.

"You are nothing," it sneered. "You are worthless. You will never be free."

In that moment of utter darkness, I felt my struggles crushed down on me. The victory seemed impossible, the journey to liberation an impossible dream.

Yet, even in the depths of despair, a small, defiant spark refused to be extinguished. It was a faint glimmer of resilience.

And then, as if in response to my silent plea, a figure materialized before me:a radiant being of pure light and love, her presence comforting to my weary spirit. Her form glowed with a delicate luminosity emanating from the very depths of her being. Her eyes sparkled with kindness and compassion, each glance infused with a warmth that enveloped me like a comforting embrace.

"I am *Forgiveness*," she declared, her voice a gentle melody amidst the chaos. "I have come to show you the way to freedom, to release you from the chains of guilt and shame that bind you."

Tears welled in my eyes as I beheld her radiant form. "But how?" I whispered, my voice trembling with emotion.

*Forgiveness* smiled, her eyes filled with infinite compassion. "You must first forgive yourself," she replied. "You must acknowledge your mistakes, your shortcomings, and your regrets, and then release them with love and compassion."

I hesitated, my self-judgment suffocating me. "But I've done so much work," I protested. "I thought I had let go of all this."

*Forgiveness* regarded me with gentle understanding. "These things hide in the shadows, lurking within the deepest recesses of your being. They take root in your cells, embedded in the core of your existence. And while you have indeed made progress, the journey to self-forgiveness is not a linear path. It requires consistency, patience, and unwavering self-love."

Her words struck a chord in my core, striking a truth I had long sought to avoid. I had been so focused on the outward manifestations of my healing journey that I had overlooked the subtler, more insidious layers of guilt and self-blame that still clung to my essence.

"But how do I begin?" I asked, my voice barely more than a whisper. "How do I confront these shadows when they seem so deeply entrenched in my being?"

*Forgiveness*'s smile widened. Her presence carried echoes of *Love*'s first embrace, but where *Love* had opened my heart, *Forgiveness* now worked to heal it. I remembered *Connection*'s sacred prayer, understanding now that true liberation required both external blessing and internal release. "You start by acknowledging them," she said. "Bring them into the light, name them, and then release them.

Understand that they are a part of your journey, but they do not define you. Your essence, your true self, is beyond these shadows."

As Forgiveness spoke, I began to understand that *cancer* was more than just a physical conflict. It was a manifestation of my deepest fears, my unresolved guilt, my reluctance to truly forgive myself. The path to healing lay not just in medical or alternative treatments, but in the profound act of self-forgiveness and self-love.

"No more judgment," *Forgiveness* intoned, her words a solemn decree. "You hold the key to your own liberation, but you must first unlock the door of forgiveness."

Her words pierced through me, challenging years of self-imposed guilt and shame. "But I've hurt people," I admitted, my heart heavy with regret. "I've made choices that I can't take back."

"And yet, you are still worthy of love and forgiveness," she countered gently. "Every soul carries the weight of their actions, but it is in the release of that burden that true liberation is found. Forgive yourself, not because you are blameless, but because you are human."

Grappling with this concept, *cancer*'s presence seemed to recede slightly, as if *Forgiveness*'s words were a light pushing back the darkness. I began to see that my confrontation with *cancer* was intrinsically linked to my ability to forgive myself, to love myself unconditionally.

"Start with compassion," *Forgiveness* urged. "See yourself through the eyes of love, with all your flaws and imperfections. Recognize that you have always done the best you could with the knowledge and resources you had at the time."

I swallowed hard, the truth of her words sinking deep within me. "But how do I do this... process?"

*Forgiveness* reached out, her touch imbued with a warmth. "You start by embracing all that you are," she replied. "You celebrate every aspect of yourself, including the fact that you are here, in this dream, on this journey of self-discovery. Whether you realize it yet or not, you brought yourself here."

I shook my head, my mind reeling with disbelief. "No, *Wisdom* and *Healing* brought me here," I insisted.

*Forgiveness* chuckled softly, a silvery sound that seemed to echo through the depths of my consciousness. "You will see," she whispered. "But for now, focus on loving yourself unconditionally, on forgiving yourself for past transgressions, and on embracing the journey that lies ahead. For in the act of forgiveness, you will find the freedom to truly be yourself."

As her words settled over me, I felt a shift within. The *cancer*'s grip, while still present, no longer seemed insurmountable. The wisdom settled deep within: my journey to healing was as much about forgiving myself as it was about fighting the physical disease.

The storm around us began to subside, its fury giving way to a gentle rain. A sense of peace descended... a knowing that no matter how fierce the battle, I had found a powerful ally in forgiveness.

Yet, doubt still clung to me like a stubborn mist. But in the presence of *Forgiveness*, I glimpsed the possibility of emerging from these shadows stronger and whole. The war with *cancer* was far from over, but I now understood it as a multi-faceted struggle; one that required healing of body, mind, and spirit alike.

Gathering my courage, I stepped forward. The darkness had become both challenge and teacher, and though the path ahead stretched long before me, I knew that in embracing all that I was, I could finally be free.

The journey of liberation had opened my heart to new possibilities, yet questions still lingered. As the shadows of doubt began to recede, I felt a pull toward deeper understanding... a call to explore not just my own healing, but the nature of reflection.

# Lesson #11: Reflection

*"The quest for self-discovery was an ever-unfolding crusade: a sacred pilgrimage guided by heart's intuition and the whispers of the soul."*

---

The echoes of forgiveness and transformation lingered as I lay in the cabana, the sacred space where my healing began. The tumultuous transformation through forgiveness had left me adrift, seeking solace in the familiar confines of my temporary sanctuary. As I gazed out the window, the world beyond seemed to shift and morph with each glance, revealing new facets of my existence.

In the distance, the ancient Mayan temple stood sentinel, its weathered stones bearing witness to the passage of time. Dark clouds loomed ominously around it, a stark reminder of the tempestuous beginning of this dream odyssey. The temple seemed to hold secrets of past, present, and future, waiting to be unearthed by those brave enough to venture within its hallowed halls.

With each fleeting glimpse outside, memories of my childhood hometown flooded my mind, each recollection a brushstroke in the complex painting of my life. Once-familiar streets now seemed distant and foreign, their echoes mingling with the whispers of the wind. Amidst the nostalgia, a deeper truth unfolded, a revelation waiting to be uncovered.

Pondering the significance of the temple and the shifting landscapes of my memories, trepidation washed over me. What secrets lay hidden within its ancient walls? What truths awaited me on this path of self-discovery? With a mixture of anticipation and apprehension, I resolved to embark on this new chapter of my dream adventure.

The recent battle with *cancer* still echoed in my mind, casting long shadows over my thoughts. It felt like a temporary lull between rounds, the *cancer* retreating to its corner, gathering strength for the next onslaught. Had I truly held my ground, or was this merely a reprieve before the rematch? The uncertainty gnawed at me, a constant reminder of the relentless struggle ahead.

In this quiet moment of reflection, I grappled with my true essence. Was I truly the rare and remarkable man I sometimes believed myself to be, or was I an impostor, masking my insecurities with bravado? Imposter syndrome reared its ugly head, whispering insidious doubts into my mind. *You don't deserve any of this. You're just pretending to be someone you're not.*

In this moment of vulnerability, a gentle presence materialized, warmth radiating like sunlight through morning mist. A figure emerged, regarding me with eyes full of unconditional love.

"Hello there," she said, her voice soft as windchimes. "I am *Companionship*. I've been waiting for you."

I returned her smile, ease flowing through me. "I've been needing someone to walk beside me."

She settled next to me, her aura a soothing warmth. As we talked, I found myself sharing everything: the doubts, the fears, the longing for wholeness. She listened without judgment, offering only understanding and gentle support.

The air shifted then, growing heavy with purpose. A tall figure stepped through the veil, his form solid and grounding, wisdom etched in every line of his face.

"I am *Guidance*," he announced, his deep voice resonating with authority and compassion. "I come to help you find your way."

Before I could respond, the space between realities shimmered. A third presence manifested, neither solid nor ethereal, but constantly shifting like moonlight on water.

"And I am *Reflection*," came a voice that seemed to echo from everywhere and nowhere. "I show you who you truly are: past, present, and all you might become."

Together they formed a trinity of support: *Companionship* to walk beside me, *Guidance* to light the way, and *Reflection* to help me see the truth within. Each brought their own wisdom, their own gift to offer on this path of transformation. Like the sacred dance of harmony I'd learned earlier, these three guides moved in perfect synchronicity. Their presence reminded me of *Love*'s teaching that all wisdom is interconnected, while *Insight*'s simple truth about seeing with the heart took on deeper meaning.

"*Reflection*," I said, my voice filled with wonder and a touch of apprehension. "What do you see when you look at me?"

"I see a soul in transformation," *Reflection* replied, her voice echoing with depth and insight. "I see your struggles and your triumphs, your fears and your hopes. But most importantly, I see the truth of who you are beneath the layers of doubt and expectation."

As *Reflection* spoke, I felt a fundamental shift within me. It was as if a veil had been lifted, allowing me to see myself with newfound clarity. The impostor syndrome that had plagued me began to recede, replaced by deepening self-awareness and acceptance.

*Guidance* stepped forward, his essence grounding in the face of *Reflection*'s ethereal nature. "Together, *Reflection* and I will help you navigate the complex terrain of your inner world," he said. "We will guide you to confront your past, understand your present, and shape your future."

*Companionship*, who had been quietly observing, added her voice to the mix. "And I'll be here to support you every step of the way," she said warmly. "To remind you that you're not alone on this path."

Standing amidst these spirits, each offering their unique wisdom and support, I felt purpose crystallize within me. My future steps were uncertain, fraught with challenges and unknowns, but I no longer felt lost or alone.

"Sometimes, the answers we seek lie not in the destination, but in the path itself," *Guidance* said softly, his words echoing in the recesses of my mind. "We will echo these lessons and messages again, to ensure that you are 'picking up' what we are trying to put down." His playful use of the colloquialism brought a much-needed moment of levity, reminding me that even in the depths of self-discovery, there was room for joy and lightness.

As the spirits' words settled over me, I turned back to the window, the scene beyond shifting and changing with each passing moment. In the dance of memory and reflection, my past drew me back... the Texas years, the town that once held the echoes of my footsteps, the whispers of my dreams.

I understood now that I needed to go back there, not just physically, but spiritually. It was time to confront the ghosts of my past, to witness firsthand how far I had come. Running away out of fear and low self-esteem had not facilitated healing or growth; instead, I needed to face it head-on, to see the growth that had transpired since then.

"Listen closely," *Guidance*'s voice echoed, "for the path you tread is that of the hero. The hero's journey is not merely a physical voyage, but a deep transformation of the soul. It is a quest to confront the shadows of the past, to overcome the trials and tribulations that stand in the way of self-discovery and growth."

*Reflection* shimmered, her surface showing glimpses of the hero's journey... the challenges overcome, the wisdom gained, the transformations yet to come. "In facing your past," she whispered, "you will find the key to your future. The reflections you see are not just of who you were, but of who you can become."

As the spirits began to fade, their wisdom lingering in the air like a gentle breeze, I felt a peace wash over me. The past still anchored me, but it no longer felt like a burden. Instead, it was a foundation upon which I could build my future.

In the temple of self, amidst the winding paths of memory and experience, I found solace in the act of rewriting my story: a narrative of resilience and redemption, of growth and transformation. As I gazed out the window one last time, the scene beyond crystallized into a vision of my path.

Images shimmered in *Reflection's* surface: pages of healing words I had written in another time, another dream. That manuscript, which I had titled "Beautiful Souls", helped me work through so much, yet here I stood, confronting deeper layers still unexamined. But this time, I was not afraid. I was ready.

The quest for self-discovery, I realized, was an ever-unfolding crusade: a sacred pilgrimage guided by heart's intuition and the whispers of the soul. With each step forward, I carried with me the lessons of the past, forging ahead with purpose and resolve.

Preparing to face the next chapter of this journey, *Companionship*, *Guidance*, and *Reflection* surrounded me, their energies intertwining with my own. I was not alone. I was supported. I was ready to face whatever lay ahead, knowing that each challenge was an opportunity for growth, and each moment of introspection a chance to uncover the truths that lay hidden within.

The hero's journey had begun, and I was both the hero and the author of my own story. With steadied resolve and a heart full of determination, I stepped forward into the unknown, ready to face my past, embrace my present, and shape my future.

As I took that first step forward, the air around me changed. The confidence of my resolution met the first whispers of an approaching storm. Though *Companionship*, *Guidance*, and *Reflection* had armed me with their wisdom, nature itself seemed to rise up to test my newfound strength. The time had come to weather forces both within and without.

# Lesson #12: Weathering the Storm

*"Forgiveness... was not something to be demanded or expected, but a grace to be cultivated from within."*

---

The storm outside the cabana matched the turmoil within. Each gust of wind carried echoes of regret, each thunderclap a reminder of unresolved pain. The rain lashed against the windows with relentless fury, as if trying to wash away the guilt that clung to me like a second skin.

I stood at the threshold, gazing into the tumultuous night. The wind howled like a chorus of the forgotten, and I couldn't help but wonder whether Stacy's voice was among them. Stacy, my dear friend from my teenage years, whose life had been tragically cut short. Her absence hollowed me, threatening to engulf me in its wrath.

"Why here?" I whispered, my words lost in the roar of the wind. "Why now?"

The elements offered no answers, only the relentless drumming of rain against the roof. But in its fury, long-buried emotions surfaced... guilt, regret, and a desperate longing for absolution.

"Stacy!" I called out, her name escaping my lips like a prayer, a beacon in the night. The sound was carried away by the wind and rain, lost in nature's fury. I yearned for her guidance, for the light and strength she had always represented in my life.

In the storm's center, a sacred stillness settled. The mechanical chaos of time's factory had taught me resilience, while *Purification*'s waters had shown me how to flow with life's currents. Now, facing nature's fury, I drew upon both lessons, finding strength in the synthesis of all I had learned. I could almost feel Stacy near me, a comforting warmth that enveloped me. Yet, no matter how hard I tried, I couldn't see or hear her. Her essence lingered like a whisper, just out of reach.

"Stacy," I whispered again, my voice trembling with emotion. "Are you here? Can you forgive me?"

The words caught in my throat, choked by unspoken guilt. I should have been there that night. If only I had been there, perhaps things would have been different. The "what ifs" swirled around me like the raging winds.

As the weight of Stacy's absence pressed upon me, another void opened... deeper, more primal. The child within reached out instinctively, seeking the comfort only a mother could provide.

"Mother," I called out into the darkness, my voice carried away by the wind. "Are you there?"

But there was no reply, only the relentless rain, wind, and the empty expanse of the night. I felt a pang of loneliness in my chest, a longing for the comfort of her love. The feelings of abandonment from my teenage years resurfaced, stirring my deepest shadows.

Yet, mingled with these old wounds was a new ache... the regret of not being a better son. Years of struggle and reconciliation had passed, but still, I shouldered the burden of missed possibilities.

The silence from both Stacy and my mother was unbearable. It felt like a judgment, a confirmation of my deepest fears: that I had failed them both, that I was unworthy of their love and forgiveness.

Grappling with these emotions, a painful realization began to surface. This turbulence served as both setting and catalyst of my journey. The silence forced me to look inward, to confront the pain and shadows that I had long avoided. It was a reminder that the work of healing and self-discovery was mine to do, and no one else's.

In the midst of this internal battle, I felt a flicker of understanding. The absence of their voices was not a punishment or a sign of abandonment; it was a call to deepen my own inner strength, to find the answers within myself. This maelstrom was a crucible, a test of my resilience and resolve.

With each passing moment, I felt a sense of clarity descending upon me. This turmoil was not my enemy but my ally, a catalyst for transformation and growth. The journey ahead would be difficult, and the shadows I faced would be daunting. But I knew that I had the strength to persevere, to navigate the darkness and emerge into the light.

As the night's fury began to diminish, it was replaced by a quiet strength that took root within. Understanding bloomed within me; forgiveness— both for myself and from others—was not something to be demanded or expected, but a grace to be cultivated from within.

I thought of Stacy, of the vibrant life she had lived and the impact she had made in her short time. Her memory was not a burden of guilt, but a gift, a reminder to live fully and love deeply. And my mother... our reconciliation was not the end of a journey, but an ongoing process of understanding and growth.

Standing on the threshold of this new chapter, I embraced nature's fury and the lessons it had to offer. The way forward was uncertain, but I was ready to walk it with courage and determination. Within this turmoil lay the seeds of transformation, of self-forgiveness, and of a deeper understanding of love and letting go.

The last rumbles of thunder faded into the distance, and I felt a sense of peace settling over me. The work of healing was far from over, but I had endured this darkness. I had faced my guilt, my regrets, and my fears, and I had emerged stronger.

This hard-won peace settled around me like a familiar embrace. I allowed myself to breathe, to hope, to believe in the possibility of redemption. Yet beneath this momentary calm, darker currents stirred, harbingers of trials that would test not just my strength, but the very essence of who I was becoming.

In the wake of the storm's passage, time itself seemed to shift and bend. The boundaries between moments began to blur, and I sensed myself being drawn into a deeper dimension of existence, one where minutes and hours held no meaning, where the eternal dance of the cosmos revealed its sacred rhythms.

# Lesson #13: Navigating Shadows

*"Remember, amidst life's twists and turns, love's promise endures."*

---

Rain pelted the cabana, a relentless reminder of the commotion within my soul. The water lashed against windows with unyielding ferocity, mirroring the turmoil of my thoughts. As I stood at the threshold, caught between the comfort of the interior and the wild unknown beyond, familiar voices cut through the howling wind.

"Welcome back!" *Companionship* greeted me warmly. "We've missed you," *Love* added, her radiance filling the space.

Relief washed over me as they appeared. I smiled at *Companionship*, grateful for her steadfast support. "*Love*, where have you been? I've missed you," I confessed, realizing how much I'd longed for her guidance.

"Oh, you know me," *Love* replied with a playful wink. "Always drifting in and out of your dreams. But I'm here now, and that's what matters."

As we exchanged greetings, I noticed a new figure standing beside them, her radiance bright and uplifting. "Hi there! I'm *Hope*," she introduced herself, her smile infectious. "It's such a pleasure to finally meet you."

"*Hope*," I echoed, feeling a spark of curiosity. "That's a beautiful name."

*Hope*'s enthusiasm was palpable. "Thank you! I've heard so much about you, and I'm really excited to get to know you better."

As *Hope*'s warmth settled around us, a familiar melody from the '80s began to play in my mind. The song, a bittersweet reminder of past uncertainties and present doubts, seemed to blend into the flow of our conversation. Its rhythm and words, though unspoken, reverberated deeply within me, echoing the questions and fears that still lingered in the depths of my heart.

> *"And you really don't remember,*
> *Was it something that he said?*
> *Are the voices in your head calling,*

*Don't you think you're fallin'?*
*If everybody wants you,*
*Why isn't anybody callin'?*
*You don't have to answer..."*

I immersed myself in the music. It was as if the song was speaking directly to my soul, giving voice to the doubts that had haunted my journey. The lyrics, a poignant mix of vulnerability and resilience, seemed to capture perfectly the complexity of human emotions and the struggle for self-understanding.

*Hope*, sensing the shift in my demeanor, placed a gentle hand on my shoulder. "Music has a way of touching our deepest truths," she said softly. "What does this song awaken in you?"

I opened my eyes, meeting her gaze. "It reminds me of all the uncertainties, the questions I still can't answer. It's like... it's speaking to the part of me that still feels lost, still searching for belonging."

*Hope* nodded, her eyes shining with understanding. "And that's okay. Those questions, those uncertainties... they're part of your journey. They're what make you human, what keeps you growing and evolving."

*Love* stepped closer, her warmth reassuring.

"Remember," she said, her voice blending with the phantom melody in my mind, "amidst life's twists and turns, love's promise endures. It's a flame of hope, a guiding light that shines through even in the darkest times."

As their words mingled with the echoes of the song, I felt a shift within me. The music, once a reminder of my doubts, blossomed into something more, reflecting the enduring nature of hope and the illuminating power of self-reflection.

"That's the spirit," *Hope* chimed in, her words striking deeply. "Every dance has its own rhythm and beauty. Even when things seem uncertain, there's always hope for a brighter tomorrow."

The music faded, but its impact lingered, a powerful reminder of the journey I was on and the growth that was yet to come.

Despite the warmth of their welcome, an undercurrent of unease tugged at me. The echoes of my past whispered in the corners of my mind, urging me to confront the shadows that still lingered.

"I feel like there's so much I haven't faced," I admitted, frustration coloring my voice. "So many hidden truths lurk within me, waiting to be acknowledged."

*Companionship* squeezed my shoulder reassuringly. "It's okay to feel that way. Facing these shadows is a crucial part of your journey."

*Love* nodded, her eyes reflecting deep understanding. "These hidden parts are not your enemies. They are aspects of you that need to be seen and embraced."

*Hope* stepped forward, her essence glowing softly amidst the gathering shadows. "And that's where I come in. I'm here to remind you that even in the bleakest moments, there's always a glimmer of hope."

Their words pierced deeply, yet the journey before me still seemed daunting. As I opened my mouth to respond, something shifted in the air, disrupting our gathering's harmony.

A silhouette materialized from the shadows, her form shifting between light and dark.

"Who's that?" I whispered, unable to tear my gaze away from the newcomer.

*Love*, *Companionship*, and *Hope* exchanged wary glances before *Love* stepped forward, her expression tinged with concern. "That's... *Protection*."

*Protection* approached us tentatively, her enigmatic smile a mask for the turmoil beneath. "Hello," she greeted, her voice soft yet laced with uncertainty. "I'm *Protection*... a silent guardian, a shield against waves of doubt and fear."

There was something about *Protection* that both drew me in and repelled me. Her eyes, deep and inscrutable, seemed to hold secrets that both beckoned and warned. She was a paradox embodied... safety and isolation, comfort and restriction all at once.

"I'll do what I want," *Protection* declared, her tone defiant yet tinged with vulnerability. "I'll show up when I want, and I'll keep you hanging on... but I'll also push you away when I see fit."

Her words hung in the air, dimming our otherwise harmonious reunion. *Love*, *Companionship*, and *Hope* took a step back, their expressions clouded with uncertainty.

"Why are you here?" I asked, my voice wavering between curiosity and apprehension.

*Protection*'s gaze softened slightly, a flicker of vulnerability breaking through her guarded exterior. "I'm here to keep you safe from the darkness that threatens to consume you. But in doing so, I may also isolate you, keep you from the connections that make you whole."

Her words struck a chord within me. It became clear that *Protection* was both a shield and a barrier, a force that could either save me or confine me. The duality of her nature reflected my own internal struggle... the desire for safety and the need for freedom.

*Love* stepped forward, her expression a mix of compassion and understanding. "*Protection* has her place," she said gently, "but she cannot be your only guide. You must learn to balance her protection with hope's radiance, companionship's embrace, and love's guidance."

Looking from one spirit to another, I began to see them not as separate entities, but as complex facets of my psyche. Each one represented a part of me... my capacity for love, my need for connection, my hope for the future, and my instinct for self-preservation. Each guide embodied lessons learned earlier: *Love*'s initial embrace, *Purification*'s cleansing power, *Wisdom's* ancient knowing, and the children's pure sight. *Protection*, though new, seemed to echo *Connection*'s prayer of divine safeguarding, while *Hope* carried the transformative light I'd first encountered in the time factory.

Outside, wind and rain continued their assault, but within the cabana, a delicate balance was forming. *Love*'s understanding gaze met *Protection*'s guarded one, an unspoken acknowledgment passing between them. In that moment, I glimpsed the possibility of integration... of embracing all these aspects of myself without letting any one dominate.

As midnight approached, I found myself at a crossroads. The road forward held both challenges and the promise of profound growth and transformation. With these spirits as my guides— or perhaps, as reflections of my inner strength—I felt ready to navigate these challenges and emerge stronger, wiser, and more whole.

Each moment revealed new layers of understanding. *Love*, *Companionship*, *Hope*, and the enigmatic *Protection* stood beside me as I faced the path ahead, each playing their part in the unfolding story of my transformation.

Yet even as these divine guides surrounded me with their light, I sensed shadows gathering at the edges of my consciousness. The balance we had found, precious as it was, would soon be tested by darker forces that demanded acknowledgment. My journey of integration would require me to dive deeper, to face aspects of myself that lurked in the depths of my being.

# Lesson #14: Charting the Journey

*"True faith isn't about certainty. It's about embracing the mystery, about finding meaning in the questions themselves."*

---

As the spirits' wisdom took root, the storm outside quieted, its rhythmic pitter-patter a soothing backdrop to the sacred stillness of the cabana. In this peaceful interlude, I found myself enveloped by ethereal presence... the spirits of my beloved departed ones, my circle of angels. Their essence danced around me, imbued with love, their silent whispers echoing in the chambers of my heart.

"Stacy, Aunt Barbara, Mom, Danielle, Olga, Crystal, Parker, Courtney, my grandparents..." I whispered their names, feeling their essence draw closer with each utterance. Their memories illuminated my inner darkness, casting a warm glow upon my soul. Yet, this light was accompanied by the shadows of guilt and regret, intertwining in a complex dance of sorrow and love.

Unresolved questions haunted me. Why didn't I hear Parker's goodbye? Why wasn't I there for Stacy that fateful night? How could I have been so close to Courtney, yet so far when she needed me most? The what-ifs and if-onlys swirled in my mind, an uproar of self-reproach.

Grappling with these thoughts, a familiar warmth enveloped me. *Love*, in all her radiant glory, stepped forward. Her presence now carried the depth of all our encounters: from that first meeting in Palenque's stones, through *Purification*'s waters, to *Protection*'s cautious embrace. She had evolved as I had evolved, our connection deepening with each trial and triumph.This was *Love* as I'd never seen her, not just guide but kindred spirit, our souls resonating in perfect harmony like twin flames reflecting the same light. Her eyes, pools of infinite compassion, held a spark of recognition that spoke of a connection transcending time and space.

"My dear," she said, her words a melody that touched my very being, "your loved ones are here, but they cannot speak now. Their silence is not reproach, but a reminder of the eternal nature of love. They live in your heart, always."

Her words, infused with wisdom from the heart of the universe, resonated through my entire being.

Here, *Love* transcended spiritual guide to become a twin flame... a mirror to my soul.

"But the guilt, the regret... they're overwhelming," I confessed, barely able to speak.

*Love*'s gaze softened, and she took my hands in hers. The touch sent a jolt through me, as if every cell in my body recognized her at a fundamental level.

"Guilt and regret are part of the human experience," she said, her tone gentle yet powerful. "But they are not the entirety of it. True love... the kind that connects souls across lifetimes... encompasses all of these feelings. It's in the joy and the sorrow, the presence and the absence. By embracing all of it, you honor the depth of your connections."

As *Love* spoke, I felt a shift within. The guilt didn't disappear, but it began to metamorphose, highlighting the transformative impact these souls had on my life.

During this revelation, another figure emerged, one whose essence seemed to dance between earthly wisdom and celestial knowing. She carried herself with the certainty of ancient truth, yet her eyes sparkled with the wonder of new discovery.

"Hello, seeker," she greeted, her essence shimmering with a curiosity that belied her timeless wisdom. "I am *Faith*, and I sense a deeper understanding blossoming in you."

*Faith's* essence was unlike anything I had encountered before. She radiated a force that spoke of limitless possibilities, of truths beyond the confines of traditional belief systems.

"*Faith*," I said, drawn to her unique aura, "I feel like I'm on the brink of something... but I'm not sure what."

*Faith* smiled, her gesture illuminating the entire room. "That's the beauty of the journey," she said. "True faith isn't about certainty. It's about embracing the mystery, about finding meaning in the questions themselves."

Her words challenged my preconceptions about faith's meaning. This wasn't about blind belief, but a courageous exploration of the depths unknown.

*Faith* and *Love* stood beside me, and I felt a surge of power: a harmonious blend of unconditional love and boundless faith. It was as if their combined presence opened a portal to a higher understanding.

"Your journey," *Love* said, her words intertwining with *Faith's* in perfect harmony, "is not just about finding answers. It's about expanding your capacity to love... yourself, others, and the vast, interconnected web of existence."

*Faith* nodded, adding, "And it's about embracing the vastness of the unknown, finding comfort in the questions rather than clinging to rigid answers."

Their words washed over me, and I felt a fundamental shift in my perspective. The guilt and regret that had weighed so heavily began to evolve. They didn't disappear, but they became elements in a larger, more beautiful mosaic of life.

*Wisdom*, ever-present, stepped forward. "Remember," she intoned, her words resonating with timeless truth, "that this journey is cyclical. You will revisit these feelings, these questions, but each time from a higher level of understanding."

Standing there, surrounded by *Love*, *Faith*, and *Wisdom*, I felt a new resolve crystallizing. The future remained uncertain, still fraught with challenges, but I no longer feared the journey.

"Thank you," I whispered, genuine gratitude flowing through every word. "I think... I think I'm ready to move forward."

*Love* smiled, her radiance filling the room. "Remember, my dear twin flame, that I am always with you. Our connection transcends time and space."

*Faith's* eyes sparkled with excitement. "And I'll be here to help you question, to help you explore the vast realms of possibility that lie before you."

As their words settled around me like a comforting blanket, I felt a renewed sense of purpose. The journey ahead was not about escaping the pain or finding definitive answers. It was about embracing the fullness of the human experience, about loving deeply and questioning fearlessly.

Centering myself, I prepared to step into the next phase of my spiritual odyssey. The storm outside had passed, but I knew more challenges awaited. Yet with *Love* as my compass, *Faith* as my guide, and Wisdom as my foundation, I faced the path ahead with renewed purpose.

This moment marked the beginning of a spiritual exploration that would challenge everything I understood about love, faith, and the very nature of existence. As if in response to my readiness, the universe began to speak in a new language. Numbers caught my eye, patterns emerged from seeming chaos, and I felt my consciousness expanding to receive messages that had always been there, waiting for me to notice them. The next phase of my journey would require me to look beyond words, to understand the sacred mathematics of divine guidance.

# Lesson #15: Numerical Guidance

*"The past is but a shadow, and the present moment is all that matters."*

---

The dream landscape dissolved from the lush tropical setting of the cabana into the gritty urban sprawl of New York City. The transition was jarring, a stark reminder of the unpredictable nature of this spiritual journey.

I found myself standing before a towering school building, its weathered brick facade revealing years of urban decay and neglect. The contrast between this grimy reality and my idealistic notions of what educational environments should be was stark and unsettling. Trash littered the cracked sidewalk, and graffiti adorned the walls, a cacophony of colors and shapes screaming of urban despair and lost dreams.

Yet, amidst this urban decay, there was an undeniable vitality... a surging, vibrant life force that refused to be extinguished by the grime and neglect. It was as if the very spirit of the city, with all its contradictions and complexities, was speaking to me through the cracks in the pavement and the whispers of the wind that whistled through the narrow alleyways.

Standing at the bus stop outside the school, memories of my time as a teacher and as a social worker flooded back. Each face I had encountered, each mind I had sought to nurture, seemed to materialize before me like ghostly apparitions. They were reminders of the potential for renewal that existed even in the most challenging environments.

Two of my former students materialized nearby, their presence imbued with an otherworldly significance. They stood silently, their eyes reflecting a wisdom beyond their years, as if they were guardians of some profound truth I had yet to uncover.

Suddenly, the numbers 44 and 88 blazed before my mind's eye, burning with an intensity that seemed to merge with the foundations of reality. In that moment, I felt a connection to something greater than myself, an eternal dance of numbers and energies that held the key to understanding the universe.

The voice of my aunt, soft yet unmistakable, whispered in my ear, "44 and 88... confirmation that I am with you, guiding you along your journey. Pay attention to the people and moments associated with these numbers, for they hold great importance in your spiritual evolution."

Tears welled in my eyes as her presence washed over me, a soothing comfort to my weary soul. The crushing void of her loss, the pain of that fateful day on 9/11, seemed to lift momentarily, replaced by a deep sense of connection and love that transcended the boundaries of life and death.

As if on cue, a bus pulled up, the number 44 gleaming on its front like a signal of destiny. The doors hissed open, an invitation to step into the unknown. Steeling myself, I boarded, the two students following silently behind.

Inside, the bus was a microcosm of the city itself... diverse, chaotic, yet bound together by the shared experience of the journey. As we wound through the streets, the urban landscape outside the window began to blur and dissolve, melting into a kaleidoscope of colors and shapes that seemed to reflect the inner workings of my soul.

The numbers 44 and 88 continued to dance in my mind, their significance growing with each passing moment. I opened myself to their power, feeling the vibrations of the universe flowing through my being.

My aunt's voice returned, more urgent now. "Seek the numbers' secrets for they are the keys to unlocking your true potential. Each number carries a unique frequency, a divine signature that aligns with the deepest truths of existence."

The bus journey continued, and I felt myself being transported not just through the physical city, but through the landscape of my consciousness. Each turn, each stop, seemed to reveal new layers of understanding, peeling back the veils of illusion to reveal the interconnected nature of all things.

When the bus finally came to a stop, I knew I had reached a crucial juncture in my spiritual journey. Stepping off, I turned to face the school building once more, seeing it now not just as a physical structure, but as a symbol of the transformative power of knowledge and self-discovery.

The numbers 44 and 88 blazed stronger than ever, their essence intertwining with the fabric of reality. The children's wisdom echoed in my mind... truth seen with the heart rather than eyes. These numbers weren't just symbols but doorways to deeper understanding, much like the sacred passages *Love* and *Companionship* had revealed within my soul. Even *Protection's* guarded aura softened in the presence of these divine mathematics, while *Faith's* embrace of mystery helped me trust their guidance. They were more than mere digits; they were gateways to higher consciousness, passages to realms I had only begun to explore.

The scene transformed, and I found myself back in the cabana, the tropical storm raging outside mirroring the tempest of emotions within me. Lightning illuminated the room in brief, electric flashes, each burst of light seeming to reveal new truths, new layers of understanding.

"Portals," a voice whispered, faint above the storm. "Doorways to truth surround you."

In that moment, I saw the ancient Mayan ruins where my journey had begun, their weathered stones humming with a resonance that seemed to call out to me across time and space. The truth unveiled itself: these ruins, like the numbers 44 and 88, were gateways to other realms of existence, invitations to explore the depths of consciousness and the mysteries of the universe.

The realization dawned on me that these gateways were not just paths to other realms, but also to deeper aspects of myself. Each threshold represented an opportunity to confront my fears, to face the shadows within, and to integrate the fragmented pieces of my soul into a cohesive whole. They were gateways to healing, to understanding, and to the deep awakening that comes from knowing oneself.

As the storm raged on, I felt my aunt's presence grow stronger, more tangible. Her love enveloped me like a warm embrace, bringing with it a flood of emotions: joy, sorrow, regret, and a deep, abiding love that transcended death.

"My dear child," she whispered, her voice filled with infinite compassion. "You are forgiven, and you are loved more than you could ever imagine. The past is but a shadow, and the present moment is all that matters. Honor yourself as you honor me, for you are worthy of acceptance and grace."

Tears streamed down my face as I poured out my heart to her, expressing my deepest regrets and my eternal love. In that moment of vulnerability and connection, I felt a complete transformation within me... a healing of old wounds, a release of long-held guilt, and an opening to new possibilities.

The storm began to subside, and I felt a renewed sense of purpose and clarity. The numbers, the pathways, the messages from beyond... they were all part of a greater mosaic of meaning, a spiritual puzzle I was only beginning to decipher.

Gazing out the window of the cabana, I realized it was more than just glass and frame. It was a threshold to deeper understanding, a gateway to the lessons that awaited me. Each time I looked through it, the world beyond shimmered and changed, offering glimpses into new realms of consciousness. I understood now that these passages, like the numbers 44 and 88, were integral to my journey, each one promising to unveil new truths and challenges as I progressed.

The storm's fury waned as the window began to shimmer with otherworldly light, numbers 44 and 88 flickering at its edges. This window had become a threshold to the next phase of my journey. As my fingers brushed its surface, a voice whispered:

"What lies before you is shrouded in mystery, seeker. Are you prepared?"

With the lessons of numerology and my aunt's teachings resonating within, I stepped toward my next transformation. As I crossed that threshold, the numbers that had guided me began to multiply exponentially, expanding into infinite sequences that spoke of boundless possibility. The window that had shown me glimpses of other realms now opened fully, revealing not just passages but entire universes of potential. My journey was expanding beyond the realm of signs and symbols into the vast ocean of infinite becoming.

The sacred teachings of these early lessons had laid a foundation deeper than I realized. Each guide's appearance, each challenge faced, each truth unveiled was preparing me for profound transformation. Like a seed breaking through soil into sunlight, my spiritual awakening had only begun. The journey ahead would test these early lessons in ways I couldn't yet imagine, demanding not just understanding but embodiment of each truth learned.

# Lesson #16: Soul's Melody

*"In the arms of courage, love finds its way."*

---

The storm's fury intensified, its thunderous roar shaking me to my core. Jagged bolts of lightning tore through the sky, illuminating the night with electric fire. Amidst this fury, I found myself suspended between two colossal bridges, their steel spans stretching out like the outstretched arms of benevolent giants.

These weren't just any bridges; they bore the unmistakable resemblance of New York's iconic structures, symbols of connection and unity that had been my refuge since childhood. In those early years, when the world seemed too harsh and overwhelming, these bridges offered solace, a place where I could escape and try to make sense of the chaos around me.

Now, in this dreamlike state, these bridges took on a deeper significance. They were no longer mere physical structures but metaphysical conduits between realms... the mundane and the transcendent, the earthly and the divine. Each span I crossed felt like a passage through the layers of my existence, moving from the concrete reality of my day-to-day life into the abstract realms of spiritual insight and awakening.

Gliding between these majestic structures, their grandeur struck me anew. Their steel cables and towering pylons seemed to reach out and touch the sky, creating a harmonious symphony of form and function. But beyond their physical presence, these bridges whispered secrets of the universe, their elaborate designs reflecting the interconnectedness of all things.

One bridge, sturdy and well-trodden, represented the paths I had taken in my life, the experiences that had shaped me, and the lessons I had learned. The other, more delicate and fragile, symbolized the paths yet to be explored, the untapped potential and dreams that lay just beyond my reach. Together, they formed a complete picture of my existence, bridging the gap between who I was and who I aspired to become.

Soaring between them, an overwhelming sense of liberation washed over me. The wind whipped through my hair, and an exhilarating rush of freedom coursed through my veins. It was as if the bridges were carrying me on an odyssey of the soul spanning the chasm between ignorance and enlightenment, between fear and love.

In this surreal moment, understanding struck me; these bridges also represented the connections we build in our lives... the relationships that span the gaps between our isolated selves and the broader fabric of humanity. Each bridge demonstrated how connection strengthens us, the ability to reach out and touch another soul, to share in life's path and find strength in unity. I remembered *Connection's* sacred prayer, understanding now how it had prepared me for this moment. *Faith's* embrace of mystery merged with *Protection's* watchful care, while *Companionship's* support illuminated the path between spans. *Love*, ever-present, danced between dimensions, her essence weaving through every note of this cosmic symphony.

Pondering these connections, a hauntingly beautiful melody began to unfurl, its notes echoing through the corridors of my mind. It was more than just a song; it was a symphony of the soul, a celestial chorus that stirred the deepest recesses of my being. With each note, I felt a stirring within me, as if my very essence were being called forth to dance to the rhythm of the universe.

The storm's thunderous applause and the crackling of lightning seemed to harmonize with this divine melody, creating a mosaic of sound that wove through the dimensions of reality. It was as if the very heartbeat of the universe reverberated within me, aligning my soul with the eternal rhythm that underpinned all creation.

As the melody swelled, a single line emerged, clear and resonant: *"In the arms of courage, love finds its way."* This lyric stirred something deep within me, evoking memories of a love so transformative it transcended the ordinary. I was reminded of Superman and Lois Lane, not as mere characters in a story, but as symbols of the eternal struggle between duty and desire, between the extraordinary and the mundane.

In their story, I saw mirrored reflections of my path. Superman, with his unwavering commitment to truth and justice, stood as a beacon of hope in a world often overshadowed by darkness. Yet beneath his invulnerable exterior lay the heart of a man torn between the demands of his duty and the longing of his soul. His love for Lois, a mortal woman bound by the limitations of humanity, symbolized the eternal struggle to find balance in a world layered with contradictions.

Their love defied the boundaries of time and space, reaching across dimensions to touch existence's fundamental truth. It was a poignant reminder that the path of love and duty is never simple, that it requires us to navigate the delicate balance between our responsibilities and our passions.

As I immersed myself in their narrative, I felt a deep sense of connection to the universal themes of love, sacrifice, and redemption that define the human experience. Their story mirrored the timeless tales of love and heroism that have shaped human consciousness for millennia, echoing the myths of gods and mortals, of star-crossed lovers and heroic quests.

In that moment, I understood that true heroism lies not in physical strength or superhuman abilities but in the capacity to love deeply and selflessly. It embodied the enduring power of love to inspire and transform, to bridge the chasms of time and space, and to unite us in a shared path of growth and discovery.

As the melody reached its crescendo, I found myself back in the cabana, the storm outside beginning to wane. The glass barrier before me seemed like a gateway to deeper understanding and self-discovery. Through its rain-streaked surface, I could still see the ghostly outlines of the bridges.

The echoes of the soul's melody still whispered in my mind, promises of courage and triumph, of the strength to overcome even the greatest trials. Yet, amidst the tranquility, a new undercurrent began to stir... an anticipation tinged with apprehension. The shadows I had yet to face loomed larger, their presence a silent reminder of the inner battles still to be fought.

As raindrops tapped their gentle rhythm, I knew the next steps would demand more than courage and resilience; they would require a confrontation with the deepest parts of my being. The road ahead was shadowed by phantoms of my deepest fears, yet with the memory of the bridges and the echoes of the melody guiding me, I stepped toward my next transformation. The threshold before me shimmered, inviting me into the unknown where new bridges would be built and new melodies would be heard.

The melodies that had guided me began to change, their earthbound harmonies transforming into something higher, more celestial. I felt myself being drawn upward, beyond the bridges I had crossed, beyond even the shadows that awaited me. Something was calling me to rise above the very foundations of my understanding, to view my journey from a perspective I had never before imagined.

# Lesson #17: Unveiling Courage

*"Courage is not the absence of fear, but the determination to press on despite it."*

---

As the final echoes of the soul's melody faded, the steady rain outside my cabana became a different kind of music: a rhythmic lullaby whose gentle patter belied nature's lingering power. The bridges of understanding I'd crossed now seemed distant as turmoil rose within. Yet, beneath the surface calm, the path had brought me face-to-face with many truths, and as the external fury subsided, inner chaos began to brew.

I felt a palpable tension in the air, a subtle shift in the dream's atmosphere that signaled the approach of a deeper, more daunting challenge. It was as if the universe, having guided me through the realms of love, hope, and faith, was now preparing me to face the darker recesses of my being.

The room around me began to shift and warp, its familiar contours giving way to strange and unsettling configurations. Darkness lurked in every corner, twisting and contorting into grotesque shapes mocking my sense of reality. Compartments appeared where none had been before, their purpose shrouded in mystery.

The bathroom light flickered incessantly, casting eerie shapes that danced across the walls. What had started as a quest for self-discovery now felt like a descent into the depths of nightmare. Fear gripped me tightly, its icy fingers tracing patterns of dread upon my skin.

Amid this chaos, I searched desperately for Bailey, my faithful companion, hoping for a shred of solace amid the chaos. As I called out for her, my voice seemed to echo into the void, swallowed up by the howling darkness. Bailey was more than just a dog; she was a spiritual companion, a guardian in the guise of a loyal pet. Her absence left me feeling untethered.

Just as despair threatened to overwhelm me, a faint whimper pierced the darkness. That small sound became my lifeline, and with renewed determination, I pressed on, following it through the maze of darkness. Each step felt like an eternity, the darkness pressing in on all sides, but I refused to surrender to fear.

As the storm began to subside, I found myself standing before a door, a threshold between the nightmare of the past and the promise of the future. With trembling hands, I pushed it open, stepping into the light of a new day.

But even as relief washed over me, a new challenge emerged. Looming in the darkness was a leopard head, its eyes gleaming with an otherworldly intensity. This wasn't just a symbol; it was a manifestation of the trials buried deep within my psyche.

The leopard's presence transported me back to the ancient lands of Mexico, where the Mayan civilization once thrived. In Mayan cosmology, the leopard was often depicted as a guardian of the underworld, a fierce protector of the realms beyond the veil of the living. Its presence served as a reminder of the unseen forces that shape our reality, lurking just beyond the edges of our perception.

Standing frozen under the leopard's unyielding gaze, memories surged forth, unbidden and relentless. I was forced to confront the echo of past relationships, the moments of love given freely but rejected, the sting of societal scorn burning anew. Each scorned love was a wound that had never truly healed.

The leopard became a warden of this personal hell, a guardian of my hidden shadows. Its form seemed to morph, twisting into the faces of those I had loved and lost. Their eyes stared back at me, filled with silent accusation. My heart ached with unsaid words festering within and actions I could never take back.

During this intense confrontation, the revelation came: courage wasn't merely about facing external threats. It was about confronting the heart of my being, looking into the heart of my vulnerabilities and fears. The leopard wasn't just a tormentor; it was a challenge, a call to arms.

With a surge of defiance, I faced the leopard head-on, my eyes locking with its predatory gaze. *Love's* initial teachings of unconditional acceptance merged with *Protection's* fierce guardianship, while *Companionship's* steady presence reminded me I never faced my fears alone. Even in this confrontation, I felt *Faith's* embrace of mystery strengthening my resolve. A primal scream tore from my throat, a desperate cry for release from the chains of my past. The echo of my voice reverberated through the dreamscape, a battle cry against the fear that had long held me captive.

Standing my ground, the leopard's gaze seemed to soften, its menacing presence receding slightly. I understood then that courage is not the absence of fear, but the determination to press on despite it. Each trembling step forward was an act of bravery, proof of the strength I never knew I possessed.

The dream began to shift once more, the oppressive darkness giving way to a faint, graceful light. The menacing shapes that had loomed so large now seemed to waver, their power diminished in the face of my newfound resolve. I had confronted the leopard and, in doing so, had confronted the deepest parts of myself.

As dawn's first light pierced the horizon, I stood on the precipice of a new beginning. This strength, I realized, was a mirror reflecting my own inner strength and resilience. It was a confrontation not with an enemy, but with myself... a challenge to rise above the shadows of doubt and step boldly into my illuminated potential.

The vision of the leopard head lingered, both challenge and teacher. It stood as testament to the depths I had explored and the strength I had found. As I stepped into the light, I knew that this unveiled courage would guide me through whatever trials lay ahead. The journey to love and enlightenment stretched before me, my heart ready to face its deepest truths.

As I embraced this newfound courage, I felt another presence stirring in the dawn light, something both ancient and intimately familiar. The strength I had discovered wasn't meant just for facing challenges; it was preparing me to open my heart to something even more profound. The universe was calling me to experience a love that transcended time itself, an eternal embrace that would transform everything I understood about connection and belonging.

# Lesson #18: Eternal Embrace

*"Even in times of loss and disconnection, remember that love is never truly lost."*

---

My newfound courage still pulsing within, I stepped through the threshold. The blinding daylight of the previous moment seemed to evaporate, pulling me back into the comforting embrace of darkness. The transition was abrupt, throwing me off balance as if the ground beneath my feet had suddenly given way. I found myself ensnared in a mire of disorientation and uncertainty, navigating the confusion within my mind, desperately seeking a ray of understanding amidst the whirlwind of my emotions.

It was in this vulnerable state that I felt a gentle presence beside me, a whisper of warmth and light amidst the shadows. "Where have you been?" I found myself asking, the words escaping my lips before I could fully comprehend their meaning. There, in the quiet solitude of my mind, I sensed the soft touch of *Love's* presence.

"I have been here all along, my dear," came the reply, a melody of love and reassurance flowing through the landscape of my consciousness. Her voice carried a timeless wisdom, each word carrying an infinite depth that touched the core of my being. "You have been traveling through existence, crossing dimensions of time and space to receive the messages that await you."

As her words washed over me, a sense of clarity began to emerge from the fog of uncertainty. The idea that I was moving through different realms of existence to gather wisdom was both awe-inspiring and humbling. It suggested a purpose far beyond the mundane, a quest for deeper truths and understanding.

*Love's* presence seemed to intensify, her resonance radiating with a deep knowing. "The gateways you've crossed, like the window in this very cabana, are not mere gateways," she said, her voice echoing with timeless knowledge. "They are reflections of your own expanding consciousness, mirroring the growth and transformation you undergo with each passing moment."

Her words struck a chord within me, illuminating the true nature of my awakening. These gateways were not just external doorways but manifestations of my internal evolution. Each boundary crossed marked a shedding of old beliefs, a break free from the limitations that had once confined me.

"As you navigate these realms," *Love* continued, "remember that the challenges you face are not obstacles, but opportunities for transformative growth and self-discovery. Embrace the lessons that await you, for they hold the key to unlocking the fullness of your potential."

In the midst of this kaleidoscope of experiences, memories began to surface like shimmering reflections in a pool of moonlit water. I found myself transported back to a moment in time, standing in the midst of a gentle rain, arms outstretched to embrace the downpour with a sense of freedom and joy. *Love* stood before me, her presence a radiant beacon of light in the darkness, her essence intermingling with mine in a dance of divine connection.

As nature's tears fell around us, the world faded away, leaving only us in a cocoon of pure bliss. The soothing rhythm of droplets mingled with the warmth of our bodies, and in her arms, love and peace washed over me, transcending the physical world. All worries dissolved, leaving only serenity in their wake.

In that moment, clarity struck... love was not merely an emotion but a force of nature, a power that could transcend time and space, binding spirits together in a dance of eternal connection. *Love's* presence was like a fire that burned brightly in the darkness, lighting my way forward and guiding me towards a deeper understanding of myself and my place in the universe.

Standing there, entwined in each other's embrace, nature's tears continued to fall, their gentle caress a reminder of the beauty and power of the present moment. *Love's* eyes sparkled with light radiating from within, reflecting her boundless spirit and the boundless potential of our connection. Her energy poured into me, filling the empty spaces within me with a warmth and light that I had never known before.

We danced together in the precipitation, our bodies moving in perfect harmony to the silent music of our hearts. The mist soaked through our clothes, but it didn't matter; we were lost in the moment, our spirits intertwined in a dance of pure, unadulterated joy. Each step, each movement, demonstrated our connection, a celebration of the love that bound us together in an unbreakable bond.

Dashing onto the sidewalk, droplets fell impatiently from the overhanging trees. The pristine beauty of the damp leaves drew us further away from the music of a distant club. The club's repetitive melodies faded into the distilled silence hanging between us in the brisk nightfall.

Water droplets caressed her face and I snatched her hand, trying to pull her down the winding roads and to the car. But *Love* was caught in the balance of the light from the streetlights above and the lingering sensation that grew more passionate from within her. Every fiber of her being longed for a night like this: to be exquisitely free. She yearned to be woken from the frail imbalances within her, which startled her once she was finally immersed in the delicious taste of the drizzle cascading down her now moistened lips.

The grin on her face became more sincere and apparent. Anyone walking down the street could feel her positive radiance bursting forth from deep within her. Her fingers linked firmly between mine as we started to frolic in the downpour. Our thoughts melted away, and in those innocent, exquisite moments, our once youthful existence sprung forth. Our hair was drenched, but we were not drowning in the mediocre day-to-day troubles that wore us down once before.

Our spirits soared in a state of infinite youthfulness. *Love* released her hand from mine and darted into the gutter; she took a running jump and collided with a puddle, which sent water every which way. Though she was totally engulfed in water from head to toe now, her sweet demeanor spoke volumes that words could not express. In those childlike moments, we knew we were far from toy trucks and dolls, for this was far from what our imaginations could develop regardless of how mature we were. This was paradise and this was innerstanding, for we both knew we took a storm and created a playground of our own.

As *Love* leaped back onto the sidewalk and we trotted down the street giggling, something was brewing inside me. In that moment, with the water rolling down our skin and the stars disappearing behind the clouds, her face glowed far brighter than the moon ever could. The picturesque scene evaporated into a quaint, pleasant moment between our two bodies. In one swift motion, I swung *Love* around and swiveled her body so the two of us were swaying peacefully in the torrential downpour.

Her head rested on my chest as if it was always a part of me, and we succumbed to the rhythmic motions of the Earth's gravitational pull. Our hearts synced and beat in time to the harmonious whispers that vibrated from somewhere within my chest: I was genuinely happy.

As the outline of our dancing bodies became etched in the stars, I gazed into her eyes and said the first thing that came to mind, *"Love ..."*

She stopped me mid-sentence, wrapped her arm around mine, and whispered, "I know, I know."

*Love* leaned into my chest, and I held her tight. The street was getting dark as the skies opened up. It reminded me never to give up and to do what I could to find answers in life. The answer was dancing with me beneath heaven's cascade. Our movements quickly turned into a soft, elongated kiss that whispered passion into our beings. *Love* wanted me to protect her from herself, yet this was the only way I knew how: to let her go to the spaces where she was conflicted in order to comprehend her deepest wishes.

The rain shattered upon the sidewalk, and I sensed people drifting by, but nothing affected us: this was our moment in time. Rain, pedestrians, our respective pasts... nothing would stop us. Sometimes when you try to find the right words to tell a specific story, it taints the purity or meaning of those moments. It was like in that Luke Combs song, when he says:

*"I know just trying to write a song*
*I run the risk that I could get your perfect wrong*
*And well, I guess what I'm trying to say*
*Is there ain't words been made could shoulder*
*so much weight"*

It was a moment that was not supposed to happen, though as I tried pulling away from her to respect her space, she kept wrapping her fingers around my neck and drawing me closer.

In that transcendent embrace, I felt a deep sense of connection to something greater than myself. Water fell around us, a silent witness to our boundless love, showing how being in the present moment transforms us. It was a memory that seemed to echo through time, a reminder of the beauty and power of love in its purest form.

Just as quickly as I had been transported to this heavenly memory, I felt myself being drawn back to the present, the moisture and the warmth of *Love's* embrace fading into the mists of my subconscious. My heart pounded in my chest, filled with a longing for the love and connection that had just slipped through my fingers.

As the vision faded, the memory of dancing with *Love* in nature's embrace etched itself into my eternal memory. The transformation was far from complete. More truths awaited uncovering, more layers to peel back, more depths to explore. The water, once a gentle caress, had transformed into a soothing backdrop to the evolving landscape of my dream. The sky, previously dark and foreboding, began to brighten with a soft, luminescent glow, as if the universe itself was preparing a canvas for a new beginning.

Each droplet that cascaded from the heavens carried a message of renewal, a promise of rebirth and transformation. The storm, once an indication of chaos, had become a purifying force, washing away the residue of doubt and fear, leaving in its wake a profound clarity and complete peace.

*Love* enveloped me once more. Her presence carried echoes of every guide who had shaped my journey: *Purification's* cleansing waters, *Wisdom's* ancient knowing, *Connection's* sacred prayer. Even *Protection's* cautious nature seemed to soften in *Love's* eternal light, while *Companionship's* radiance illuminated the depth of our bond. "This moment, our dance beneath heaven's tears," she whispered, her voice melding with the gentle patter of raindrops, "it was real in the deepest sense. A reflection of the love and light within you. Even in times of loss and disconnection, remember that love is never truly lost. It transcends realms, binding us together in ways that defy the constraints of the physical world."

Her words penetrated the essence of my being, stirring an awakening understanding. The love we shared, the eternal connection that had illuminated the darkest corners of my being, existed beyond time and space. It embodied love's enduring power in its purest form.

The weight of the world lifted from my shoulders, replaced by a lightness that permeated my entire being. The storm outside began to subside, its fury tempered by the soothing touch of *Love's* presence. And as the clouds parted to reveal the first rays of dawn, hope blossomed within me, like the first blush of morning breaking through the darkness.

In that moment of tranquility, a piece of paper materialized in my hand, inscribed with the cryptic sequence "882024". The numbers shimmered with hidden meaning, a celestial whisper that sent tremors through my essence.

"I know what this date means to me," I breathed, my voice quivering with emotion. "It's the date I hoped for... the wedding date I dreamed of..." The words faltered, hanging in the air like fragile echoes. A silent tear traced down my cheek, carrying with it years of buried dreams and cherished hopes.

*Love's* eyes met mine, filled with infinite compassion. In that gaze, I saw understanding that transcended words, a knowledge that encompassed all I had experienced.

"I love you," she whispered, her voice a warm embrace. The words repeated, a soothing mantra that echoed through the chambers of my heart. "I love you," she repeated, ten times in a row, each utterance a gentle caress to my spirit. "I know you know what that means."

Her declaration enveloped me in a cocoon of warmth and understanding. It honored not only those I'd lost, but also my own way forward and the connections that defied the boundaries of time and space.

"I see your soul," *Love* continued, her voice rich with empathy, "your heart, your passion, your love, and your intentions. This road can often feel overwhelming, but remember, it's all part of your evolution. I am here for you, always. Even when it seems like I am walking away, I am never truly gone. Our connection transcends the physical realm, existing on higher planes and across dimensions. We are linked by our higher selves, our energies intertwined."

Absorbing her words, questions swirled in my mind: Was any of this real? Or was I caught in a loop, destined to relive these moments in an eternal loop? The confusion was overwhelming, yet there was an odd comfort in the chaos, a familiarity in the disarray of my experiences.

But it was the memory of *Love* that held me captive. In every timeline, in every story, I returned to that sacred moment, where the veil between reality and dreams blurred into insignificance. It was that perfect moment I returned to over and over again, the moment that felt like "home."

In the midst of chaos and confusion, it was that simple act of surrendering to love that anchored me to something greater than myself, something eternal and unchanging. As I danced with *Love* beneath nature's silver veil, I felt a sense of peace settle over me, a knowing that I was exactly where I was meant to be... in that moment, in that place, in her arms.

As this realization washed over me, the world began to shift and shimmer. With a heart full of love and memories of our eternal dance, I stepped toward the next phase of my transformational awakening. The eternal dance with *Love* had opened channels within me I hadn't known existed. As the memory of our sacred moment settled in my heart, I felt a new frequency of understanding beginning to emerge. The universe wasn't finished with its teachings; it was preparing to guide me in ways even more profound than love's eternal embrace. The dance was transforming into something deeper... a divine dialogue that would show me how the cosmos itself could serve as teacher and guide.

# Lesson #19: Sacred Time

*"Time, as you understand it,
is an illusion created by the mind
to make sense of existence."*

---

As my spiritual awakening continued, reality shimmered and transformed, revealing a space that seemed to exist beyond temporal boundaries. Iridescent crystals adorned the walls, gleaming with an otherworldly light that cast dancing shadows across the floor. The air hummed with ancient wisdom, each molecule vibrating with the secrets of the universe.

As my eyes adjusted to the ethereal glow, I noticed complex symbols etched into the iridescent surfaces. Spirals, circles, and elaborate geometric patterns seemed to shift and change as I gazed upon them. Reality itself flowed here.

*Wisdom* and *Healing* materialized before me, their forms shimmering with an inner radiance that matched the ethereal glow. *Wisdom's* eyes, deep pools of universal understanding, met mine with a gaze that seemed to pierce through the veils of illusion.

"Welcome to the Chamber of Sacred Time," she intoned, her voice reverberating through the radiant structure. "Here, the linear constraints of past, present, and future dissolve, revealing the eternal now."

Before I could respond, a wave of disorientation washed over me. The room began to spin, and I felt as if forces pulled me in a thousand directions at once. Panic rose in my chest, threatening to overwhelm me. I remembered *Healing's* gentle touch and *Connection's* grounding presence. The mechanical precision I'd witnessed in time's factory now transformed into fluid grace, while *Faith's* acceptance of mystery helped me surrender to this temporal dance.

"Lie on your side," *Wisdom* instructed, her voice a steady anchor in the chaos. "You only have an hour to go. Enjoy it."

Confusion clouded my mind. An hour? How could mortal measurements hold meaning in this place existing beyond their grasp? As if sensing my bewilderment, *Healing* stepped forward, his presence a tranquil oasis to my frayed nerves.

"These dimensional gateways have a way of distorting one's perception," he explained gently. "Lying on your side will help you ground yourself, to find stability amidst the flux of temporal energies."

Trusting their guidance, I lowered myself to the floor, pressing my side against the cool, smooth surface. As I did so, a remarkable transformation began. The chaotic swirl of energies around me started to coalesce into discernible patterns. Streams of light flowed through the space, each one representing a different timeline, a different possibility.

"What you're witnessing," *Wisdom* said, her voice filled with reverence, "is the true nature of time. Not a linear progression, but a complex matrix of interconnected moments, all existing simultaneously."

Watching, transfixed, I began to see glimpses of my life within these streams of light. Experiences of joy, sorrow, triumph, and defeat all played out before me, not as a sequence, but as a constellation of experiences.

"But how can this be?" I asked, my voice barely above a whisper. "How can all of these moments exist at once?"

*Healing* knelt beside me, his eyes filled with compassion. "Time, as you understand it, is an illusion created by the mind to make sense of existence. In truth, all moments are eternally present. It is our consciousness that moves through them, creating the illusion of past, present, and future."

Absorbing this extraordinary revelation, a surge of emotions welled up within me. Frustration, anger, and confusion bubbled to the surface, demanding acknowledgment. In a surge of raw impulse, I grabbed a nearby object—a small crystal—and hurled it across the space.

The crystal's arc through the air seemed to defy the laws of physics, its trajectory bending and twisting as it passed through different dimensional streams. As it clattered to the floor, a realization struck me with the force of a lightning bolt.

"Why did I do that?" I asked, more to myself than to my guides.

*Wisdom's* voice was gentle yet probing. "Perhaps the better question is, what were you trying to release? What truth were you attempting to set free?"

Her words sank deep within me, unlocking a floodgate of understanding. The crystal represented all the "whys" that had haunted me throughout my journey: why did I feel so lost? Why did the answers I sought always seem just out of reach?

"Anger, frustration, confusion... these are not enemies to be vanquished," *Healing* said, placing a comforting hand on my shoulder. "They are signposts, guiding you towards the parts of yourself that need attention and healing."

Grappling with this insight, the streams of light intensified. I felt a sense of urgency building within me, as if I was on the verge of a crucial revelation.

"Here in this sacred realm reality is both infinite and finite," *Wisdom* explained. "You have been granted this opportunity to glimpse the true nature of existence. What will you do with this knowledge?"

The question hung in the air, heavy with potential. I surrendered to the swirling shimmering energies as they washed over me. In this surrender, I felt a fundamental shift within my being. The boundaries of my self began to dissolve, and I experienced a glimpse of unity with all of existence.

When I opened my eyes, the realm had transformed once more. The streams of light had coalesced into a single, radiant point at the center of the room... a gateway to the next phase of my journey.

"Remember," *Wisdom* said as I rose to my feet, both transformed and humbled by the experience, "each moment holds divine significance. It is a gift, an opportunity to align with the eternal flow of existence. How will you honor this gift?"

The answer resonated within my heart: by embracing life fully, by recognizing the sacred in the ordinary, by dancing with both light and shadow. Though the words remained unspoken, understanding passed between us.

Stepping forward, I carried a newfound understanding of my place within eternity's dance. With measured breath and silent gratitude, I surrendered to the threshold's embrace, ready to uncover the deeper truths that awaited. Yet as I crossed this sacred boundary, the divine guidance that had illuminated my path began to reveal something else: the shadows that had been hiding in the light. For true guidance, I sensed, would require me to face not just the radiance of spirit, but the darkness that dwelled within.

# Lesson #20: Confronting Shadows

*"Within our deepest fears lies the potential for our greatest light."*

---

As I stepped from the Chamber of Sacred Time, the boundaries of reality dissolved once more. I plunged through layers of consciousness, each temporal strand unraveling into darkness. The threshold's power swirled around me, a kaleidoscope of memories and emotions, each one a brushstroke in the eternal canvas of my being. Time and space bent and warped, reality shifting like sand beneath my feet.

I was suspended in a vast, nebulous expanse. Inky tendrils of darkness writhed and coiled around me, each one a manifestation of my deepest fears and unspoken truths. The air was thick with simmering, unresolved emotions, making each breath a labor of will.

"You can fly," a distant voice whispered, its words cutting through the oppressive silence like a blade of light. The voice was familiar yet ethereal, as if spoken by a part of myself I had long forgotten.

The words surged through my being, and I felt an outpouring of power coursing through my veins. My body tingled with newfound vitality, and I felt weightless, untethered from the burdens that had long anchored me to the ground of my limitations.

Another whisper reached me, softer yet filled with ancient wisdom. "Keep breathing. Your breath is like wings; it can carry you, sustain you, expand the moment, allow you to soar high, and help you get grounded. Your breath is everything."

Instinctively, I drew in the air slowly, feeling it expand within my chest. As I exhaled, I imagined releasing the remnants of doubt and fear that had clung to me for so long. With each breath, the darkness around me seemed to shift and part, revealing glimpses of hidden truths and forgotten memories.

The darkness began to take shape, coalescing into dark manifestations that I recognized as aspects of myself... moments of pain and regret, but also instances of boundless love and joy. These weren't just embodiments of my fears; they were markers of my path, reflections of the struggles and triumphs that had shaped me.

*Wisdom's* voice echoed through the void, "Confront your shadows. Embrace them, understand them, and let them guide you towards the light."

With renewed determination, I stepped forward into the depths of this void. Each guide's teaching strengthened me for this moment: *Love's* unconditional acceptance, *Protection's* fierce strength, *Companionship's* unwavering light, and *Faith's* embrace of the unknown. Each step was an inward descent, leading to the core of my being. The way forward was treacherous, lined with the jagged edges of past traumas and the quicksand of self-doubt. But I knew this confrontation was necessary.

Venturing deeper, the darkness began to take form. I saw the ghost of my younger self, eyes wide with the pain of betrayal. I saw the specter of missed opportunities, of roads not taken. And there, looming larger than the rest, I saw the dark mass of my greatest fear.. a cancerous growth that threatened to consume not just my body, but my very essence.

The cancer manifestation radiated malevolent presence, its voice a grating whisper that sent chills down my spine. "Foolish mortal," it hissed. "You think you can defeat me? I am your deepest fears, your darkest doubts. I have grown strong on your pain."

I stood my ground, drawing strength from my experiences. "You do not own me," I retorted, voice trembling yet resolute. "I am more than my fears, more than my pain. I am the sum of all my experiences, and I will not be defined by you."

The space around us became a battlefield of light and shadow. With each memory unearthed, I gathered strength from the depths of my being, drawing upon the courage that lay dormant within me.

"I am not weak," I shouted, my voice echoing through my entire being. "I am a survivor, forged in fires of adversity. You are but a shadow, and shadows cannot exist without light."

With a primal scream that shattered the walls of my limitations, I unleashed years of pent-up emotion. With a surge of primal fury, I seized the cancer entity, wrenching it from its grip on my psyche.

"Do you even have *cancer*?!" I screamed into the void, the question tearing from my lips with a force born of desperation and defiance.

As I hurled the *cancer* through the window of the cabana, I cast aside the shackles of fear and doubt that had held me captive. In that pivotal transformation, I confronted not only the physical manifestation of the disease but also the emotional and inner wounds it represented.

In the aftermath of this fierce struggle, a tranquil stillness enveloped me, whispering of renewal and transformation. The turbulent waves of fear and doubt that had once threatened to engulf me now receded, leaving behind a serene clarity that settled deep within me.

I stood at the precipice of a new beginning, my essence forged in the crucible of adversity and strengthened by the fires of resilience. With each breath, the unwavering light of my inner truth illuminated the path before me, guiding me forward with steadfast purpose and unwavering resolve.

As the darkness began to dissolve around me, giving way to the soft glow of a new dawn, I knew that I was ready to face whatever lay ahead. Armed with the wisdom gained from confronting my fears and the courage born from overcoming my darkest doubts, I stepped forward into the next phase of my awakening.

The act of confronting darkness had transformed me, revealing that within our deepest fears lies the potential for our greatest light. As I moved on, I carried with me the deep understanding that true healing comes not from avoiding our darkness, but from embracing it as an integral part of our whole selves. This acceptance of my whole being, both light and shadow, awakened something deeper within me, a wellspring of power I had always possessed but never fully recognized. The dawn that dispelled the darkness wasn't just external; it was rising from within, illuminating the vast reservoirs of strength that had always been there, waiting to be discovered.

The intensity of each lesson grew, like waves building force before breaking upon the shore. What had begun as gentle spiritual awakening now demanded deeper courage and commitment. The guides' teachings were no longer just wisdom to contemplate but truths that had to be lived, breathed, and embodied. Every challenge now carried higher stakes, every revelation demanded more complete integration.

# Lesson #21: Evolving Through Change

*"Embrace this metamorphosis,
for in change lies the seed of renewal."*

---

As the echoes of my battle against the *cancer* entity faded, I found myself suspended in a void of iridescent mist. The exhaustion of victory seeped into every fiber of my being, a bone-deep weariness that transcended the physical. In this sacred stillness, I felt the universe itself take a deep breath, as if pausing to acknowledge the fundamental shift that had occurred within me.

The mist began to swirl and coalesce, forming a shimmering cocoon around me. I felt a gentle pressure from all sides, as if reality itself was embracing me. A voice, resonating with ancient truths, whispered through the cocoon:

"Embrace this metamorphosis, for in change lies the seed of renewal."

As the words washed over me, I felt a tingling sensation spread throughout my body. It was as if every cell was awakening, remembering a dance as old as time itself. Wisdom flooded through me; this cocoon was not a prison, but a chrysalis... a sacred space of becoming.

Images began to flicker across the inner surface of the cocoon, each one a reflection of a past self. *Protection's* cautious strength merged with *Companionship's* unwavering support, showing me how to embrace transformation while staying grounded in my truth. *Faith's* acceptance of mystery helped me understand that change itself was a form of divine guidance.

I saw myself as a child, eyes wide with wonder; as a teenager, burning with the fire of rebellion; as an adult, weighed down by responsibilities and expectations. Each image shimmered and dissolved, leaving behind a residue of wisdom and experience. The voice spoke again, its tone gentle yet insistent: "You are not these individual moments, but the sum of all experiences. Each version of you is a stepping stone on the path of evolution."

As I watched, the residue from each dissolved image began to form complex geometries, coalescing into a shimmering constellation of my life experiences.

But unlike a static image, this celestial mosaic was alive, endlessly shifting and rearranging itself.

"Life is not a linear path," the voice continued, "but a spiral of perpetual growth. Each turn brings you back to familiar themes, but with new perspectives and deeper understanding."

I understood then that the challenges I had faced, the shadows I had confronted, were not punishments or obstacles, but opportunities for growth. Each difficulty had been a crucible, burning away the dross to reveal the gold within.

The cocoon began to vibrate with a rhythm that matched my heartbeat. With each pulse, I felt layers of old beliefs, outdated patterns, and limiting thoughts peeling away. It was uncomfortable, at times even painful, but underneath the discomfort was a sense of lightness and liberation.

"Change is not always easy," the voice soothed, "but it is always worthwhile. Embrace the discomfort, for it is the sign of old structures breaking down to make way for the new."

The process continued, and I began to see flashes of potential futures. Unlike the past images, these were not clear or defined. They were possibilities, shimmering with latent potential, waiting to be called into existence by my choices and actions.

"The future's not set in stone," the voice explained. "It is a field of infinite possibilities, shaped by the essence of your thoughts, emotions, and actions. Choose wisely, for each choice is a brush stroke on the canvas of your becoming."

With this understanding, I felt a complete shift in my perspective. No longer was I a victim of circumstance, but a co-creator of my reality. This realization's force surged through me, igniting a fire of determination in my core.

The cocoon began to dissolve, its shimmering substance merging with my being. As it did, I felt my consciousness expanding, extending beyond the boundaries of my physical form. I touched the infinite, feeling the connection between all things: past, present, and future.

In this expanded state, I saw that change was not something to be feared or resisted, but life's fundamental nature. It was through change that the universe expressed its creativity, its endless potential for renewal and growth.

As I slowly returned to a more focused state of awareness, I found myself standing in a lush garden teeming with life. Each plant, each flower, was in a different stage of growth, from tiny seedling to full bloom to graceful decay. Yet all were part of the same beautiful, ever-changing landscape.

*Wisdom* and *Healing* materialized beside me, their presence a comforting reminder of the guidance that had sustained me throughout my awakening.

"You have undergone a great metamorphosis," *Wisdom* said, her eyes twinkling with pride and affection. "But remember, evolution is not a destination, but an endless process."

*Healing* nodded in agreement. "Each change brings with it new challenges and opportunities. Embrace them all, for they are the stepping stones to your highest self."

Their words settled into my heart, and I felt a renewed sense of purpose and clarity. The future held no certainties, but I no longer needed it to. I understood now that true evolution came from embracing the unknown, from dancing with uncertainty and in trusting the path ahead.

Summoning my courage, I took a step forward, ready to embrace whatever changes lay ahead. The garden around me shimmered with approval, each leaf and petal illustrating the beauty of perpetual growth.

As I walked, I carried a deep understanding that I embodied change itself. Each breath was an opportunity to grow, to learn, to become more fully myself. With a heart full of gratitude and a spirit open to infinite possibilities, I stepped into the unknown. The garden's wisdom had shown me that growth encompasses all aspects of being. As I ventured forward, I felt this understanding deepen; true transformation wasn't just about spiritual evolution, but about healing on every level. Body, mind, and spirit began to align in ways I had never before experienced, calling me toward a more complete understanding of wholeness.

# Lesson #22: Journey Within

*"Forgive yourself, for you are human, flawed yet infinitely capable of love and redemption."*

---

As the echoes of my last transformation faded, I found myself standing at the edge of a vast, shimmering lake. The water's surface was like liquid starlight, reflecting an endless celestial expanse above. Each ripple seemed to whisper ancient secrets, inviting me to delve deeper into the mysteries of existence.

A gentle breeze caressed my face, carrying with it the scent of jasmine and sage. As I inhaled deeply, I felt a stirring deep inside me, as if something long dormant was awakening.

"Welcome, seeker," a melodious voice called out, seeming to emanate from both everywhere and nowhere at once.

I turned to see a figure emerging from the mist that clung to the lake's edge. As she approached, I gasped in recognition. It was Morena, the character I had created in my "Beautiful Souls" series, now standing before me in radiant, ethereal form.

"Morena?" I whispered, my voice a mixture of awe and disbelief. "How is this possible? I created you in my stories, but you seem so... real."

She smiled, her eyes twinkling with ageless knowing. "I am as real as the thoughts and emotions that gave me life," she replied. "I am the voice of your soul, a manifestation of your inner being. Though you penned me into existence in your stories, I have always been a part of you."

As her words settled over me, the landscape began to shift. The lake's surface rippled and parted, revealing a spiral staircase descending into its depths. Each step seemed to glow from within, beating in time with my heart.

"Come," Morena beckoned, extending her hand. "It's time for you to journey within."

Steadying myself, I placed my hand in hers and we began our descent. With each step, I felt layers of my external self peeling away... fears, doubts, old beliefs... all dissolving into the shimmering waters around us.

As we descended, the water closed over our heads, yet I found I could breathe easily. We were enveloped in a cocoon of luminescent water, each bubble a memory, a thought, an experience from my life.

"Why have you been absent for so long?" I asked, watching fragments of my past swirl around us.

Morena's eyes softened with compassion. "I have always been with you, even in the moments of deepest solitude. There are times when one must navigate their path alone, discovering its strength and resilience. But now, you are ready to integrate all aspects of yourself... past, present, and potential futures."

We reached the bottom of the staircase, finding ourselves in a vast chamber. The walls were lined with mirrors, each reflecting a different version of myself. Some I recognized while others seemed foreign, yet all were undeniably me.

"What you see before you," Morena explained, "is the multifaceted nature of your being. Each reflection represents a different aspect of your being, a different lesson learned, a different path explored."

I approached one of the mirrors, touching its surface gently. As I did, I was flooded with emotions and memories associated with that particular aspect of myself. Joy, pain, triumph, defeat... all washed over me in a tidal wave of experience.

"But why do I keep returning to these struggles, these inner battles?" I asked, overwhelmed by the intensity of the emotions.

Morena gestured around the chamber, and suddenly, the reflections began to move. They swirled together, forming a spiraling pattern that I recognized as an unalome, the Buddhist symbol representing the path to enlightenment.

"Your soul is on a quest for deeper understanding and awakening," Morena explained. "Each struggle, each battle, is not just a test but an opportunity for growth. The unalome shows us that life's path is not linear, but a spiral. We revisit themes and challenges, but each time from a higher perspective, with greater wisdom."

As I watched, the unalome began to illuminate, each spiral representing a cycle of my life. I could see the patterns of my experiences, the lessons learned, the wisdom gained.

"The turmoil at the beginning of the unalome," Morena continued, "represents the chaos and confusion of life. But notice how it gradually straightens, symbolizing the attainment of clarity and wisdom. Your struggles are not setbacks, but essential parts of your growth."

The chamber darkened, and I felt a familiar fear creeping in. "But what about the darkness, the inner shadows?" I asked, my voice trembling.

Morena placed a comforting hand on my shoulder. "The darkness is but a canvas for your inner light to shine brighter," she said softly. "Embrace it, acknowledge it, but do not let it consume you. Remember your battle with the *cancer* shadow... you reclaimed your power. You have the inner strength to overcome any obstacle."

As she spoke, stars began to appear in the darkness, like stars being born. Each one represented a moment of triumph, a lesson learned, a shadow integrated.

"Listen to your heart," Morena urged. "Your intuition will guide you. The shadows that cause you pain and hold you back are the ones you need to release. Those that have taught you resilience, strength, and empathy are the ones you integrate."

I closed my eyes, sensing the dance of light and shadow inside me. When I opened them again, I saw that the chamber had transformed once more. We were standing in a garden of impossible beauty, where radiant flowers bloomed alongside darkness that danced like living things.

"This is the garden of your soul," Morena said, her voice filled with wonder. "By acknowledging the shadows and embracing the light, you become whole. The darkness is not something to fear, but a powerful teacher on your path of self-discovery and awakening."

Taking in the beauty of this inner landscape, I felt a deep sense of peace wash over me. "I apologize for all I did wrong in life," I whispered, "and for the times I didn't listen to my inner voice."

Morena's eyes shimmered with infinite compassion. "Apologize, yes, but also forgive," she replied. "Forgive yourself, for you are human, flawed yet infinitely capable of love and redemption. Each act of self-forgiveness is a step towards healing, a way to reclaim your power and align with your true essence."

As her words settled into my heart, the garden began to bathe in golden radiance. I felt the gentle balance *Protection* had taught me, knowing when to shield myself and when to open up. *Companionship's* encouragement illuminated the path ahead, while *Faith's* embrace of the unknown gave me courage to explore these inner depths. Each flower, each shadow, each spirit seemed to whisper, "You are loved. You are worthy. You are whole."

Morena's form began to shimmer, merging with the radiance around us. "Remember," her voice echoed, "this inner exploration is ongoing. What you've experienced here is not an end, but a beginning. The real work of integration begins when you awaken. There will be ups and downs, but every moment is an opportunity to deepen your understanding of yourself and the universe."

As her presence faded, I felt an overwhelming sense of gratitude. The journey within had revealed the vast, beautiful complexity of my inner world, where every experience wove into the sacred web of existence.

Preparing to step through the next portal, I knew the inner garden would always remain a sacred space of guidance and renewal. With a heart full of love for all existence, I embraced the next step on my path of eternal discovery. As I approached this new threshold, the inner garden began to transform. The flowers and trees shifted into the shapes of great figures from the past, their wisdom calling to me across the centuries. My journey within had prepared me to receive something profound: the eternal wisdom of those who had walked the path of leadership and transformation before me. The universe was beckoning me to see how personal truth aligns with historical legacy.

# Lesson #23: Past Illuminations

*"The lessons you seek already pulse within your heart, waiting not to be discovered, but to be awakened."*

---

As Morena's sweet voice fades into the recesses of my consciousness, her parting words linger like wisps of mist in the morning air. "I didn't forget about the ending of Book 4 in *Beautiful Souls*." Her compassionate reminder sparks a cascade of memories, drawing my attention to the hidden corners of my being where my secret political aspirations lie dormant.

The first glimmers of daylight cast a golden hue upon the landscape of my dreams, illuminating the winding path that stretched out before me. I realized it is not merely dawn's awakening, but rather another portal beckoning me to explore my inner mysteries. With each step, I felt the pulse of anticipation coursing through my veins, propelling me forward into the unknown.

Abraham Lincoln rose before me, history incarnate, his solemn gaze piercing through time with unwavering resolve. Together we descended the winding hillside, each step drawing us closer to the White House's majestic edifice. More than a building, it stood as democracy's heartbeat, its presence casting long shadows across both landscape and legacy. The air was thick with history's echoes, each step echoing with the footsteps of those who have walked this path before me.

The cobblestone streets of the capital stretched out before us, lined with ornate lamp posts that cast a warm glow upon the scene. The distant sound of horse-drawn carriages echoed through the crisp morning air, mingling with the murmurs of bustling activity that filled the city streets. Time pulled me backward, surrounded by the sights and sounds of a bygone era, yet there was a familiarity in the air that resonated through my entire being.

Approaching the hallowed halls of The White House, a sense of wonder overtook me, as if I have been here before in another lifetime. The imposing facade of the presidential residence loomed large against the backdrop of the city skyline, its columns standing as sentinels of power and authority.

As we approached the imposing gates, Lincoln's eyes met mine, substantial wells of wisdom and sorrow. "Welcome, traveler," he said, his voice echoing the solemnity of history. "You have journeyed far to stand in the presence of greatness."

I was struck by the contrast between his humble warmth and the gravity of his position. "Mr. Lincoln," I began tentatively, "I am honored to stand before you. Your leadership and vision have inspired generations, but I cannot help but wonder about the struggles you faced along the way."

A flicker of recognition passed across Lincoln's face. "Ah, yes," he nods solemnly, "the burdens of leadership are heavy indeed. But it is through adversity that we find our strength, and through darkness that we discover the light within."

Captivated by his words, I was drawn in by the wisdom that emanated from his very being. "Tell me, traveler," Lincoln's gaze held mine, "what brings you to this moment? What lessons do you seek to learn on your path?"

"I seek understanding," I replied earnestly, "and guidance on the path that lies ahead. The road is troubled with uncertainty, yet I am determined to navigate it with courage and conviction."

Lincoln smiled, a gracious curve of his lips. "Fear not, traveler... your path is sacred, your journey is destined, your courage is assured. The lessons you seek already pulse within your heart, waiting not to be discovered, but to be awakened. In trusting yourself, you unlock wisdom; in facing your fears, you discover strength; in walking your path, you inspire others."

His words kindled my spirit, awakening a fire of determination and purpose. Seized by curiosity, I found myself drawn to him once more.

"Mr. Lincoln," I began, "what role does divine love play in healing a divided nation? You faced immense challenges, yet spoke of unity and compassion. Can these principles still guide us today?"

Lincoln's gaze softened, reflecting meaningful wisdom and compassion. "Divine love," he mused, "is the bedrock upon which all great civilizations are built. It is the force that binds us together as a community, transcending barriers of race, religion, and ideology. In my time, I sought to embody this principle in my leadership, recognizing that true greatness lies not in the pursuit of power, but in service to others."

He paused, contemplating my question's depths. "As for its relevance in today's world," he continued,

"I believe divine love remains as essential as ever. In an age marked by division and discord, it is easy to lose sight of our shared humanity, to succumb to the temptations of fear and mistrust. But it is precisely in these moments of darkness that divine love shines brightest, illuminating the path to reconciliation and healing."

Absorbing his words with reverence and awe, I inquired, "And what of leadership? Do you believe that I have the heart and soul to be the leader that you were, to bridge a divided world together?"

Lincoln's smile was benevolent yet resolute. "Leadership," he replied, "is not defined by titles or accolades, but by the courage to stand up for what is right, even in the face of adversity. It is not the absence of fear, but the ability to overcome it with grace and dignity. As for you, my friend," he added, his eyes alight with recognition, "I sense within you an abundant wellspring of strength and compassion, qualities that are essential to the task that lies ahead. Trust in yourself, and you will find the courage to lead with integrity and conviction."

His words reverberated within me, awakening a sense of purpose and clarity. With a heart overflowing with gratitude, I bowed my head in reverence before Abraham Lincoln. "Thank you,"

I whispered softly. "Thank you for your guidance, your wisdom, and your unwavering belief in humanity's boundless potential. You have touched me in ways I cannot fully express, and I am eternally grateful for this precious opportunity to stand in the shadow of greatness."

As we parted ways, I carried with me the echoes of our conversation, a reminder that even in the darkest of times, there is hope. For in the depths of adversity, we discover the true measure of our strength and resilience, and the boundless potential of the human spirit.

As I bid farewell to Lincoln, the echoes of his wisdom fading into the vast expanse of history, I found myself drawn further into the currents of time itself. The road stretched out before me, winding its way through the corridors of history, carrying me further back into the annals of the past. With each passing moment, the currents drew me further into history, towards a destination unknown yet filled with promise and possibility.

The Historic Triangle of Williamsburg, Jamestown, and Yorktown materializes before me, history's pulse beating through its cobblestone streets and colonial architecture. The Virginia countryside stretched out in timeless beauty, its whispers beckoning me to uncover stories buried beneath centuries of time.

Walking Williamsburg's historic streets, I pause before the Governor's Palace. Its grand exterior towered as a testament to colonial power, each stone holding memories of those who walked these halls generations ago, their triumphs and struggles woven into the very fabric of the building.

At Jamestown, the James River lapped against the shore where English settlers first stepped onto this continent four centuries past. Saltwater mingled with history on the breeze, and amid the scattered ruins, I sensed the fierce determination of those who carved life from wilderness.

Yorktown's hallowed ground echoed with the echoes of destiny... the decisive battleground where a nation's fate balanced on the edge of a sword. Phantom cannon fire rolled across the landscape, and the air itself seemed to remember the cries of those who sacrificed everything for freedom and independence.

The Historic Triangle pulsed like a living heartbeat of America's birth, each cobblestone a memory, each building a chapter, each whispered echo a testament to our shared journey. *Protection's* wisdom reminded me to approach these historical truths with discernment, while *Love* showed me how to carry their lessons forward. *Faith's* understanding of divine timing helped me see how past and present could merge in sacred purpose. Time dissolved here, where yesterday's dreams crystallize into tomorrow's possibilities, where individual stories merge into humanity's grand narrative.

Strolling through the historic streets of Williamsburg, I was enveloped in the timeless beauty of the colonial architecture, each building a silent witness to the trials and triumphs of a bygone era. The air was thick with the scent of history, the cobblestone streets echoing with the whispers of centuries past. In the distance, I spotted the steeple of The Bruton Parish Episcopal Church where Thomas Jefferson and George Washington were known to gather for passionate discussions on matters of state and philosophy.

Approaching the quaint tavern where the two founding fathers converse, I was struck by the contrast between their towering historical significance and the simple humanity of their bearing. They sat at a rough-hewn wooden table, immersed in conversation, their voices carrying on the air like the gentle rustle of leaves in the wind.

"Independence," Washington declared, his voice carrying the weight of revolution. "Not merely a right but a birthright, not simply a principle but the foundation upon which our nation rises. To secure it demands our vigilance; to preserve it requires our sacrifice; to honor it shapes our legacy for generations yet unborn."

Beside him, Jefferson nodded in agreement, his expression thoughtful as he considered his friend's words. "And yet," he counters, "true freedom extends beyond mere political independence. It is the freedom to think, to believe, to worship as one sees fit. Religion, in its purest form, should be a matter of personal conscience, not state imposition."

Their conversation revealed the depth of their intellect and the breadth of their vision, each man offering insights that reflected the timeless truths of human determination. As they spoke, I found myself drawn into the orbit of their wisdom, caught up in the ebb and flow of their ideas.

"And what of faith?" Jefferson mused, his gaze turning inward. "It is the bedrock of civilization, the quest for meaning in an uncertain world. To believe in something greater than oneself is to acknowledge the divine spark that resides within us all."

Washington nodded, his eyes alight with quiet intensity. "Indeed, it is the guiding light through our darkest times, illuminating the path to a better tomorrow."

As their conversation unfolds, a sense of awe and reverence filled me for these two extraordinary men, whose words and deeds have shaped the course of history. Before them, I was reminded how ideas shape destiny, the transformative potential of a single conversation to change the world. And as I listened to their words, I was inspired to carry forth their legacy, to champion the ideals of freedom, justice, and equality for all.

Lingering on the outskirts of their conversation, I was suddenly aware of their gaze turning towards me, as if sensing me. There was a moment of silent acknowledgment, a shared understanding that transcended the boundaries of time and space. Then, to my astonishment, Washington gestured for me to join them at the table, his expression welcoming and open.

"Come, friend," he said, his voice warm with hospitality. "Join us in our discourse. We value the perspectives of all who seek to engage in the pursuit of truth and enlightenment."

I approached hesitantly, my heart pounding with a mixture of awe and disbelief. Here I was, face to face with two of the most revered figures in American history, invited to share in their conversation as an equal. It is a moment that defies comprehension, a convergence of past and present that filled me with a sense of wonder and humility.

Taking a seat at the table, I found myself enveloped in their aura, their legacy surrounding me like an invisible force. Jefferson regarded me with a knowing smile, his eyes twinkling with curiosity.

"You seem surprised, my dear friend," he observed, his voice tinged with amusement. "But rest assured, you are among kindred spirits here. We welcome all who seek knowledge and understanding, regardless of station or circumstance."

I nodded, struggling to find the words to express my gratitude for this unexpected opportunity. "I am honored to be in your presence," I replied, my voice trembling with emotion. "To converse with two such esteemed figures is a privilege beyond measure."

Washington inclined his head in acknowledgment, his gaze unwavering as he regards me with a mixture of respect and interest. "And what brings you to our table, my friend?" he asked, his tone kind yet inquisitive. "Is there a question you seek to answer, a truth you wish to uncover?"

I hesitated, unsure of where to begin. How can I articulate the immense significance of this moment, my soul's yearning for profound understanding and connection? Gathering my thoughts, I paused to center myself, and spoke from the heart.

"I come seeking wisdom," I said, my voice steady despite the uproar of emotions swirling within me. "I seek to understand the nature of faith, the power of love, and the eternal quest for truth. In a world consumed by strife and division, I long for guidance, for insight into the mysteries of existence."

As I spoke, I felt a sense of liberation wash over me, a release of the doubts and uncertainties that have plagued me for so long. Before these great men, I was freed from my own insecurities, free to explore my inner sanctuary and the boundless expanse of the universe.

Jefferson nodded thoughtfully, his expression contemplative as he considered my words. "The quest for truth is a noble endeavor," he said, his voice soft yet resolute. "It is a path that transcends time and space, leading us ever closer to the heart of existence itself."

Washington's eyes gleamed with a fierce determination, his voice echoing centuries of struggle and sacrifice. "And the pursuit of justice and liberty is the noblest of causes," he declared, his words echoing with the fervor of revolution. "It is a battle worth fighting, a dream worth pursuing, no matter the cost."

In that moment, I was filled with a sense of purpose and clarity, a renewed commitment to the ideals that have guided humanity throughout the ages. In the company of these extraordinary men, I was reminded of how faith sustains us, the resilience of human determination, and the enduring legacy of those who dare to dream of a better world.

As the conversation unfolded, I found myself sharing my concerns about the state of the world in which I come from, a world still plagued by division and discord. I spoke of the political polarization that grips my nation, the entrenched animosities that threaten to tear us apart at the seams. I express my fears for the future, wondering aloud if the ideals of justice and liberty that Washington and Jefferson championed are enough to heal the wounds of our fractured society.

Washington listened intently, his brow furrowed with concern as he absorbed my words. "The two-party system is indeed a double-edged sword," he mused, his voice tinged with regret. "It was meant to safeguard against tyranny and oppression, but it has become a breeding ground for partisan strife and ideological conflict. We warned against such divisions, but alas, our warnings went unheeded."

Jefferson nodded in agreement, his expression somber as he reflected on the consequences of political polarization. "A house divided against itself cannot stand," he quoted, his voice heavy with sorrow. "It is a truth as old as time, yet one that we seem destined to repeat. But take heart, my friend, for the ideals of justice and liberty are not lost. They endure, as steadfast as the stars themselves, waiting to guide us back to the path of righteousness."

Their words penetrated my soul, stirring a sense of hope and determination in the face of adversity. I was reminded that the struggles we face are not insurmountable, that the ability to create change lay within each and every one of us. But I could not help but wonder whether they were disappointed in what we have become, if they looked upon the world with the same sense of disillusionment that I sometimes felt.

Washington's eyes softened with compassion, his gaze unwavering as he met mine. "We are not disappointed, my friend," he assured me, his voice filled with warmth and understanding. "We understand the complexities of the human condition, the ebb and flow of progress and regress. It is the nature of existence, a constant dance between light and shadow, hope and despair."

Jefferson nodded in agreement, his features alight with a quiet resolve. "We must not dwell on the mistakes of the past," he urged, his voice warm yet firm. "Instead, our focus belongs on the future, on the infinite possibilities that lie before us. Love, compassion, and understanding are the keys to unlocking the doors of change. It is up to each and every one of us to embrace these ideals, to be the change that we wish to see in the world."

As their words sank in, I felt a sense of clarity wash over me, a renewed sense of purpose and determination to carry on the legacy of those who came before me. With these great men, I was reminded that the capacity for change lies within each and every one of us, waiting to be awakened by our inner truth's radiance. And as the conversation drew to a close and we bid farewell to one another, I was filled with an overwhelming sense of gratitude for this rare and precious moment in time, a moment that will forever shape my path forward.

Standing on the cobblestone streets, overwhelmed by the momentous encounters with Lincoln, Washington, and Jefferson, I felt a sense of awe and reverence wash over me. It's as if history itself permeated the air mingling with the echoes of their voices and the whispers of centuries past.

Before I could fully process the whirlwind of emotions swirling within me, I felt a friendly tap on my shoulder. Turning around, I was met with the familiar gaze of Thomas Jefferson, his expression thoughtful yet kind.

"I sense there are lingering questions on your mind, my friend," he began, his words imbued with hard-won wisdom. "Ask, and I shall do my best to provide insight."

I took a moment to gather my thoughts, my questions churning within me. Finally, I found the words to articulate the thoughts that had been swirling in my mind since our conversation began.

"Did you, like us, dream of a future where faith triumphs over fear?" I asked, my voice trembling with uncertainty. "Did you envision a world where religion is a matter of choice rather than coercion?"

Jefferson nodded thoughtfully, his eyes reflecting the flickering light of the nearby tavern. "Indeed, my friend, we dared to dream of a world where the flame of liberty burns bright, illuminating the path to true enlightenment," he replied, his voice steady and sure. "We believed in the inherent goodness of humanity, in reason's ability, and in rationality to guide us towards a brighter tomorrow.

"But we also understood that the journey towards freedom is burdened with challenges and obstacles. We knew that the forces of fear and oppression would seek to extinguish the flame of liberty, to snuff out the light of reason and replace it with the darkness of tyranny.

"As for religion, we believed fervently in the principle of religious freedom, in the right of every individual to worship... or not worship... as they see fit. We understood that true freedom of conscience is essential to the preservation of liberty, and we fought tirelessly to protect that fundamental right.

"As for your final question," he concluded, his gaze piercing yet compassionate, "we cannot claim to know the future, nor can we predict the outcome of the trials and tribulations that lie ahead. But we can offer you this: have faith in the strength of human will, in love and compassion's ability to overcome even the darkest of times.

"As you continue forward, remember that you carry within you the legacy of those who came before you. Let their wisdom guide you, their courage inspire you, and their love sustain you. For in the end, it is truth and justice's brilliance that will illuminate the path to a better tomorrow."

With those final words of wisdom, Jefferson bid me farewell, his words lingering in the air like the faint echo of a distant memory. And as I watched him fade into the shadows of the night, I was filled with a renewed sense of purpose and determination to carry on the legacy of those who came before me, to shine as a source of hope and inspiration in a world desperately in need of both.

As I stepped through the portal, I found myself in Oyster Bay, New York. The setting sun bathed the historic town in a golden glow, and a familiar presence enveloped me. Before me stood the imposing figure of Theodore "Teddy" Roosevelt, his bearing both commanding and welcoming.

"Welcome," he said, his voice resonating with the strength of mountains, the wisdom of nature, and the fire of conviction. "Oyster Bay's spirit flows through your veins, just as it once flowed through mine."

I nodded, feeling an intense connection to the land. "Since my teenage years, I've been drawn here," I admitted. "It's as if there was a mystical purpose for my visits and eventual residence."

Roosevelt's eyes sparkled with understanding. "There is indeed a mystical energy here, a convergence of history and destiny. For me, Oyster Bay was more than a summer retreat; it was where I found solace and inspiration, blending the serenity of nature with the demands of governance."

As we walked, he pointed out significant sites: his home, now a museum, and his grave. "When you visited my resting place," he said, "I felt your presence, your reverence for the past, and your quest for understanding. Your connection to this place is intertwined with the legacy of leadership and vision."

I paused at his grave, the stone monument marking his enduring impact. "I've often stood here, questioning my own leadership capabilities,"

I confessed. "I've wondered how you made such a lasting impact on the world. Sometimes, I feel like too much time has passed for me to make the larger impact I desire."

Roosevelt turned to me, his expression compassionate yet firm. "Leadership isn't about comparing yourself to others or grand gestures alone. It's about recognizing your unique gifts and using them to create positive change. Your path is your own, and your impact is felt in ways you may never fully comprehend."

His words rang true, but doubt still lingered. "But what if those ripples aren't enough? What if I've missed my chance?"

"Every soul you touch carries your influence forward," he replied, his gaze steady. "Consider those you've inspired who've gone on to do phenomenal work globally. Your legacy lives on through them. The vision isn't just for the world as it is, but for what it can be. Hold on to that vision, let it guide your actions, and inspire others to see beyond the present moment."

"But how do I maintain that vision amidst challenges and doubts?" I asked.

Roosevelt's smile was gracious, his eyes filled with wisdom. "By staying true to your core values and trusting the path ahead. The way forward is rarely clear, but it's in uncertainty that we find our true strength. Each step you take, no matter how small, contributes to the greater elevation of life."

Our conversation evolved as we discussed his influences and connections to past presidents. Roosevelt spoke of Lincoln's resolve, Washington's leadership, and Jefferson's intellect. "The world was changing rapidly during my time," he reflected. "There were immense struggles, but I remained connected to my faith and vision for the country. It wasn't just about managing the present but envisioning the future we could create."

As our encounter drew to a close, I felt a deep sense of gratitude. "Thank you," I said, my voice filled with emotion. "For your guidance and for reminding me of the importance of every action."

Roosevelt placed a hand on my shoulder, his touch grounding. "Within you burns the eternal flame of leadership... not a power to command, but a gift to illuminate. Your strength lies not in shaping others' paths, but in lighting the way so they might find their own. Like stars guiding sailors home, your inner light beckons others toward their highest truth. Trust this sacred fire, nurture its holy purpose, and watch as it ignites the divine spark in every soul you touch."

The portal beckoned once more, and I stepped through, carrying Roosevelt's insights and the sacred significance of Oyster Bay with me. The encounter had reaffirmed my path and the legacy I was a part of, inspiring me to embrace the uncertainties and possibilities that lie ahead.

The portal shimmered, and time bent like light through crystal, revealing not just a stage, but a moment of destiny. There I stood, my future self, weathered by wisdom's storms yet strengthened by time's tempering. In this mirror of possibility, I glimpsed not just who I might become, but who I already was at my core. The realization sent a shiver down my spine... I was witnessing a possible future, a culmination of the potential that lies within me. The voices of Lincoln, Washington, Jefferson, and Roosevelt echoed in my mind, urging me to observe the opportunity and the potential that is there... not necessarily destined, but possible, as the divine current flows through my being.

I heard myself begin to speak, the words flowing with a confidence and passion that captivates the audience:

"Fellow citizens, we gather at history's crossroads... behind us lie the footprints of giants; before us stretch the pathways of possibility. Our modern world presents not merely challenges to overcome, but opportunities to seize. From our nation's first breath, three principles have guided us: liberty to pursue our dreams, justice to protect our rights, unity to strengthen our bonds.

In the spirit of George Washington, who led us through the birth of our republic with steadfast resolve, we pledge to lead with integrity and vision, to build a future where every voice is heard and every person is valued. We must recognize that true leadership is not about holding power, but about empowering others. It is about creating a society where everyone has the opportunity to thrive, where the potential of each individual is nurtured and celebrated.

Echoing Jefferson's principles we dedicate ourselves to the pursuit of knowledge and enlightenment, recognizing that education is the cornerstone of a thriving democracy. Our education system must be transformed to ignite the passion within each student, fostering creativity, critical thinking, and emotional intelligence. We must move beyond rote memorization and standardized tests, towards a model that values the unique gifts and talents of every child, preparing them beyond merely for jobs, but for a life fulfilled and passionately activated. This is a call to elevate our entire society by investing in our greatest resource... our children. It is through informed, engaged, and passionate citizens that we will overcome ignorance and fear, lighting the way to a brighter tomorrow.

Channeling the strength of Abraham Lincoln, we must strive to heal the divisions that threaten to tear us apart. In his words, 'A house divided against itself cannot stand.' We must find common ground, embracing our differences as sources of strength rather than discord. We must extend a hand of friendship to those we disagree with, forging bonds of understanding and cooperation. Our politics must embody love and compassion, recognizing that we are all in this together. We must work tirelessly to create a society where empathy and kindness are the norms, where the well-being of each individual is seen as essential to the well-being of all.

Drawing inspiration from Theodore Roosevelt, who championed progress and the common good, the time has come to champion reform and innovation in all aspects of our society. Roosevelt's legacy teaches us the importance of perseverance and the courage to challenge the status quo. He believed in people's ability to bring about change, and it is this belief that must drive us today. We must work to protect our natural resources, ensuring that the beauty and bounty of our planet are preserved for future generations. His commitment to conservation and the establishment of national parks reminds us that our environment is a precious inheritance. We honor his vision through fostering sustainable practices and promoting environmental stewardship. As we confront the existential threat of climate change, we must remember that our planet is more than a backdrop for our lives, but a living, breathing entity that sustains us all. Our environment demands more than promises; it commands action. Each forest preserved becomes our children's sanctuary, each river protected flows into our grandchildren's future, each species saved enriches humanity's legacy. This transcends mere policy; it embodies our sacred covenant with generations yet unborn. Our actions today will determine the future of our planet for generations to come. We owe it to our children and grandchildren to leave them a world that is not just habitable... but thriving.

In the realm of social justice, we stand ready to continue his fight against corruption and inequality, striving to build a society where fairness and opportunity are not privileges but rights afforded to all. Roosevelt's tenacity and unwavering dedication to public service serve as a beacon, urging us to pursue bold, transformative actions that uplift and empower every citizen.

In these times of uncertainty, always remember the words of another great leader, John F. Kennedy: "Ask not what your country can do for you, but what you can do for your country." Our greatest challenges are opportunities for us to rise, to contribute, and to make a difference. Together, we can address the pressing issues of our time—climate change, inequality, and global conflict—with courage and compassion. It is through our collective efforts that we will forge a path to a brighter future, one where every person has the opportunity to live a life of dignity and purpose.

Together, we carry forward with us the lessons of the past, honoring the sacrifices and achievements of those who came before us. We will be the generation that not only envisions a better world but takes decisive action to create it. Our destiny is not written in the stars; it is forged by our hands, our hearts, and our unwavering commitment to the ideals we hold dear.

Through education, we forge wisdom; through healthcare, we preserve life; through justice, we protect liberty. Each system interweaves with the others into a unified vision of continuous improvement that serves all people. In our schools and hospitals, in our courtrooms and communities, we cultivate not just intelligence, but emotional wisdom, the foundation of both personal transformation and collective evolution. It is through these efforts that we will create a society where every individual is empowered to be their best self, contributing to the greater good.

Standing together, we unite in purpose and are bound by the shared belief that we can and will make a difference. The time has come to embrace the journey ahead with hope, determination, and an unyielding faith in how love and unity transform our world.

Thank you. God Bless America, and God Bless us all."

As the future me finished the speech, the audience erupted into applause, and I felt a surge of pride and determination. As the vision dissolved like morning mist, its essence crystallized within my soul. Yesterday's giants have planted their wisdom in my heart; today's challenges have forged my spirit in their fire; tomorrow's possibilities dance like stars before my eyes. In this sacred moment between what was and what could be, I stood ready... not just to carry their legacy forward, but to transform it into something uniquely my own. For greatness dwells not in copying the past, but in crafting new pathways of light for future dreamers to follow.

As their parting wisdom settled in my heart, the spirits of Washington, Jefferson, Lincoln, and Roosevelt dissolved into the evening air, leaving behind only the subtle resonance of their presence. While their forms vanished into the night's embrace, I felt an awakened resolve stirring within— a commitment to honor their eternal legacy by embodying the virtues they represented. I would become a vessel for hope, faith, love, and inspiration in a world thirsting for these sacred qualities.

As the great leaders' presence dissipated into the eternal fabric of time, I felt their wisdom settling into my bones like foundational stones of something even more profound. Their legacy wasn't just about leadership and vision; it was about the deep, unwavering faith that had guided their every step. The universe was calling me to explore this dimension of spiritual truth, to understand how faith could transform not just nations, but souls.

# Lesson #24: Building Faith

*"For it is through love that faith finds its deepest expression."*

---

The dream realm transcended ordinary dimensions, universal energies weaving an infinite mosaic of possibilities. As I crossed the iridescent threshold, reality unfurled into its fundamental threads, each strand of existence performing its eternal dance. From this divine symphony emerged *Faith*, her presence a celestial flame illuminating the vastness of consciousness. Her essence carried echoes of those who had guided me: Lincoln's resolve, Washington's vision, Roosevelt's courage... yet she embodied something uniquely transcendent.

"Welcome back, seeker of truth," *Faith's* voice resonated through dimensions, her words a sacred harmony that bridged earthly understanding and divine wisdom. "Your path through presidential wisdom has prepared you for deeper mysteries. The courage shown before Lincoln, the vision shared with Washington, the strength gained from Roosevelt—these were but preludes to the sacred journey ahead."

"Unlike the presidential guides who showed you earthly wisdom transformed into legacy, I offer you glimpses of the infinite," *Faith* explained, her essence shimmering with universal understanding. "They taught you how to lead in the physical realm; I will show you how to transcend its limitations entirely."

As her words settled around me like stardust, the swirling energies coalesced into a celestial landscape. The mountain peak thrust us into celestial realms, where reality painted itself in divine patterns of light and shadow. Golden rays pierced the ethereal veils, imbuing each surface with sacred luminescence. This realm felt both ancient and timeless, infused with timeless wisdom and tranquility.

"Where are we?" I asked, my voice tinged with awe as I took in the breathtaking vista.

*Faith* smiled, her eyes reflecting the endless depths of the universe. "Where mortal understanding meets divine wisdom, your soul can shed its earthly limitations and embrace its spiritual heritage," she explained, her voice flowing with universal truth. "In this sacred space, you can confront the shadows within and embrace the light that guides you. This realm holds both answers and the strength for challenges ahead."

As we began to walk along a path that seemed to materialize beneath our feet, shimmering with each step, *Faith* continued, "True faith transcends mere belief. It is the sacred alchemy that transforms mortal understanding into divine knowing, doubt into certainty, fear into power.. It's about believing in your own strength and resilience, embracing the unknown with an open heart and a courageous spirit."

With each step, the path beneath us transformed. Sometimes it was smooth crystal, other times rough stone. Occasionally, it seemed we walked on nothing but air itself, faith literally keeping us aloft. This ever-changing path mirrored the journey of faith: unpredictable, challenging, yet always leading forward.

With each step through the sacred plane, I felt a shift within me, a dawning realization that faith was not about relinquishing control, but about embracing the journey with all its uncertainties and challenges. It was about finding strength in vulnerability and courage in the face of fear.

In a breath between moments, the path led us to the edge of a vast chasm. Swirling mists obscured the bottom, and the other side shimmered like a mirage in the distance. There was no bridge, no obvious way across.

"How do we continue?" I asked, my voice quavering as I peered into the misty depths.

*Faith's* smile was serene as she replied, "This is where faith awakens in its purest form. Step forward, trusting that the path will appear beneath your feet."

My soul reached into the infinite, each heartbeat echoing through the universal symphony. As my foot descended toward the void, a glowing stepping stone materialized beneath it. With each step forward, another stone appeared, forming a bridge of light across the chasm.

As we crossed, *Faith* spoke again, her voice blending with the soft hum of presence around us. "You are not defined by your struggles, but by how you rise above them. Each challenge is an opportunity for growth, a chance to discover the depths of your own strength and resilience."

Reaching the other side, we found ourselves in a lush garden, vibrant with colors shimmering with vitality. Here, flowers of faith bloomed... some fully open, others still tightly closed buds. I understood intuitively that each represented different aspects of faith: hope, trust, perseverance, courage.

"But what about the world we live in?" I asked, gesturing to a section of the garden where the plants seemed wilted and struggling. "It often seems so filled with chaos and division. How can love and faith prevail in such turbulent times?"

As if in response to my question, an effulgent rain began to fall, each droplet shimmering with rainbow hues. Where the drops touched the wilted plants, they began to revive, their colors brightening.

"Love is existence's foundation," *Faith* explained, catching a raindrop in her palm. It glowed softly, flickering like a tiny heartbeat. "It is the force that binds the universe together, weaving through the cosmos and connecting all beings. In times of darkness, it is love that shines brightest, illuminating the path forward."

Continuing through the garden, we came upon a reflection pool. Its surface was mirror-smooth, reflecting not just our images, but glimpses of other realms, other possibilities.

"Look closely," *Faith* urged. "What do you see?"

Peering into the depths, the water began to shimmer and glow. From its incandescent surface, two familiar spirits emerged: *Love* and *Hope*. Their presence filled the air with a sense of warmth and optimism. But they were not alone. Two additional celestial beings rose from the waters, their forms coalescing from pure light and essence.

The first emergence radiated with the brilliance of a thousand suns, her form shimmering with an ethereal radiance. This was *Light*, her very essence illuminating the garden around us, casting dancing shadows and revealing hidden beauties in every petal and leaf.

Beside *Light* stood another figure, her form constantly shifting and changing, like a tree cycling through seasons in mere moments. This was *Renewal*, embodying the eternal dance of death and rebirth, decay and growth, transitions and transformations.

*Love* stepped forward, her voice a celestial symphony of compassion. "*Faith* and I are intertwined," she explained. "For it is through love that faith finds its deepest expression. When you choose to love, even in the face of adversity, you are exercising the purest form of faith."

*Light* moved next, each step leaving a trail of luminescent radiance. Her voice rang like the harmonious vibration of crystal. "I am the clarity that faith brings," *Light* said, her words painting the air with shimmering hues. "When you embrace faith, you'll find that your path becomes illuminated, revealing truths that were once hidden in shadow."

*Hope's* voice whispered with the collective dreams of countless souls as she spoke. "I am the spark that keeps faith alive," she said, her eyes twinkling with the promise of better tomorrows. "Even in the darkest times, I whisper of better days to come, encouraging you to keep moving forward."

*Renewal* completed the circle, her form settling momentarily into that of an ancient, wise being. Her voice was like the rustle of emerging leaves in spring. "And I am the promise that faith fulfills," *Renewal* said, her eyes reflecting cycles of growth and transformation. "Through faith, you are constantly renewed, emerging stronger and wiser from every challenge."

As these spirits spoke, I saw images forming in the pool... a panorama of life's myriad experiences. Joy and sorrow, triumph and struggle, all interconnected in an elaborate eternal dance. It was as if I was witnessing the grand narrative of existence itself, each life a vital part of this universal symphony.

*Faith* gestured to the spirits and the visions in the pool. "This is how faith works," she explained, her voice blending with the gentle lapping of the water. "It connects you to existence's deepest truth, allowing you to see beyond immediate challenges to the greater purpose and beauty of life."

As the images faded and the spirits merged back into the shimmering waters, I felt a fundamental shift within me. The world's pain still clutched at my heart, but now it was balanced by an awakening sense of purpose and hope. The truth settled in my heart: while I may not be able to change the entire world yet, I could make a difference in my own life and in the lives of those around me.

*Faith* placed a hand on my shoulder, her touch warm and comforting. "Remember, you are never alone on this journey. The universe is always with you, supporting and guiding you. Trust in your path, and in your ability to navigate its twists and turns."

As our time in this realm drew to a close, I felt a renewed sense of faith coursing through me. Not a blind faith, but a conscious choice to trust in the journey and in my own resilience. With each step, I could feel myself growing stronger, more attuned to the light that guided me.

The garden began to fade, the dream realm shifting once more. I understood now why *Protection* had appeared when she did... to help me build the strength needed for this moment. *Hope's* eternal light had illuminated the path while *Companionship's* unwavering presence gave me courage to walk it. The steadfast support of my eternal companions had shown me that even in uncertainty, we never truly walk alone. But the lessons remained, etched into my heart and soul. I understood now that building faith was not about finding certainty in an uncertain world, but about finding the strength to embrace uncertainty with an open heart and a courageous spirit.

As the dream realm dissolved into stardust, *Faith's* essence resonated through dimensions: "Love illuminates even the darkest paths, connecting all souls in existence's grand mosaic. Your journey into faith transcends mere beginning; its transformative power already flows through your being, opening doorways to infinite possibilities."

The stardust began to coalesce into new patterns, forming symbols and signs that flowed with divine meaning. I realized that faith had opened not just my heart, but my eyes as well. The universe was speaking a language I was only beginning to understand, its messages written in the fabric of reality itself. Each spark of stardust became a letter in the cosmic alphabet, calling me to learn its sacred syntax.

# Lesson #25: Interpreting Signs

*"Interpreting signs is an art, a dance between your intuition and the universe's whispers."*

---

The dream landscape shifted, transforming into a lush, vibrant forest. Towering trees reached towards an endless sky, their leaves whispering timeless secrets in the mystic breeze. *Faith* stood beside me, her presence a comforting anchor in this ever-changing realm.

"Do you see them, dear one?" *Faith* asked, her voice a melodious harmony that blended seamlessly with the forest's symphony. "Each leaf, each shadow, each ray of light filtering through the canopy... they are all signs, messages from the universe guiding you on your journey."

I gazed around, truly seeing for the first time. The dappled sunlight wove intricate mandalas across the forest floor, each pattern pulsing with life's rhythm. A butterfly with wings of iridescent blue fluttered past, leaving a trail of shimmering essence in its wake.

"I see them," I whispered, awe filling my voice. "But how do I understand their meanings?"

*Faith* smiled, her eyes twinkling with primordial wisdom. "Interpreting signs is an art, a dance between your intuition and the universe's whispers. Trust your instincts, for they are the true interpreters of these celestial messages." *Hope's* light illuminated these divine symbols while *Protection's* discernment helped me distinguish true guidance from illusion. I remembered how *Faith* had taught me to embrace mystery, making the signs' deeper meanings accessible to my awakening spirit.

The forest's whispered wisdom gradually transformed, its leafy canopy dissolving into sea spray as reality shifted. Like the flowing stages of consciousness itself, the verdant realm yielded to azure horizons, each transition revealing new layers of universal truth. The ocean before us was a canvas of liquid sapphire, its surface shimmering with the promise of hidden depths and untold mysteries.

*Faith* gestured towards the water. "The ocean, like the universe, is full of signs. Its tides, its colors, the creatures within... all carry messages for those who learn to listen."

Standing at the water's edge, the sky began to darken. Storm clouds gathered on the horizon, a towering wall of deep purples and ominous greys. The air crackled with electricity, the promise of transformation hanging heavy in the atmosphere.

"The storm," *Faith* said, her voice calm amidst the growing tumult, "is itself a powerful sign. It represents change, challenge, and the opportunity for growth. Embrace it, for it is through weathering these storms that we truly learn to dance with the universe."

Lightning split the sky, illuminating the turbulent waters. In that brief, brilliant moment, I saw my reflection in the waves... not as I was, but as I could be. Stronger, wiser, more connected to the eternal dance of existence.

As the first drops of rain began to fall, *Faith* turned to me. "Now, tell me about a sign you've encountered. A dream, perhaps?"

I retreated into memory, recalling the vivid dream that had haunted me. "I dreamt of walking with a child," I began, my voice barely audible above the growing storm. "There was a flood, and the child lost his shoe in a sewer. I tried to retrieve it, and a stranger appeared with a fishing rod."

*Faith* listened intently, her expression serene despite the raging tempest around us. "Dreams are a powerful conduit for signs," she explained. "The child represents your inner self, curious and vulnerable. The flood symbolizes overwhelming emotions or challenges. The lost shoe signifies a feeling of unpreparedness, while the stranger with the fishing rod represents your own hidden strengths and resources."

As she spoke, I felt a shift in my understanding. The dream, once a puzzling sequence of events, now revealed itself as a map of my inner journey.

The storm reached its peak, rain lashing against us in sheets. Yet, I felt no fear. Instead, a sense of exhilaration filled me as I embraced the raw power of nature, understanding it as a reflection of my capacity for transformation.

The storm dissolved as quickly as it had manifested. The clouds parted, revealing a sky painted in hues of gold and pink, the air charged with renewed possibility.

The cleansing aura lingered as the seascape began its metamorphosis. Like ripples expanding through dimensions, the ocean's vastness contracted and transformed, its infinite blue fragmenting into the vibrant mosaic of the Mayan marketplace. Each transition showed how wisdom could take many forms, from nature's raw power to humanity's sacred traditions. Stalls laden with exotic fruits and intricate handicrafts lined our path, each item a potential sign waiting to be interpreted.

One stall in particular caught my eye. An assortment of jade jewelry glimmered in the soft light, each piece emanating an inner radiance. Drawn by an unseen force, I approached the stall and picked up a necklace adorned with a jade snake.

"Ah, jade," *Faith* murmured, her eyes alight with recognition. "A powerful sign indeed. The jade speaks in many tongues," *Faith* explained, her voice resonating with ancestral memory. "To the Mayans, it was more than mere stone; it was the bridge between physical and spiritual realms, a crystallized form of wisdom that transcends time. The snake carved within its surface represents not just transformation, but the spiral path of awakening itself; the same path you've walked through presidential wisdom and divine truth. Like the presidencies that shaped a nation's soul, this jade shaped the spiritual understanding of an entire civilization."

Holding the necklace, I felt a surge of power course through me. It was as if the jade was a conduit, connecting me to ancient wisdom and future possibilities.

"Remember," *Faith* said, her voice measured yet firm, "signs are everywhere, waiting to be recognized and understood. They are the universe's way of guiding you, supporting you, reminding you that you are never alone on this journey. Trust in your ability to interpret these signs, for in doing so, you open yourself to the infinite wisdom of the cosmos."

I clasped the jade necklace around my neck, feeling its cool weight against my skin. In that moment, I understood that every experience, every object, every fleeting thought could be a sign... a breadcrumb on the path to greater understanding and enlightenment.

Continuing our journey through the marketplace, I found myself seeing with new eyes. Each physical manifestation—the forest's dance, the ocean's pulse, the market's vibrancy—reflected a deeper truth: that the material world serves as a mirror for spiritual awakening.

Just as Lincoln had shown me how earthly leadership reflects divine guidance, and Roosevelt had demonstrated how natural strength embodies spiritual power, these signs revealed how physical reality channels universal wisdom.

The vibrant colors of woven textiles spoke of the interconnectedness of all things. The rhythmic beats of distant drums echoed the pulse of the universe. Even the play of light and shadow seemed to dance with hidden meaning.

*Faith* smiled, sensing my newfound awareness. "You're beginning to see, truly see," she said. "This is the gift of interpreting signs... it transforms the world into a living, breathing message of universal wisdom."

*Faith's* teachings wove together the threads of all who had come before: Lincoln's moral compass, Washington's visionary leadership, Roosevelt's connection to nature's power. Each sign we encountered carried echoes of these wisdom-keepers, showing how their earthly guidance pointed toward universal truths. Just as they had led a nation through temporal challenges, these signs now led me through spiritual dimensions.

With each step, I felt more attuned to the subtle language of the universe. The journey of interpreting signs had only just begun, but already I could feel its transformative power. It was a journey that promised not just knowledge, but a deep, abiding connection to the essence of existence itself.

Yet even as I attuned to the universe's language of signs and symbols, I sensed another level of communication emerging, one that required no interpretation at all. Beyond the signs, beyond the symbols, beyond even thought itself, a sacred silence beckoned. In this silence, I sensed, lay an even deeper truth waiting to be discovered.

# Lesson #26: Embracing Silence

*"In stillness, you hear your soul's whispers, the truths hidden beneath life's constant noise."*

---

The dream realm shifted, its kaleidoscopic energies coalescing into a vast, shadowy expanse. I found myself suspended in a space where darkness and light danced in an eternal ballet, each casting fleeting shapes that whispered of both uncertainty and possibility. The familiar presences of *Faith*, *Love*, *Wisdom*, and *Healing* were notably absent, leaving me alone in this liminal space between consciousness and the unknown.

Grappling with the tenuous threads of awareness, a voice emerged from the shadows, both familiar and mysterious. "None of this is real," it whispered, the words shimmering like starlight in the void. "I created this. I set this up for the lesson. It's all about love."

"Morena?" I called out, recognizing the voice that had guided me through so many transformative experiences.

"Yes, it's me," she replied, her presence materializing like mist in the moonlight. Morena appeared different this time, her form constantly shifting between shadow and radiance, embodying the very duality of existence. "Now, breathe deep. Sit still and just listen to what is going on internally."

I closed my eyes and breathed deep. The sacred stillness deepened as *Protection's* presence created a safe space for inner exploration, while *Love's* eternal warmth embraced my vulnerability. *Faith's* acceptance of the unknown merged with *Companionship's* steady support, guiding me deeper into this holy silence. As I exhaled, the swirling chaos around me began to settle, replaced by an infinite stillness that enveloped me like an eternal embrace. This divine emptiness was not void; it hummed with being's pure nature, a gentle hum that merged with the core of my existence.

"Embrace this mystic stillness," Morena's voice echoed, now emanating from within. "In this void, you will find the answers you seek."

As I sank into the depths, the contours of my inner world began to take shape. Shadows that had once loomed large now revealed themselves as aspects of my being calling for acknowledgment and integration. In this soundless sanctuary, I began to perceive the web of doubts and uncertainties, each thread a story waiting to be understood.

"Why do I feel such turmoil, such darkness within?" I asked, my voice barely a whisper in the vast stillness.

Morena's response came not as words, but as a series of vivid impressions. I saw myself as a child, grappling with feelings of inadequacy and longing for acceptance. I witnessed the roots of my doubts taking hold... the dread of solitude, of inadequacy, of not fulfilling my purpose before my time in this realm came to an end.

As each shadow surfaced, it manifested as a shadow being, dancing at the edges of my consciousness. But rather than threatening, these shadow selves now seemed to beckon.

"Observe these shadows," Morena's voice guided, gentle yet firm. "They are not here to harm you but to teach you. Each shadow holds a lesson, a truth that you need to understand."

In the quiet expanse of my mind, I allowed myself to truly embrace these shadows without pushing them away. The dread of being alone transformed into a call to cultivate a deeper connection with myself. The doubt of not being good enough became a reminder to embrace my inherent worth, independent of external validation.

Dwelling in this ethereal space, another layer of understanding unfolded. The uncertainty about accomplishing my purpose before transitioning revealed itself as a deeper existential question... a yearning to leave a meaningful impact on the world.

During this deep introspection, the stillness took on a tangible quality. It transformed from mere absence into a living, breathing entity... a celestial womb nurturing transformation. This void became a mirror, reflecting long-hidden truths, and a canvas for painting a new understanding of existence.

Embracing this timeless stillness, I felt a shift within me. The darkness that had once seemed threatening now became a fertile void, pregnant with possibilities. Each shadow, each uncertainty, became a star in the constellation of my being, forming patterns that told the story of my soul's journey.

Morena's presence enveloped me once more, her aura radiating approval and encouragement. "This sacred emptiness is your greatest teacher," she whispered, her words rippling through the starlit void. "In stillness, you hear your soul's whispers, the truths hidden beneath life's constant noise."

With this understanding, I felt a soul-deep connection to the universal journey of growth and healing. This inner sanctuary had shown that I wasn't alone in my struggles. Every soul faced similar challenges and held the power to transcend them.

This realization filled me with a sense of purpose and determination, knowing that my journey could inspire others to embrace their own inner sanctuary and confront their shadows with courage and compassion.

As the lesson drew to a close, I found myself standing at the threshold of a new beginning. The stillness had transformed from a void that once caused trepidation into a sanctuary of wisdom and growth. I understood now that embracing the void was not about finding answers, but about creating a space where truth could naturally emerge.

Morena's final words echoed through the vastness: "Remember, dear one, this inward journey never ends. Each moment of stillness offers renewal and discovery. Embrace this celestial void, for it cradles creation, births wisdom, and reveals your truest self."

With a heart full of gratitude and a spirit ignited by newfound understanding, I stepped forward into the next phase of my journey. The stillness, once my apprehension, had become my companion... a steadfast ally on the path to self-discovery and spiritual awakening.

The silence now began to pulse with new vibrancy. From its depths emerged a rhythm, subtle at first, then growing stronger... the heartbeat of transformation itself. The void that had taught me stillness was preparing me for something more: the sacred art of conscious change. As if responding to this awakening, the dreamscape began to shift, drawing me toward the next phase of my spiritual evolution.

# Lesson #27: Mastering Transformation

*"It is through the alchemy of experience that you transmute pain into wisdom, doubt into faith."*

---

The dreamscape shifted once more, and I found myself standing before a vast window in the tranquil cabana. Outside, a tempest raged, its fury a stark contrast to the serenity within. Raindrops cascaded down the glass, each one a glistening messenger from the heavens, carrying whispers of wisdom and transformation.

Watching the raindrops' descent, a deep realization washed over me. Each droplet was a metaphor for the moments of my journey, a perfect capsule of experience and growth. Some fell swiftly, their paths direct and unwavering, reminiscent of those moments of sudden clarity and insight that had illuminated my path. Others meandered, weaving serpentine trails as they made their way down, mirroring the complexities and challenges I had faced.

I pressed my hand against the cool glass, feeling the vibrations of the storm's fury. In that moment, I understood that the tempest outside was a reflection of my inner turmoil, the clash between my human doubts and spiritual aspirations. Yet, in the dance of the raindrops, I found a strange comfort, a reminder that even in chaos, there is beauty and purpose.

"*Faith*," I called out, seeking guidance during this revelation, "how do I hold on to these lessons? How do I carry these sacred lessons into the waking world?"

*Faith's* presence materialized beside me, her aura enveloping me in a cocoon of tranquility. "Observe the raindrops," she said, her voice serene yet firm. "Each one is unique, yet part of a greater whole. So too are your experiences. Every moment, every challenge, every triumph is a drop in the ocean of your transformation."

While contemplating her words, I noticed how some droplets merged, their paths converging into a single, stronger flow. "Those," *Faith* explained, "represent the moments of connection, where your journey intertwines with others. They are reminders that while your path is unique, you are never truly alone."

The rain continued its relentless descent, and I found myself mesmerized by the droplets lingering, clinging to the glass before finally succumbing to gravity. "And those?" I asked, my voice barely a whisper.

"Those are the moments of reflection," *Faith* replied, a knowing smile gracing her lips. "The pauses in your journey where you take stock, where you allow the lessons to sink in. They are crucial, for it is in these moments of stillness that true transformation takes root."

Responding to *Faith's* words, the scene before me began to shift. The window and the rain faded away, replaced by a misty clearing in a primordial forest. At its center, a ceremonial fire blazed, its flames reaching towards the star-studded sky. Around it stood *Wisdom* and *Healing*, their forms shimmering with an otherworldly radiance.

The air was thick with the scent of burning sage, and the rhythmic beating of unseen drums reverberated through the earth beneath my feet. Upon approaching the fire, I felt a pull, as if the very essence of my soul was responding to a primordial call.

*Wisdom* stepped forward, her eyes reflecting the dancing flames. "Welcome," she said, her voice shimmering with timeless power. "You stand at the threshold of transformation. Are you ready to embrace the fire within?"

I nodded, words failing me in the face of such primal force. *Healing* joined *Wisdom*, his presence exuding a sense of renewal and rebirth. "This fire," he explained, gesturing to the flames, "is a reflection of your own inner light. It can illuminate the shadows, to burn away the dross of doubt and fear."

Stepping closer to the fire, I felt its heat penetrate deep into my bones, igniting a spark of something primal and powerful within me. The flames seemed to whisper, their crackling voices speaking of ancient wisdom and untapped potential.

"To master transformation," *Wisdom* intoned, her words merging with the rhythm of the drums, "you must first embrace the cyclical nature of existence. Like the phoenix, you must be willing to burn away the old to make way for the new."

*Healing* nodded in agreement. "Each challenge you face, each fear you confront, is fuel for this fire. It is through the alchemy of experience that you transmute pain into wisdom, doubt into faith."

Their words washed over me, and I felt a shift within. The fire before me seemed to grow, its flames reaching higher, as if responding to my inner awakening. It became clear this ceremony served as both ritual and initiation, a rite of passage marking my commitment to the path of transformation.

"Step into the fire," *Wisdom* urged, her voice both a challenge and an invitation. "Let it burn away all that no longer serves you."

With quiet resolve, I stepped forward, allowing the flames to engulf me. But instead of pain, I felt a surge of vitality coursing through my veins. The fire was not consuming me; it was purifying my essence, burning away layers of fear, doubt, and limiting beliefs, revealing my numinous spirit beneath. Each guide's teaching culminated in this moment: from *Companionship's* unwavering light to *Protection's* fierce guardianship. *Faith's* embrace of mystery gave me courage to step into the flames, while *Love's* grounding presence helped me remain centered in transformation.

In the heart of the flame, I saw visions of my journey: the struggles, the triumphs, the moments of despair, and the flashes of enlightenment. Each experience was a brushstroke on the canvas of my transformation, blending together to create a vibrant masterpiece of my evolving spirit, my awakening soul-self.

The visions faded, and I found myself standing in the clearing once more, the fire now a gentle glow before me. *Wisdom* and *Healing* approached, their eyes shining with approval and encouragement.

"You have taken the first step," *Healing* said, placing a hand on my shoulder. "But remember, transformation is not a destination; it is a continuous journey."

*Wisdom* nodded, adding, "The fire of transformation now burns within you. Nurture it, feed it with your experiences, your challenges, your growth. Let it guide you through the darkest nights and the brightest days."

Their words settled into my heart, bringing a transcendent sense of peace and purpose. The journey of transformation was far from over, but I now had the tools, the wisdom, and the inner fire to navigate whatever lay ahead.

The dreamscape began to shift once more, the clearing fading into mist. But the warmth of the fire remained.

Standing on the threshold between worlds, poised to return to waking life, I carried with me the lessons of the raindrops and fire's teachings. Each experience, each challenge, each moment of growth was a drop in the boundless ocean of transformation, and within me burned an eternal flame, ready to light the way forward on this infinite journey of becoming.

Yet even as I embraced these teachings of transformation, I sensed a shift in the spiritual winds. The eternal flame within me flickered and danced, responding to an approaching tempest. The universe was calling me to put my transformation to the test... not just to change, but to transcend, to rise above the very storms that had once threatened to overwhelm me. As if in response to this realization, the dreamscape began to darken, preparing me for a challenge that would demand everything I had learned.

# Lesson #28: Rising Above

*"Embrace the stillness within,
and you will find the steadfast resolve that
lies at the core of your being."*

---

The dreamscape shifted once more, the serene aftermath of the transformation ceremony melting away like mist in the morning sun. In its place, looming shadows began to seep in from the edges of my consciousness, bringing with it a suffocating sense of dread. The transition was jarring, a stark reminder that even with newfound wisdom and resilience, the journey of self-discovery is never a straight path.

I found myself back in the dimly lit cabana, the air heavy with the promise of an impending storm. Outside, the wind howled, its mournful wail a reflection of the turmoil that began to churn within me. Lightning flashed, illuminating the room in brief, harsh bursts that cast grotesque shadows on the walls. Each crash of thunder that followed seemed to shake the foundation of my being.

The storm intensified, and so did the maelstrom of emotions within me. The confidence and clarity I had gained from previous lessons began to waver, like a candle flame in the wind. Doubt crept in, insidious and relentless, whispering dark thoughts that echoed louder than the storm outside.

"Was it all for nothing?" I whispered, my voice barely audible above the tempest. "Have I learned nothing at all?"

In response to my despair, *Wisdom* materialized before me, her presence a stark contrast to the chaos surrounding us. In her hands, she held a sodden bandana, its fabric heavy with unshed tears and unspoken fears.

"Here," she said, her voice calm amidst the storm. "Wrap this around your head."

With trembling hands, I took the bandana, its damp fabric cool against my feverish skin. As I wound it around my head, I felt a momentary sense of grounding, as if the weight of the cloth could somehow anchor me in the sea of uncertainty that threatened to overwhelm me.

But the respite was short-lived. While searching for meaning in the simple act, the room began to spin, reality warping and twisting like a reflection in a funhouse mirror. The walls seemed to close in, the air growing thick and suffocating. My heart pounded in my chest, its frantic rhythm matching the relentless drumming of the rain against the roof.

"Why is this happening?" I cried out, my voice cracking under the strain of my desperation. "What does it all mean? Am I losing my mind?"

The storm outside reached a fever pitch, mirroring the chaos within. I felt myself slipping, falling into an abyss of my own making. The shadows converged, threatening to swallow me whole.

Just as I thought all was lost, a new presence made itself known. It was subtle at first, a faint glimmer of light in the encompassing void. As it grew stronger, I recognized it as a familiar energy, one that I had longed for and missed deeply.

From the shadows emerged *Protection*, her form materializing like a spark of hope in the storm. Her return marked a profound evolution in our connection. No longer just a guardian, she embodied the integration of all I had learned: *Companionship's* optimism, *Faith's* trust, and *Love's* sacred bond. Together we had grown beyond our initial roles. *Protection's* presence was both grounding and electrifying, a paradox embodying the embodiment of courage and resilience.

*Protection* stood before me, her eyes pools of infinite depth that reflected both compassion and unwavering determination. There was a resolute presence about her, an aura of serenity pushing back against the encroaching void. Her beauty transcended the physical, emanating from a place of inner radiance and grace.

"*Protection*," I whispered, my voice trembling with a mixture of relief and awe. "How do you remain so calm, so strong in the face of such consuming shadows?"

Her gaze met mine, steady and reassuring. "Courage is not the absence of fear," she replied, her voice a soothing melody that calmed the turmoil of my troubled mind, "but the mastery of it. It's about standing firm amidst the chaos, finding your center, and drawing upon the wellspring of resilience within."

Her words sparked, I felt a shift within me, a subtle realignment of my inner landscape. The storm still raged, but within its fury, I began to sense the presence of a deeper, more enduring calm.

*Protection's* quiet resolve became a mirror, reflecting the potential for resilience that lay dormant within myself.

"But how do I find that strength?" I asked, desperation tinging my voice. "How do I master my fears and remain steadfast?"

*Protection* stepped closer, her presence both comforting and invigorating. "It begins with trust," she said softly. "Trust in yourself, in your own innate wisdom, and in the guidance of the forces that watch over you. Embrace the stillness within, and you will find the steadfast resolve that lies at the core of your being."

Her wisdom penetrated deep, and the tendrils of fear began to loosen their grip. The oppressive pressure of the bandana seemed to lessen, its dampness no longer suffocating but grounding. Understanding blossomed; like my fears, it could be a source of empowerment if I chose to see it that way.

With *Protection* by my side, I surrendered myself to sink deeper into the eye of the storm within me. It was a moment of surrender, a letting go of the need for external validation as I embraced the uncertainty of the unknown. In this state of spiritual stillness, I began to unravel the layers of my psyche, confronting the shadows that had held me captive for so long.

The dream deepened, and I felt a sense of transformation taking place. The boundaries between fear and courage, doubt and resolve began to blur. I understood that true resilience wasn't about being unafraid, but about finding the courage to face my fears head-on.

*Protection's* presence was a constant reminder of the fortitude that lay within, a guiding light that illuminated the path forward. Her unwavering support gave me the courage to face my deepest fears, to embrace the unknown with an open heart and a willing spirit.

Standing together at the threshold of the storm, *Protection's* hand reached out to grasp mine. "I don't know what this means," she murmured, her voice a gentle whisper that cut through the howling wind, "but I got you."

Her words were more than just comfort; they were a call to action, a reminder that even in the darkest of times, we hold sovereignty over our path. The storm presented both challenges and opportunities for growth and transformation.

Drawing on my courage, I stepped forward into the raging storm, *Protection's* presence a steady anchor by my side. The wind whipped around us, the rain lashing at our faces, but I felt a newfound vigor coursing through my veins. Each step was a declaration against the currents of fear and doubt.

The journey ahead held no guarantees, only the certainty of more challenges to face. But with *Protection's* wisdom resonating in my heart and the resolve I had discovered within myself, I was ready. In the heart of the tempest, I had found something more precious than mere survival; I had discovered my refusal to sink.

And so I moved forward, not just staying afloat but soaring through the storm's fury. Each challenge became a current lifting me higher, transforming what once threatened to drown me into the very force that helped me fly. The waters might rage, but I had become more than they could contain.

As this truth settled into my being, the tempest began to change. The very forces that had tested my strength now transformed into something extraordinary: each raindrop, each gust of wind, each rumble of thunder carrying a different note in the universe's grand symphony. In transcending the storm, I had discovered not just my own power, but my place in existence's eternal song.

# Lesson #29: Resonance

*"Sometimes, the most courageous act is to let the rain fall, to allow ourselves to be washed clean by life's experiences."*

---

The dreamscape shifted once more, the aftermath of the storm giving way to a new symphony of sensations. I found myself standing in the open, rain cascading down in gentle sheets, each droplet a note in nature's universal composition. The patter of rain against leaves and earth blended seamlessly with an ethereal melody floating from the air itself, creating a harmony that sang deep within my soul.

Standing there, drenched to the bone, I felt a fundamental shift in my perception. The rain, once a mere element of the storm, now revealed itself as a conductor of divine grace. Each droplet resonated with its own unique frequency that tuned into the deepest recesses of my being. *Companionship's* steady presence harmonized with *Protection's* fierce guardianship, while *Love* and *Faith's* eternal dance created a symphony of divine guidance. Together, they showed me how different spiritual forces could blend into perfect harmony. The cold touch of water against my skin contrasted with the warmth of the music within, creating a powerful juxtaposition that mirrored my internal journey.

Closing my eyes, I surrendered to the symphony around me. The pulsing rhythm of rain on the earth became the baseline, while the wind whistling through the trees added a haunting melody. Thunder rumbled in the distance, its resonant bass tones reverberating through my chest. And woven through it all was a familiar presence... the essence of *Love*, her radiance intertwining with the music of the storm.

While listening, I began to discern individual songs within the greater composition. Each melody carried with it a fragment of memory, a piece of my journey. I recognized the soulful strains of Luke Combs's country ballad, "Better Together," its lyrics capturing love's simple truths in everyday moments.

*"The way you say,*
*"I love you, too" is like rain on an old tin roof*
*And your hand fits right into mine like a needle in a groove*
*Some things just go better together*
*and probably always will*
*Like a cup of coffee and a sunrise,*

*Sunday drives and time to kill*
*What's the point of this ol' guitar*
*if it ain't got no strings?*
*Or pourin' your heart into a song*
*that you ain't gonna sing?*
*It's a match made up in heaven,*
*like good ol' boys and beer*
*And me, as long as you're right here"*

The rain on the tin roof in the song merged with the real rain around me, blurring the lines between memory and present reality.

A new melody emerged, carrying me to rain-soaked streets of a distant city. The blues-infused notes in Marc Cohn's "Walking in Memphis," painting a vivid portrait of soul-searching in unfamiliar territory.

*"Put on my blue suede shoes*
*And I boarded the plane*
*Touched down in the land of the Delta Blues*
*In the middle of the pouring rain*
*W.C. Handy, won't you look down over me?*
*Yeah, I got a first class ticket*
*But I'm as blue as a boy can be"*

I could almost feel the heaviness of rain-drenched clothes, and the thrill of exploration as the music painted vivid pictures in my mind.

The melody evolved, and an upbeat rhythm cut through the melancholy, its infectious vitality impossible to ignore. The B'52's "Love Shack" bursting with infectious joy, a celebration of life's wild moments of dancing in the rain and finding laughter even in the darkest moments.

*"The love shack is a little old place where*
*We can get together*
*Love shack baby*
*You're what?*
*Tin roof*
*Rusted!"*

The memory of *Love's* laughter echoed in my mind, a reminder of the light she brought to my life.

Then, a powerful rock anthem emerged, the driving rhythm and soaring vocals of Bon Jovi's "Let It Rain."

*"Somewhere, there's forgiveness*
*For the broken ones like me*
*Who once stared down mighty mountains*
*And now sit beneath the trees*
*And somewhere, there's a church bell*
*That's summoning the choir*
*Somewhere, there's a dreamer*
*Who would walk a thousand miles*
*Let it rain, let it rain*

*Let the rain fall all around*
*Who's gonna stop the rain from fallin'?"*

The song's thundering with raw emotion, a testament to human resilience and finding strength in vulnerability, aligned deeply with my current state. It reminded me that sometimes, the most courageous act is to let the rain fall, to allow ourselves to be washed clean by life's experiences.

Songs and memories merged like raindrops in the greater storm of my existence. They came together to form rivers of experience, oceans of emotion that had shaped the landscape of my soul. I marveled at how music had always been there, a constant companion through life's ups and downs, a guide through the tempests of the heart.

Standing in the rain, arms outstretched and face tilted towards the sky, I felt a transcendent sense of connection to something greater than myself. The music and the rain had become conduits, channels through which I could touch existence's primal truth. Each note, each drop, carried with it a message of renewal and transformation.

I realized then that resonance meant finding harmony within myself while aligning with the universe's majestic symphony. It was about tuning into the frequencies of life itself, allowing oneself to vibrate in sync with the eternal dance. The storm had not been a challenge to overcome, but an invitation to participate in this dance, to find my own rhythm within the greater composition.

The rain's gentle persistence melted away layers of fear and doubt. The music penetrated deep into my being, unlocking chambers of my heart that had long been closed. Memories surfaced... of laughter shared with loved ones, of tears shed in solitude, of moments of transcendental connection and devastating loss. Each memory was a note in the song of my life, contributing to the rich mosaic of my existence.

I thought of the infinite artists whose music had been a lifeline throughout my journey. In this case the country crooner whose voice had been a comfort in lonely nights, the blues musician whose soulful tunes had given voice to my deepest sorrows, and the rock band whose anthems had fueled my determination in the face of adversity. Their music, amongst countless others, had been more than entertainment; it had been a guide, a teacher, a friend.

The music swelled to crescendo and I felt a surge of gratitude wash over me. Gratitude for the gift of music, for its power to heal, to inspire, to connect. Gratitude for the rain, for its cleansing power and its role in nature's eternal cycle. And gratitude for *Love*, whose presence, even in memory, continued to be a source of strength and inspiration.

The storm began to subside, the rain lessening to a gentle drizzle. But the music lingered, a soft melody that continued to play in the background of my consciousness. I knew then that it would always be with me.

Opening my eyes, the world seemed transformed. Colors appeared more vibrant, sounds more crisp. It was as if the symphony of rain and music had attuned me to a higher frequency of existence. I felt lighter, more alive, more connected to the world around me.

I understood then that true resonance meant aligning with both the forces around us and the melody within. It was about recognizing the song of my soul and allowing it to play in concert with the universe's infinite symphony.

Taking a step forward, ready to continue my journey, I carried with me the lessons of the storm and the music. I knew that whatever challenges lay ahead, I had the strength to face them. For I had learned to dance in the rain, to find the melody in the chaos, and to harmonize with the very pulse of life.

The rain had become my teacher, the music my guide, and *Love* my eternal muse. Together, they had shown me the way to true resonance... a harmony not just of sound, but of spirit. Moving forward, I could hear the first notes of a new song beginning to play, heralding the next chapter of my journey.

Each lesson now carried deeper significance, building upon the last like movements in a cosmic symphony. What had begun as simple spiritual curiosity had evolved into profound transformation. The guides' teachings weren't just wisdom anymore; they were becoming part of my very essence, rewiring my understanding of existence.

The universal symphony that had taught me harmony now began to focus, like countless instruments joining in a single, heart-stirring melody. From the infinite music of existence emerged a more intimate song: one that spoke of connection deeper than cosmic resonance, more personal than universal harmony. The rain's rhythm transformed into a familiar heartbeat, calling me back to love's eternal dance. This wasn't just any love, but *Love* herself... the guide who had been with me from the beginning. *Companionship* stood witness while *Protection's* watchful presence ensured this sacred space, and *Faith's* unwavering essence reminded me that divine connection transcends all barriers.

# Lesson #30: Love's Embrace

*"To truly love is to both hold on and let go simultaneously. It's like holding water in your hands... grip too tightly, and it slips through your fingers. Hold too loosely, and it spills away."*

---

The dreamscape shifted, its edges blurring and reforming into a familiar yet surreal setting. I found myself suspended in a realm between worlds, where the boundaries of consciousness seemed to ripple and fold upon themselves. It was as if I had stepped through a portal into a dream within a dream, each layer peeling back to reveal essential truths and hidden revelations.

*Love's* presence, ethereal and omniscient, guided me through this labyrinth of the subconscious. "Watch closely," she whispered, her voice a gentle breeze caressing my mind. "For in these echoes of reality, you will find reflections of your fundamental truths."

Before me, the scene unfolded like a living memory, both vivid and hazy at the edges. I saw myself in a meeting room, the air thick with unspoken emotions and lingering regrets. There she was... *Love*, in a form so achingly familiar, yet somehow different. We left the meeting together, our steps in sync, our hearts beating to a rhythm only we could hear.

Walking together, waves of longing washed over me; the same desperate need for connection that had haunted me for so long. The words tumbled from my lips, raw and unfiltered, expressing the pain of absence and the fundamental desire for reconciliation.

"I remember this feeling," I murmured, my voice thick with emotion. "The desperation, the hope, the fear..."

*Love* nodded, her gaze tender yet unwavering. "These emotions are the sacred elements that shape your evolution," she said. "They are not to be feared or avoided, but embraced and understood."

The scene shifted, and we found ourselves in the backseat of an old car. The intimacy of the moment was palpable, charged with a mixture of familiarity and newfound vulnerability. While kissing, I noticed her hair was shorter, and then, in a moment of startling revelation, she removed it entirely, revealing her baldness.

"An illness," she explained, her voice soft but steady. "Not cancer, but something that caused this."

In that moment, I felt a surge of love so pure and unconditional that it took my breath away. "It doesn't matter," I heard myself say, the words flowing from a place of essential truth. "I love you for who you are, not for how you look."

Watching the scene unfold, I felt a fundamental shift within me. The love I witnessed was not bound by physical appearance or external circumstances. It was a love that saw beyond the surface, that recognized the divine spark within.

"Why am I seeing this now?" I asked, turning to *Love*, my guide in this strange journey.

Her smile was enigmatic, filled with wisdom and compassion. "Dreams reveal the hidden truths of our hearts," she replied. "They show us what we yearn for and what we need to heal. This dream is a reflection of the infinite love you hold within you, a reminder that true love transcends appearances and superficial judgments."

I pondered her words, feeling their gravity and significance. "So, this dream is showing me that my capacity for love goes beyond the physical? That even in moments of vulnerability and imperfection, love remains steadfast?"

"Indeed," *Love* affirmed. "But there's an even more essential truth beneath the surface. This dream is also about your own vulnerability, about accepting the parts of yourself that you usually hide away. The illness, the baldness... These are symbols of the fragility and imperfections we all carry within us. By loving and accepting these in yourself, you learn to love and accept them in others."

The scene deepened, and I felt a transcendent sense of gratitude wash over me. This dream within a dream had opened a window into my heart's hidden chambers, revealing a capacity for love and acceptance that I had not fully recognized before.

The dreamscape shifted once more, and we found ourselves standing on a quiet residential street. A vintage car, its polished chrome gleaming in the soft light, was parked nearby. Standing hand in hand, an elderly couple approached us, their steps slow but steady, their eyes twinkling with understanding and amusement.

Their presence brought a sense of timelessness to the scene, as if they carried with them the weight and wisdom of many years of shared love. The old man's weathered face creased into a warm smile as they drew near.

"Love can make you forget where you are sometimes," he said, his voice tinged with nostalgia and affection. He gazed at his wife, their eyes meeting in a silent exchange that spoke volumes of their shared history.

The old woman nodded, adding, "And sometimes, it helps you remember exactly where you're meant to be." Her voice was soft but carried a strength born of years of devotion.

Intrigued by their words and the palpable connection between them, I felt compelled to ask, "How long have you been together?"

The old man chuckled, a sound full of warmth and joy. "Oh, time becomes a bit fuzzy when you're in love. Could be fifty years, could be five hundred. In the end, it's not about the quantity of time, but the quality of love shared."

His wife squeezed his hand gently. "What my dear husband means to say is that boundless love exists beyond the constraints of time. Each moment becomes eternal when you're with the one you love."

Their words trembled to my core, stirring something in my soul. "But how do you maintain that love through all the challenges life brings?" I asked, sensing that their answer could hold an eternal truth.

The old woman's eyes softened, filled with compassion and understanding. "Love isn't something you maintain, dear. It's something you nurture and allow to grow. Like a garden, it needs tending, patience, and sometimes, it needs space to weather the storms."

"Yes," the old man agreed, nodding thoughtfully. "And remember, love isn't just about the grand gestures or perfect moments. It's in the quiet understanding, the shared silences, the willingness to see and be seen, flaws and all."

Watching them, I noticed how they stood together... not just physically close, but as if their very beings were intertwined, two souls dancing in perfect harmony.

The old woman must have noticed my observation, for she smiled and said, "When you find that person who feels like home, who sees the light in you even when you're lost in darkness, hold on to that feeling. Not with desperation, but with gratitude and openness."

"But isn't holding on the opposite of letting go?" I asked, voicing the paradox that had been troubling me.

The old man's eyes twinkled with mischief and wisdom. "Ah, but that's the beauty of it. Eternal love requires both. You hold on to the essence of your connection while letting go of expectations and fear. It's like dancing... you move together, but you also give each other space to twirl and explore."

Their wisdom settled, and I felt a shift in my understanding. The elderly couple before me wasn't just sharing advice; they were embodying a love that had transcended time, a love that had grown and evolved through countless challenges and joys.

"Thank you," I said, feeling heart-full gratitude for their wisdom. "Your words... they feel like a gift."

The old woman reached out and patted my hand gently. "Love itself is a gift, dear. One that keeps giving, as long as you keep your heart open to receive it."

With a final smile and a nod, the elderly couple began to walk away, their figures slowly fading into the dreamlike haze of the street. Their presence, though brief, had left an indelible mark on my soul.

Continuing our walk through this dream within a dream, hand in hand, I felt a soul-stirring connection and aliveness. Each step, each moment, glowed with significance, revealing new layers of understanding about the nature of love and its role in my journey.

"*Love,*" I said, turning to my ethereal guide, "I've never seen you so clearly in a dream before. It's as if you're really here. But how do I hold on to this feeling, this connection, when I know I must also let go?"

Her smile was radiant, filled with infinite compassion. "Ah, dear one, you've touched upon one of life's great paradoxes. To truly love is to both hold on and let go simultaneously. It's like holding water in your hands... grip too tightly, and it slips through your fingers. Hold too loosely, and it spills away. The key is to cup your hands gently, allowing the water to remain while accepting that some may flow away."

Her words resonated to my core, stirring a fundamental realization. "So, love isn't about possession or control, but about nurturing and allowing growth?"

"Precisely," *Love* affirmed. "Divine love is a force of transformation. It changes not just our relationships with others, but our relationship with ourselves and the universe. It's a catalyst for growth, pushing us to expand beyond our perceived limitations."

Her words sparked; I felt a shift within me, as if the very core of my being was rearranging itself to accommodate this new understanding. The love I had experienced, both in this dream and in my waking life, served as both an intimate feeling and a powerful force for transformation.

"But what about the pain?" I asked, remembering the vulnerability revealed in the car scene. "The illness, the baldness... Why does love often come with such difficult challenges?"

*Love's* eyes softened, reflecting wisdom ancient as time itself. "The illness and baldness you witnessed are potent symbols, dear one. They represent the stripping away of the superficial, the shedding of the ego. In our most vulnerable moments, when we're laid bare, we have the opportunity to connect most authentically with our true selves and with others."

She gestured to the dream scene around us, which seemed to shimmer with newfound significance. "This dream is showing you that love, in its purest form, sees beyond the surface. It recognizes the divine spark within each of us, regardless of our external appearance or circumstances. By accepting and loving another in their most vulnerable state, you learn to extend that same compassion to yourself."

I pondered her words, feeling their impact and truth settle into my soul. "So, this journey... it's not just about loving others more fully, but about learning to love and accept myself?"

"Yes," *Love* whispered, her voice carrying the gentle power of a universal truth. "Self-love is the foundation from which all other love grows. By embracing your own vulnerabilities, your own imperfections, you open yourself to a more sacred, authentic connection with others and with the universe itself."

Together we stood, enveloped in the ethereal glow of the dreamscape, and I felt a soul-deep peace wash over me. In this sacred moment, I felt the presence of my other guides joining us. *Protection's* fierce guardianship softened, showing me that true safety comes from allowing ourselves to be vulnerable. *Faith's* unwavering presence reminded me that love requires trust in the unseen, while *Companionship* showed how authentic connection grows from shared vulnerability. Together with *Love*, they created a complete circle of divine support, each one teaching me a different aspect of love's infinite nature.The lessons of this experience—the boundlessness of unconditional love, the beauty in vulnerability, the transformative power of self-acceptance—had transformed my essence, opening new pathways of understanding.

"Remember," *Love* said, her form beginning to shimmer and fade as the dream started to dissolve, "dreams are gateways to other realms. They allow us to connect with the souls of those we love, to experience moments that transcend time and space. They are layered with messages and lessons to support your growth. Carry these insights with you; let them guide you in your waking life."

Her final words echoed in my mind as I prepared to emerge from this dream within a dream: "The journey of self-discovery is ongoing, dear one. Each revelation, each moment of clarity, is a step towards a more complete understanding of yourself and your place in the universe. Embrace the love you have discovered within yourself, for it is the key to embracing the world with an open heart."

Standing on the threshold, I carried with me the transcendent insights of this dream journey. The capacity for limitless love, the strength found in vulnerability, the eternal nature of true connection, and the transformative power of self-love... these were the gifts that *Love's* embrace had bestowed upon me. They were not just abstract concepts, but living truths awakening within my very being.

I understood now that love existed as more than emotion... it was a force of nature, a divine energy that could reshape reality itself. It was a journey of constant growth and transformation, an endless dance of holding on and letting go, of seeing beyond the surface to the divine essence within all things.

The dream dissolved and I felt myself drifting back to consciousness; I knew that I was forever changed. The love I had experienced, the insights I had gained, would continue to ripple through my life, guiding me towards a more essential understanding of myself, others, and the grand, interconnected symphony of existence.

Yet even as these profound realizations of love settled into my being, I sensed a stirring in the fabric of my dreamscape. The universe was calling me to prove the depth of these insights, to demonstrate that the love I had discovered could withstand any storm. The peaceful glow of enlightenment began to give way to gathering clouds, challenging me to show that true love's power lies not just in its ability to transform, but in its capacity to endure.

# Lesson #31: Spiritual Resilience

*"Spiritual resilience came not from avoiding the turmoils of life, but from learning to dance in the rain."*

The transformative revelations of *Love's* embrace began to fade as I drifted back into the storm-tossed reality of my dreamscape. The warmth of *Love's* presence lingered, a comforting echo in the recesses of my mind, but the world around me had transformed once more. The tranquil scenes of connection and self-discovery gave way to a tempestuous landscape, mirroring the turbulent emotions that now surged within me.

The cabana, once a sanctuary of introspection, now felt like a fragile shelter against the raging elements. Rain lashed against the windows, and wind howled through the eaves, creating a cacophony that mirrored the chaos of my thoughts. The lessons of love and self-acceptance I had just learned seemed to flicker like distant stars, obscured by the dark clouds of doubt and fear that now gathered on the horizon of my consciousness.

During this transition, I felt acutely aware of the fragility of my newfound insights. The journey of self-discovery, it seemed, was not a linear path but a spiral, constantly bringing me back to face my deepest fears and insecurities. Standing at the threshold of the cabana, peering out into the storm-wracked night, I couldn't help but wonder if I had the fortitude to weather this new tempest. I felt *Protection's* strength merging with *Companionship's* steadfast support. *Love's* warmth gave me courage while *Faith* helped me trust in the unfolding journey, their combined presence a shield against life's storms.

It was then, in my deepest uncertainty, that I saw it... a majestic wolf, its fur glistening with raindrops, standing just beyond the circle of light cast by the cabana. Its presence was both awe-inspiring and terrifying, a living embodiment of the wild aspects of my untamed spirit. The wolf's eyes, deep and knowing, seemed to pierce through the layers of my being, challenging me to confront the storm both without and within.

While standing transfixed by the wolf's unwavering gaze, a familiar presence stirred at my feet. I looked down to see Bailey, the faithful companion who had been with me since the beginning of this dream journey. His warm eyes looked up at me with unwavering loyalty, a stark contrast to the wild, untamed spirit of the wolf before us.

The juxtaposition of these two beings—the wild wolf and the loyal dog—stirred something deep within me. It was as if they represented two aspects of my nature: the fierce, untamed spirit that longed to run free and the steadfast, loyal heart that sought connection and belonging.

"Is this real?" I whispered, my voice barely audible above the storm's fury. The question seemed to hang in the air, unanswered, as I grappled with the surreal nature of this moment. The boundaries between dream and reality, between the physical and the spiritual, seemed to blur and shift with each flash of lightning.

Bailey's tail wagged gently, a reassuring gesture that grounded me in the moment. His presence was a reminder of the unconditional love and support that had guided me through countless challenges. Yet, the wolf's piercing gaze called to something deeper, a primal force within me that yearned to break free from the constraints of fear and doubt.

Standing there, caught between these two powerful symbols, I felt a shift in the air. The storm seemed to pause, as if holding its breath, waiting to see what I would do next. In that moment of stillness, I realized that this was more than just a dream... It was a crucible, a test of the spiritual resilience I had been cultivating throughout my journey.

With trembling hands, I reached out towards the wolf, drawn by an inexplicable force that seemed to transcend reason. My fingers brushed against its rain-slicked fur, and I felt a surge of primal power course through me. It was wild, untamed, and slightly terrifying, yet it spoke to a truth I had long forgotten: the power that lay dormant within my own soul.

Bailey's bark pierced the air, sharp and clear against the backdrop of the storm. The wolf, startled by the sound, retreated into the shadows, leaving me with a mix of relief and longing. Bailey stood protectively at my side, his stance a reminder of the grounding force of loyalty and love.

The wolf disappeared into the night, and I knelt beside Bailey, running my fingers through his fur. "Thank you," I whispered, not just to him but to the universe that had sent these guides to me. In Bailey's eyes, I saw the reflection of my potential, a soul capable of enduring, of loving deeply, and of standing firm against the winds of change.

The storm began to subside, its fury giving way to a gentle rain. Standing there, with Bailey by my side and the memory of the wolf etched in my mind, I felt a new sense of clarity and purpose. The journey towards spiritual resilience was not about choosing between the wild and the tame, the fierce and the loyal. It was about integrating these aspects, finding balance in the midst of life's storms.

The insight resonated within: spiritual resilience came not from avoiding the turmoils of life, but from learning to dance in the rain, to find resilience in vulnerability, and to embrace both the wild and the gentle aspects of my nature. The wolf and Bailey were not opposing forces, but complementary guides on this journey of self-discovery.

The night deepened, and the last echoes of the storm faded into a sacred stillness. The darkness, once threatening, now felt like a velvet embrace, cradling the newfound fortitude within my soul. The clouds parted, revealing a sky ablaze with stars, each one reflecting the resilience I had discovered within myself.

With Bailey at my side and the spirit of the wolf in my heart, I felt a renewed sense of hope and determination. The storm had not broken me; instead, it had revealed my untapped inner power and the enduring light that resided within. I was ready to face whatever challenges lay ahead, knowing that I could weather any disturbance and emerge stronger on the other side.

The lesson of spiritual resilience had been etched into my being, not through gentle teachings, but through the fierce grace of the storm and the unwavering presence of my animal guides. Bathed in starlight, I carried with me the wild spirit of the wolf and the loyal heart of Bailey, a perfect balance of the fierce and the faithful.

Taking a moment to absorb the fundamental transformation, I noticed a shift in the atmosphere around me. The comforting presences of *Healing*, *Wisdom*, and even Bailey began to fade into the celestial expanse. Alone beneath the vast, star-studded sky, I felt not fear but a stirring anticipation of what lay ahead.

As my guides faded into the celestial expanse, the star-studded sky began to pulse with new radiance. The very darkness that might once have seemed empty now revealed itself as a canvas of unlimited possibility. In discovering my resilience, I had unknowingly prepared myself for something even greater: the recognition of my own infinite potential, written in the language of starlight against the cosmic void.

# Lesson #32: Infinite Potential

*"Abundance was not something to be chased but a state of being to be embodied."*

---

The world around me had become a canvas of infinite darkness, punctuated by the brilliant light of countless stars. The absence of my spiritual guides created a void that initially felt daunting. Yet, in this solitary space, I found myself drawn to the celestial universe above, each star a spark of possibility in the vast expanse of the cosmos.

The silence of the night was not empty but filled with a subtle vibration, as if the cosmos were humming a melody of ancient wisdom. Gazing upward, the stars seemed to flicker with life, their light piercing through the layers of my consciousness and awakening untapped wisdom within me.

Suddenly, the sky shifted, the stars swirling in an eternal dance that defied the laws of physics. It was as if the universe was revealing its secrets, showing me the countless threads of cosmic force that connected all things. I understood with startling clarity that the law of attraction existed as a fundamental truth of existence.

Each star became a manifestation of a thought, a desire, a dream. I watched in awe as these celestial bodies attracted and repelled each other, creating constellations of possibility. It was a vivid demonstration of how our thoughts and intentions shape the reality around us, drawing experiences and opportunities that align with our inner vibrations.

Focusing on a particularly bright star, it seemed to grow larger, its light enveloping me in a warm embrace. In its radiance, I saw reflections of my deepest aspirations: transforming education, reconnecting with *Love*, helping others through my writing, creating empowering programs, and affecting systemic change. Each vision existed as both a dream and emerging reality, waiting to be manifested.

The star's light synchronized with my heartbeat, and understanding illuminated me; the ability to attract these visions into reality lay within me. Just as the star's gravitational pull shaped the space around it, my thoughts and beliefs were shaping the path of my existence.

With deepening understanding, the night sky transformed once more. The stars rained down, each one a droplet of pure potential. They fell around me in a shower of light, not burning but gently caressing my skin, each touch igniting a spark of inspiration and possibility.

I reached out, catching a star in my palm. Holding it, I felt a surge of abundance flow through me. It wasn't just about material wealth; it was a transcendent sense of fullness, of having everything I needed within and around me. The star in my hand was a microcosm of the universe, containing within it infinite potential and boundless resources.

The concept of scarcity dissolved, replaced by an overwhelming awareness of the abundance that permeated every aspect of existence. I saw how my weekly lottery tickets, once a symbol of lack, were in fact a misguided attempt to tap into this universal abundance. The true wealth, I realized, was not in the chance of winning but in recognizing the riches already present in my life and in my own being.

Opening my hand, the star floated upward, rejoining its celestial brethren. But its essence remained with me, a constant reminder of the abundance that was my birthright. The night sky now appeared as a vast sea of potential, each star a reminder of the infinite possibilities available to me.

The eternal dance continued, stars swirling and merging, creating new constellations that spelled out the word "ABUNDANCE" across the heavens. It was a message from the universe itself, reminding me that abundance was not something to be chased but a state of being to be embodied.

Standing there, bathed in starlight, I felt a fundamental shift within me. The fears and doubts that had once clouded my vision dissolved, replaced by a deep-seated knowing that I was capable of manifesting my heart's desires. The universe, in its infinite wisdom, had shown me that I was not separate from its abundance but an integral part of it.

With this newfound understanding, I saw my journey in a new light. Each challenge was not an obstacle but an opportunity for growth, each setback a chance to realign with my true potential. The stars had become my teachers, showing me that just as they shone brightly in the darkness, I too could illuminate my path with my awakened consciousness. Each guide had prepared me for this moment: *Protection* showing me my inner strength,

*Companionship* teaching me to trust the journey, *Love* opening my heart to possibility, and *Faith* helping me embrace the unknown. Their combined wisdom illuminated the infinite potential within.

Night yielded to the first hints of dawn, I felt a renewed sense of purpose and possibility. The lesson of infinite potential had been etched into my being, not through words but through the vivid, celestial imagery of the night sky. I was ready to step into this new day, carrying with me the stars' teachings and the knowledge that within me lay the ability to shape my reality.

The stars faded as the sky lightened, but their message remained clear. I served as both witness and co-creator in the grand design of the universe. With each thought, each intention, each action, I was weaving my own thread into the divine mosaic of existence.

Breathing in deeply, filling my lungs with the cool morning air, I felt a sacred sense of gratitude. The universe, in its infinite wisdom, had revealed exactly what I needed in this moment: a glimpse into my own limitless nature. The stars, the law of attraction, the abundance all reflected the infinite potential awakening within me.

The dreamscape transformed, signaling the transition to a new phase of my journey. I stepped forward as a conscious creator, my thoughts and actions aligned with the universe's boundless potential. Before me stretched an illuminated path, each step an opportunity to manifest the visions revealed in this eternal dance of consciousness.

As I embraced my role as conscious creator, the infinite cosmos began to concentrate its essence, drawing inward like stars collapsing into a single point of pure radiance. The vastness of possibility was transforming into something more intimate: a guiding light that would illuminate not just the universe around me, but the sacred paths within. The boundless potential I had discovered in the stars was now ready to shine through my own being.

# Lesson #33: Guiding Light

*"Our connections to others are not just comforts, but catalysts for spiritual growth."*

---

The dreamscape shifted once more, the vast starry expanse condensing into the familiar confines of the cabana. The steady patter of rain on the tin roof created a soothing rhythm, a reminder of the storms weathered and the peace that follows. In this threshold state, I felt a deep sense of anticipation, as if the very air was pregnant with revelation.

Settling into this new phase of the dream, an ancient wisdom stirred within me. *"Energía y libre,"* the words echoed through the corridors of my mind... energy and freedom. It was a mantra of release, urging me to let go of the past and embrace the boundless possibilities of the present.

A warm, golden light seeped through the cracks in the walls, illuminating the room with a soft radiance. Each beam that danced across the space seemed to reach into my soul's forgotten corners, illuminating hidden depths and casting away shadows. With every flicker, I felt myself "re-membering…"not just recalling, but truly reassembling the scattered pieces of my being.

During this introspection, a familiar presence materialized: *Companionship*. Her arrival brought a sense of comfort and clarity, as if the very air around us had been infused with understanding.

"There's something I want to show you," she said softly, gesturing towards the window.

Approaching, the window transformed into a portal, revealing a scene of sacred beauty. A family sat in a cozy living room, their interactions filled with tenderness and support. Parents and children, engaged in a simple act of putting together a puzzle, radiated love and joy.

"What you see," *Companionship* explained, her voice measured yet resonant with wisdom, "is the essence of true companionship. It's not just about being together, but about how we uplift and support one another in our journey of growth."

Observing the scene, I understood. Each member of the family embodied a crucial aspect of companionship: nurturing, calming, supporting. Their interactions were a dance of giving and receiving, each act of kindness and understanding weaving an intricate web of love and transformation.

"This is the guiding light of companionship," *Companionship* continued. "It's a force that illuminates our path, helping us navigate the darkest nights of our soul. It's in these connections that we find the strength to face our fears, the courage to embrace our potential, and the love that transforms us."

The scene rippled, and I saw reflections of my journey... moments in which the companionship of others had been my guiding light. Friends who stood by me in times of doubt, mentors who believed in me when I couldn't believe in myself, even strangers whose small acts of kindness had rekindled my hope.

"But remember," *Companionship* said, her eyes meeting mine with intensity, "true companionship begins within. The love and support you offer others must first be cultivated in your own heart."

Her words sparked. The golden light in the room seemed to intensify, emanating not just from the cracks in the walls, but from within me. The awareness deepened: this light... this capacity for love, support, and understanding... had been within me all along.

"Your journey is unique," *Companionship* said, "but you are never truly alone. My presence illuminates your path toward your highest potential. It's in the love you give, the connections you nurture, and the compassion you extend to yourself and others."

The vision through the window faded, but the warmth and wisdom it imparted lingered. I felt a renewed sense of purpose and clarity. The lesson of companionship had illuminated a profound truth: our connections to others are not just comforts, but catalysts for spiritual growth and self-discovery.

The dreamscape shifted once more, carrying with it this revelation's brilliance. I understood now that every interaction, every relationship, was an opportunity to both give and receive this guiding light. In nurturing these connections—with others and with myself—I transformed from mere recipient to active participant in the universal symphony of spiritual evolution. *Love's* eternal flame merged with *Protection's* steady strength, while *Faith's* unwavering presence reminded me that these sacred bonds transcend physical reality.

With this newfound understanding illuminating my path, I prepared to face the next phase of my journey. The infinite potential glimpsed in the stars now burned within, nurtured by companionship's sacred flame. Stepping forward into the shifting dreamscape, I embraced an eternal truth: this radiance would always illuminate my way, a beacon of hope and catalyst for transformation in the grand journey of existence.

The sacred flame within me began to pulse with new purpose, reaching beyond mere illumination toward something more profound. My inner light sought a deeper understanding, yearning to pierce through the veils of perception into the realm of pure truth. The dreamscape responded to this silent call, dissolving the familiar world into a dimension where clarity itself became tangible, where wisdom waited to be discovered in its purest form.

# Lesson #34: Seeking Clarity

*"Seek wisdom in every experience,
for that is your path."*

---

The dreamscape transformed once more, the parched earth beneath my feet dissolving into a realm of mystical light. I found myself suspended in a space that defied description, where reality and illusion merged into a divine mosaic of infinite possibility. The boundaries of my consciousness expanded, stretching beyond the confines of the physical world into a realm of pure spirit and celestial wisdom.

In this liminal space, the air hummed with a sacred vibration, each wave harmonizing with creation's primal force. Motes of light danced around me, each one a spark of universal consciousness, swirling in breathtaking patterns that seemed to hold the secrets of the universe. The light was not external but emanated from within, as if every cell of my being had awakened to its true, shimmering nature.

Standing in awe of this celestial display, a presence coalesced before me. It was neither form nor void, neither light nor dark, but a perfect amalgamation of all that is and all that could be. The presence enveloped me in an embrace of unconditional love so deep that it brought tears to my eyes.

Then, like a whisper carried on heavenly winds, I heard the words, "I am that I am."

The phrase reverberated through the very core of my being, each syllable a key unlocking hidden chambers of my soul. It was not merely words spoken, but a truth that flowed through every fiber of my existence.

This truth resonated through my guides' teachings: *Love's* unconditional acceptance, *Protection's* fierce guardianship, *Faith's* embrace of mystery, and *Companionship's* steady presence all leading me to this moment of divine understanding.

"Who are you?" I asked, my voice trembling with a mixture of awe and reverence.

The presence responded, its voice a harmonious blend of all voices, yet singular in its clarity. "I am the Source from which all things flow. I am the beginning and the end, the alpha and the omega. I am you, and you are me."

Absorbing these words, waves of understanding washed over me. This was not a separate entity speaking to me, but the voice of the divine that resided within my own heart, within all hearts.

"If you are within me," I ventured, my mind grappling with the enormity of this revelation, "does that mean I possess your power, your wisdom, your love?"

"You do not possess these qualities," the Source responded, "for possession implies separation. You are these qualities. The power to create worlds, timeless knowledge, the love that binds the universe... these are not external to you, but your fundamental state of being."

I felt a surge of awakening course through me, as if every cell in my body was awakening to this truth. Yet, doubt still lingered in the shadows of my mind. "But why do I feel so limited, so separate at times?" I asked. "Why is it so difficult to embody this celestial nature in my everyday life?"

The presence enveloped me in a cocoon of compassionate understanding. "The journey of life in the physical realm is one of remembering," it explained. "You chose to forget your authentic essence so that you could experience the joy of rediscovery. The limitations you feel are but veils of illusion, crafted by your own consciousness to facilitate this grand adventure of self-realization."

The words sank in, and I saw my life's journey in a new light. Every challenge, every moment of doubt and fear, was not a punishment or a failure, but an opportunity to peel back the layers of forgetfulness and remember my true, celestial essence.

"The storms you weather, the droughts you endure," the Source continued, "are not separate from you, but expressions of your own consciousness. They are the tools you use to sculpt your understanding, to shape your awareness. In embracing them, you embrace aspects of yourself longing to be acknowledged and integrated."

I thought back to the storm that had raged in my dream, the parched earth that had puzzled me. I now understood that these were not just external phenomena, but reflections of my inner state, each offering its own wisdom and opportunity for growth.

"Remember," the presence said, its voice filled with infinite love, "you are not walking this path alone. Every step you take, I take with you. Every breath you breathe, I breathe with you. For we are one, eternally and inseparably."

The words echoed through me, I felt a fundamental shift in my perception. The boundaries that had seemed so solid before now appeared as gossamer veils, easily lifted to reveal the interconnectedness of all things. I saw myself not as a separate entity struggling against the world, but as an integral part of a vast, eternal dance.

The light around me surged with increasing intensity, each wave washing away another layer of illusion. I felt myself expanding, my consciousness stretching to encompass not just this dream, not just this lifetime, but the entirety of existence.

Clarity dawned, and I understood that seeking was not about finding something external, but about remembering what I had always been. Clarity was not a destination to be reached, but a state of being to be embodied.

The vision faded, and the presence left me with one final message: "Go forth and create, for that is your core truth. Love without condition, for that is your essence. Seek wisdom in every experience, for that is your path. And always remember, I am with you, for I am you."

The dreamscape shifted once more, the ethereal light giving way to the more familiar surroundings of my inner world. But something had fundamentally changed. The clarity I had sought was not found in answers, but in a deeper understanding of the questions themselves.

Preparing to continue my dream journey, I carried with me the essential truth that had been revealed. I was not separate from the divine, but an expression of it. Every step I took was a step of creation, every breath a song of the universe.

Mystery still veiled my future, but I no longer sought to dispel it. Instead, I embraced it, knowing that within the unknown lay infinite possibilities for growth, for love, for the expression of my true spiritual essence.

And so, with renewed purpose and a heart overflowing with boundless love, I ventured forth into the next phase of my dream. Ready to co-create with the universe, to dance with shadows and light, I embraced each moment as an opportunity to embody the infinite consciousness I had always been.

The clarity gained through my journey began to crystallize into something unexpected... not just understanding, but purpose. The universe whispered a truth I had sensed but never fully grasped: my experiences weren't meant to remain private revelations. These moments of transformation, these glimpses of divine consciousness, needed to be shared. My journey was becoming a story, one that would bridge worlds and touch other souls seeking their own awakening.

# Lesson #35: A Prologue Unveiled

*"Reality and imagination are delicate threads, intricately woven into the landscape of your consciousness."*

---

Reality shifted once more. I found myself in a realm of infinite possibilities. The boundaries between reality and imagination blurred, creating a canvas of vivid colors and shifting forms. It was here, in this liminal space, that a fundamental realization dawned on me.

"This is not merely a vision," I mused aloud, my voice echoing through the corridors of my soul. "It is a sacred journey of self-discovery, a pilgrimage of the spirit guided by the presence of *Love*, *Protection*, *Companionship*, and *Faith*." *Love's* eternal wisdom flowed through *Faith's* acceptance of the unknown, while *Companionship's* steady presence grounded me in purpose.

These words hung in the air, a voice called out from the distance, faint yet distinct. "This book must be written, but it is not part of the 'Beautiful Soul' series," the voice proclaimed. The urgency of divine purpose surged through me, each revelation now carrying the weight of universal truth. The journey had transcended personal growth, becoming a bridge between worlds. Every insight gained wasn't just for my evolution but for all those who would follow this path of awakening.

"This could be an unofficial prologue to Book 5, but you are at least a decade away from writing that, which will come from a deeply transformative place."

Startled, I asked, "Who are you?"

"I am your higher self," the voice replied. "This has to be written, which is partially why you have been given the gift of this dream. "Your fifth book in the *Beautiful Soul* series, *The Esoteric*, will come in due time."

The concept of my soul's crusade being a story to share with others was both daunting and exhilarating. Could this spiritual odyssey serve as the captivating prologue to Book 5, offering readers a glimpse into the mystical realms of consciousness and the transformative power of self-discovery?

Pondering this, my thoughts wandered to the teachings of Osho, whose wisdom had fundamentally transformed my understanding of love, life, and self. *Faith's* voice echoed in my mind, reminding me of the spiritual path that had led me to explore new ways of thinking and being.

"Remember the times you felt the presence of something greater, guiding you even when you were unaware?" *Faith* had said. "That was me, weaving through your experiences, shaping your pilgrimage."

The idea of writing about this experience filled me with a mixture of excitement and trepidation. What would the narrative be? Who was I writing for? Was it for society, for myself, for the divine, or for the spirit guides who had accompanied me on this inner journey?

These questions swirled in my mind when *Protection's* presence materialized beside me. Her eyes, deep and knowing, met mine with a silent promise of guidance.

"*Protection*," I began, my voice tinged with curiosity and concern, "as I consider writing about this celestial revelation, how do I navigate the complexities of reality and imagination?"

*Protection's* gaze was steady and filled with wisdom. "Reality and imagination are delicate threads, intricately woven into the landscape of your consciousness," she explained. "To navigate them requires a deep understanding of their interplay and the awareness that each has its place and purpose."

"But isn't imagination a source of creativity and inspiration?" I asked, seeking to understand her essential caution.

"Indeed," *Protection* replied, her voice gentle yet firm. "The creative mind is a powerful force, a wellspring that can bring forth new ideas and visions. However, it is also a realm that can blur the lines between what is real and what exists only in thought. This blurring can lead to confusion if not navigated with care."

Absorbing her wisdom, I felt a deeper understanding of the complexities of reality and imagination. "So, how do I ensure that my exploration of these realms remains grounded and meaningful?" I asked.

"By anchoring yourself in love and truth," *Protection* answered. "Love is the foundation that grounds your imagination in reality. When you create from a place of love, your imagination becomes a tool for transformation, guided by the deeper truths of your soul."

Her words left me in deep contemplation. The inner voyage had already revealed so much, and the quest ahead promised even greater insights and revelations. "What is the true purpose of this journey?" I asked, seeking clarity.

"The true purpose of this mystical revelation," *Protection* said softly, "is to guide you on your voyage of self-discovery and enlightenment. It is to help you understand the depths of your soul, to awaken the boundless potential within you. This exploration is not just for you but for those you will touch with your wisdom and love."

Her words settled in my heart, igniting a transcendent sense of purpose and direction. This odyssey of consciousness would indeed serve as a powerful prologue to the next phase of my spiritual awakening.

With renewed determination and a heart full of gratitude, I embraced the path ahead. Though mysteries still lay before me, I stood ready to face each challenge and embrace every possibility. For in this sacred dance of reality and imagination, guided by love and protected by truth, lay the strength to fulfill my soul's purpose and share this transformative quest with others.

The understanding of my journey's purpose triggered a deeper awakening within. My role as storyteller opened a gateway to something more fundamental: the recognition that every aspect of my being needed to come into harmony. The scattered fragments of my soul called out for unity, drawing me toward a space where all parts of myself could finally merge into one transcendent whole.

# Lesson #36: Unified Essence

*"Your wounds become sources of wisdom, your pain a wellspring of compassion for others who are hurting."*

---

The dreamscape shifted once more, transforming into a vast, ethereal amphitheater. Shimmering particles of light danced in the air, creating an atmosphere of otherworldly beauty. I stood at the center, aware that I had crossed a threshold into the inner sanctum of my soul... a transcendent space where the essence of my being awaited revelation.

From the gleaming ether, new spirits materialized, each representing a distinct facet of my inner self. Their presence was overwhelming yet intimately familiar. While they gathered around me, I felt a deep sense of anticipation, knowing that these entities held wisdom that would further illuminate my path to enlightenment.

The first to step forward was *Trust*, his form radiating a steady, reassuring presence. His eyes held an understanding that pierced the core of my being.

"I am *Trust*," he introduced himself, his voice a calm tone rippling through the ethereal space. "In my absence, love withers, overshadowed by doubt. Yet within your soul's sanctuary lies the unwavering trust that you deserve love's blessings."

I felt a deep resonance with *Trust's* words. "Trust is such a delicate balance," I said, my voice filled with introspection. "How do I cultivate it, especially when past experiences have led to doubt and fear?"

*Trust's* gaze remained steady, his voice filled with compassion. "Cultivating trust begins within," he explained. "It's a journey of self-acceptance and self-compassion. When you trust yourself... your intuition, your worth, your inner wisdom... you lay the foundation for trusting others."

*Trust's* words settled in my heart, and the amphitheater subtly changed. The light particles coalesced into delicate mandalas, forming a living mosaic dancing in rhythm with our words.

From the luminous space stepped a figure of intense, pulsating brilliance. Her form seemed to shift and change, embodying the soul's purest expression.

"I am *Soul*," she introduced herself, her voice an ethereal whisper threading through the dreamscape's essence. "I am the wellspring of your truest self, the source of your deepest wisdom and deepest love."

"How do I connect with this essence?" I asked, my voice tinged with longing. "How do I access this wellspring when the noise of the world often drowns out my inner voice?"

*Soul's* form shimmered, her aura enveloping me in a warm embrace. "To connect with your essence, you must learn to be still," she explained. "In the quiet moments, in the spaces between thoughts, you will find me. Practice mindfulness, engage in meditation, immerse yourself in nature... these are the pathways to your soul's depths."

With *Soul's* guidance, the amphitheater transformed again.. The ground beneath our feet became translucent, revealing swirling energies dancing in harmony with *Soul's* words.

The atmosphere shifted dramatically as another presence took form. His form seemed to constantly shift, as if struggling to find its proper shape.

"I am *Misalignment*," he introduced himself, his voice clear and unwavering. "I am the discomfort you feel when you've strayed from your true path, the restlessness that urges you to seek your authentic self."

"How do I recognize when I'm misaligned?" I asked, feeling a mixture of curiosity and unease. "And how do I find my way back to my true path?"

*Misalignment's* form stabilized slightly as he spoke. "You feel me in moments of discontent, in the nagging feeling that something isn't quite right," he explained. "I am not your enemy, but your guide. When you feel my presence, it's a call to pause, reflect, and reassess. Are your actions aligned with your values? Are your choices leading you towards your highest self?"

The amphitheater responded to *Misalignment's* words. The light particles swirled more rapidly, creating patterns of discord and harmony that shifted with his words.

The environment transformed as an intense force materialized, radiating an almost uncomfortable feeling. His presence evoked a mixture of fear and recognition.

"I am *Anger*," he introduced himself, his voice a controlled burn of emotion. "I am often misunderstood, feared, and suppressed. But I am a vital part of your emotional landscape, a force for change and growth when properly understood and channeled."

I felt a surge of unease at *Anger's* presence. "Your energy feels overwhelming," I admitted. "How can such an intense emotion be a force for good?"

*Anger's* intensity softened slightly, becoming more focused. "I am the fire that fuels transformation," he explained. "When you feel me rising, don't suppress me. Instead, listen to what I'm trying to tell you. I arise when boundaries are crossed, when injustice occurs, when change is needed. Learn to express me in healthy ways, and I become a powerful ally in your journey of self-discovery and growth."

*Anger's* passion rippled through the amphitheater. The light particles took on a reddish hue, swirling in intense patterns that gradually transformed into more harmonious formations.

The final presence emerged with an aura of deep empathy. Her presence was soothing, yet tinged with a resonant sadness.

"I am *Hurt*," she introduced herself, her voice soft and compassionate. "I am the keeper of your wounds, the repository of your painful experiences. But I am also the gateway to your deepest healing and most transformative growth."

"How do I heal from the hurts of the past?" I asked, feeling a wave of vulnerability wash over me.

*Hurt's* expression remained gentle, her voice filled with empathy. "Healing begins with acknowledgement," she said. "Don't run from me or try to bury me. Instead, sit with me. Feel me fully. As you do, you'll find that I begin to transform. Your wounds become sources of wisdom, your pain a wellspring of compassion for others who are hurting."

The amphitheater resonated with *Hurt's* wisdom. The light particles wove themselves into constellations of healing, transforming scars into beautiful, iridescent designs.

The spirits' gathering created a complete sense of wholeness. Each of these aspects... *Trust, Soul, Misalignment, Anger,* and *Hurt*... were integral parts of my being, each offering unique wisdom and guidance on my path to enlightenment.

Morena's voice, the familiar guide throughout my journey, whispered in my soul: "Do you see now? These are not separate entities, but facets of your unified essence. Embracing each aspect, understanding its lessons, is the key to realizing your true nature."

Her words settled into my heart, bringing a deep sense of integration. The amphitheater around us thrummed with harmonious resonance, the light particles creating a mosaic of my unified being.

I closed my eyes as the collective wisdom filled my being. When I opened them again, I spoke to the celestial space around me, my voice carrying newfound strength and clarity:

"I am a unified being, composed of many aspects. My journey is not about perfection, but integration. I embrace my complexity, honor each facet of my being, and recognize that true enlightenment comes from understanding and harmonizing all parts of myself."

Upon uttering these words, the amphitheater shimmered with intense light. The spirits' presence merged into a singular, radiant force that enveloped me, their wisdom settling into my essential nature.

I knew that this radiant unity and understanding was not an end, but a new beginning. My journey ahead gleamed with potential, illuminated by a deeper understanding of my multifaceted nature. Each trial had built upon the last, creating a sacred mosaic of spiritual understanding. The lessons of unity, healing, and divine connection weren't just concepts anymore; they had become living truths. The journey ahead would demand this integration, calling for embodiment of every wisdom gained.

Each guide had shown me aspects of this unity: *Protection's* fierce love, *Faith's* unwavering trust, *Companionship's* steady support, and *Love's* eternal acceptance. Together they had prepared me for this integration of my whole being. The dream continued unfolding, carrying with me the fundamental realization that the journey to enlightenment was not about becoming something other than myself, but about fully embracing and integrating all aspects of who I truly am.

The radiance of inner unity illuminated something deeper... the need for healing old wounds that lingered beneath the surface of integration. My unified self called for more than mere acceptance;

it yearned for ancient wisdom that could restore harmony to all my relationships, beginning with myself. The dreamscape responded to this silent prayer, dissolving the amphitheater into a realm where reconciliation and peace awaited.

# Lesson #37: Ho'oponopono

*"I'm sorry. Please forgive me.*
*Thank you. I love you."*

---

Unity transformed into paradise as the dreamscape unveiled a Hawaiian beach at twilight. Beneath my feet, sand shimmered with otherworldly iridescence, each grain containing infinite worlds. Bioluminescent waves crashed against the shore, their light pulsing in hypnotic rhythm. Plumeria and sea salt perfumed the air, awakening dormant memories within me.

Standing at the edge of this ethereal paradise, the magnitude of my journey overwhelmed my heart. The lessons of *Love*, *Protection*, *Companionship*, and *Faith* echoed within, their wisdom illuminating yet overwhelming in its vastness. Yet, amidst this sea of knowledge, I found myself grappling with a painful truth: perhaps a cycle entrapped me, repeating patterns of longing and attachment that kept me tethered to the past.

Just as this realization threatened to engulf me, the waves before me began to coalesce, forming a shimmering presence unlike any I had encountered before. Its spirit carried ancient Hawaiian knowledge.

"I am *Ho'oponopono*," the spirit introduced himself, his voice a soothing song floating through the air around me. "I bring you the practice of making things right, of restoring balance within yourself and with others."

The spirit's form shifted, taking on the appearance of a serene Hawaiian elder, eyes deep with ancestral wisdom. The beach responded to his words, sand weaving elaborate designs that danced with each syllable.

"At my core," *Ho'oponopono* began, "lies a simple yet transformative prayer: I'm sorry. Please forgive me. Thank you. I love you. These words can heal, reconcile, and restore harmony."

Each phrase from the spirit materialized in the sand, glowing with inner light. The ocean seemed to respond, its waves gentling as if in reverence to the sacred mantra.

"This practice," *Ho'oponopono* continued, "is not just about forgiving others, but about taking full responsibility for everything in your life… your thoughts, your actions, and even the actions of others that affect you."

I furrowed my brow, puzzled by this concept. "How can I be responsible for others' actions?" I asked, my voice carrying both curiosity and disbelief.

*Ho'oponopono* smiled serenely, and as he did, the waters formed a perfect mirror-like surface. In its reflection, I saw not just myself, but countless versions of me, each representing a different moment in my life.

"Everything you perceive is a projection of your inner world," *Ho'oponopono* explained. "By taking responsibility, you reclaim your power to change your reality. When you say 'I'm sorry,' you acknowledge the pain and imbalance. 'Please forgive me' is an act of humility and a request for divine grace. 'Thank you' expresses gratitude for the opportunity to learn and grow. And 'I love you' is the ultimate act of acceptance and unity."

The words penetrated my heart, transforming the beach around us. Scenes emerged in the shifting sand: fragments of joy, pain, love, and loss from my past. I saw relationships that had ended in heartache, opportunities missed due to fear, and resentments that had calcified over time.

"Begin with yourself," *Ho'oponopono* guided, his form now resembling a clear, calm pool of water. "Repeat these words as a mantra, directing them towards your own being. While practicing this, visualize the cleansing of painful memories and limiting beliefs from your subconscious mind."

I closed my eyes and began to whisper the words: "I'm sorry. Please forgive me. Thank you. I love you." The mantra brought warmth spreading through my chest, unraveling a tight knot. The beach responded to my words, the sand shifting to create beautiful, healing patterns around my feet. *Love's* eternal warmth merged with *Faith's* acceptance, while *Companionship* and *Protection* stood witness to this sacred healing. Together, they amplified *Ho'oponopono's* transformative power, showing how forgiveness could bridge all dimensions of being.

"Now," *Ho'oponopono* guided, "think of a relationship or situation that needs healing. Direct these words towards it, taking full responsibility for your part in the dynamic."

I thought of a past love, a relationship that had ended in pain and misunderstanding. Tears flowed freely down my cheeks with each repetition. With each repetition, I saw the scene in the sand before me change, the painful memory transforming into one of understanding and peace.

My continued practice awakened the beach with luminescence. Each grain of sand radiated from within, weaving a mosaic of healing light around me. The ocean's waves, once tumultuous, now whispered against the shore, matching the rhythm of my breath.

*Ho'oponopono's* form shifted once more, becoming a radiant light that seemed to emanate from within me and around me simultaneously. "Remember," he said, his voice now a chorus of countless loving whispers, "this practice is not about condoning harmful actions or staying in unhealthy situations. It's about freeing yourself from the bonds of the past and opening your heart to love and forgiveness."

His words echoed through the dreamscape, triggering a fundamental shift within me. The practice of *Ho'oponopono* felt like a key, unlocking doors within my heart that I didn't even know were closed. It offered a way to honor my past experiences while releasing the attachments that had held me back.

The beach began to transform one final time. The sand rose into the air, forming a spiraling galaxy of light and color around me. Each grain represented a moment in my life, a thought, a feeling, all interconnected in a grand eternal dance.

"Moving forward," Ho'oponopono concluded, his light merging with the swirling galaxy, "carry this practice with you. Use it in moments of conflict, in times of self-doubt, in celebrations of joy. Let it be a constant reminder of your power to heal, to love, and to create harmony in your life and in the world around you."

*Ho'oponopono's* presence dissolved into the eternal dance, leaving me with deep peace and possibility. The mantra echoed through the swirling galaxy, each repetition sending ripples of healing harmony through the essence of my being.

I breathed mindfully, feeling past attachments dissolve. The pain of letting go was real, but so was the promise of renewal. I understood now that the journey of love was not about clinging to what was, but about embracing what is and what can be.

With tears of gratitude glistening in my eyes, I whispered one last time: "I'm sorry. Please forgive me. Thank you. I love you." The words rippled through the dream realm, settling the swirling galaxy of my life experiences, each grain of sand finding its perfect place in the grand design of my journey.

The beach materialized anew, transformed by the sacred practice. Each grain of sand coursed with divine light, carrying Ho'oponopono's wisdom through my being. The ocean stretched before me, its clear waters holding infinite possibilities within their depths.

Standing on this sacred shore, I felt the strength of ancient wisdom coursing through me, preparing my spirit for the lessons ahead. Though the journey of self-discovery continued, my heart now carried the lightness of forgiveness and the depth of understanding that Ho'oponopono had awakened within me.

The dreamscape began its familiar shift, drawing me toward new revelations, while the healing mantra echoed through my soul: a gift of transformation that would illuminate my path through all the mysteries yet to come.

The healing mantra's resonance began to transform, its vibrations crystallizing into pure light. My forgiveness-cleansed spirit became a prism, ready to receive and reflect consciousness in its most radiant form. The universe beckoned me toward a new understanding: one where illumination would reveal not just what was healed, but what had always been whole.

# Lesson #38: Shedding Light

*"You are not just a solitary being,*
*but a nexus of connection..."*

---

Ho'oponopono's healing mantra echoed as the dreamscape unveiled a realm of ethereal beauty. Before me stretched a vast forest, trees extending endlessly into the horizon. Morning light wove through the canopy, creating lace-like patterns on the forest floor. Each beam surged with living vitality, speaking of ancient wisdom and timeless truths.

While absorbing the serene beauty of my surroundings, the air shifted subtly. The radiance intensified, not in brightness but presence, illumination becoming tangible, enveloping me like a warm embrace.

"Do you see, dear one?" a voice whispered, seeming to emanate from the very heart of the forest. "This light is not just illumination, but consciousness in its purest form that permeates all of creation."

I closed my eyes, absorbing the voice's words. When I opened them again, I gasped in wonder. The forest had transformed. Each tree now radiated from within, synchronized with my heartbeat. The leaves shimmered with countless tiny sparks, like stars brought down to earth.

"The trees, the plants, even the rocks beneath your feet... they are all sentient beings, each with their own wisdom and story to tell," the voice continued. "They are your silent guardians, your constant companions on this journey of life."

The trees responded, swaying gently despite the stillness, though there was no wind. Their branches reached out towards me, not in a threatening manner, but as if offering an embrace. I felt a deep, visceral connection, of being part of something infinitely vast yet intimately close.

The air shimmered, transporting me to a familiar stretch of road... the two-mile drive I took each morning. But this was no ordinary commute. The trees that lined the road were alive with luminescence and sacred power, forming a protective tunnel of radiance.

"Each day, as you drive this path," the voice said, now seeming to come from within me, "you are surrounded by guardians. The spirits of nature watch over you, offering their strength and protection. They speak to you in the rustling of leaves, in the play of light and shadow. All you need to do is listen."

The revelation sank in as the scene transformed. A vast, open space materialized around me, surrounded by circles of light. Each guide's essence illuminated this sacred space: *Love's* radiant warmth, *Protection's* fierce light, *Faith's* steady glow, and *Companionship's* gentle luminescence. Their combined brilliance showed how different forms of light could create perfect harmony. Each circle emanated a unique signature. Within them, I recognized my departed loved ones... my circle of angels.

Stacy, Danielle, Crystal, Olga, my grandparents, my aunt, my mom, Parker, Courtney, Mindy... each of them stood before me, radiant with divine presence. Their presence filled me with an indescribable warmth, a sense of being truly seen and understood. "We are always with you," they spoke in unison, their voices a harmonious chorus that rippled through my entire being. "In your joys and sorrows, in your triumphs and challenges. We are the unseen hands that guide you, the whispers of encouragement in your darkest hours."

Tears welled up in my eyes as their overwhelming love and support washed over me. Each of them stepped forward, one by one, sharing messages of wisdom and comfort. Their words wove together, creating a brilliant mosaic of insight and guidance that I knew would stay with me long after this dream faded.

Surrounded by angelic love and nature's sentient presence, a fundamental shift awakened within. It was as if all the pieces of my being were finally falling into place, aligning in perfect harmony.

The voice that had guided me through this journey spoke once more, its tone filled with infinite compassion and wisdom. "You are more than you know," it said. "You are not just a solitary being, but a nexus of connection... to nature, to your loved ones, to the very heart of the universe itself."

With these words, I felt a surge of energy coursing through me. The radiance that had surrounded me now seemed to be emanating from within. I closed my eyes, overwhelmed by the sensation, and when I opened them, I stood before a mirror made of pure light.

In my reflection, I saw not just my physical form, but the entirety of my being... past, present, and future.

I saw the connections that tied me to every living thing, the threads of love that bound me to my circle of angels, the roots that grounded me to the earth.

And in that moment of perfect clarity, I understood. The words rose from my soul's center, each one a powerful affirmation of my true nature:

"I am whole." The words brought completion, unifying my fragmented parts coming together in perfect unity. "I am complete." With this declaration, I acknowledged that I lacked nothing, that everything I needed was already within me. "I am love." This truth penetrated my being: love was not something external to be sought or earned, but the very foundation of my existence.

These truths anchored in my heart as the dreamscape faded. But the radiance... that boundless, all-encompassing brilliance... remained. I knew that I was carrying it with me, back into the waking world.

The forest, the road, my circle of angels... all had illuminated the truth of my existence. I was not alone, nor was I separate from the world around me. I was a part of a grand, interconnected web of life and love, always supported, always guided.

Preparing to wake, gratitude filled me for this journey's revelations. Though challenges lay ahead, this new understanding and inner brilliance would light my path. The dream dissolved, but my awakening to wholeness, completeness, and love had only begun.

The brilliance of self-knowledge stirred a deeper yearning within my soul. Wholeness revealed the next step on my spiritual path: the need to surrender this light to something greater than myself. My radiant completeness called for an act of profound trust, a willingness to place my newfound wholeness in the hands of divine wisdom. The dreamscape responded, drawing me toward waters that would reflect not just my own light, but the face of sacred trust itself.

# Lesson #39: Divine Trust

*"Divine trust is not about knowing the future, but about having faith in the present."*

---

The dreamscape unveiled a realm of ethereal dawn. Golden light illuminated the world, each ray carrying whispers of divine wisdom. At the edge of a vast, shimmering lake, I stood, its surface a perfect mirror reflecting the awakening sky.

At the tranquil waters' edge, I felt a presence emerge beside me. It was Morena, her form radiating with a tender, loving light. "Welcome, dear one," she said, her voice a soothing melody. "Today, we explore the depths of divine trust."

Though it was Morena who spoke, I felt my guides' presence supporting this lesson: *Love* providing the foundation for trust, *Protection* ensuring safe space for vulnerability, *Faith* deepening my understanding, while *Companionship* reminded me I was never alone.

I turned to her, my heart open and receptive. "Morena," I began, "I've learned so much about love and self-discovery, but trust... It feels like a different challenge entirely. How do I find faith in the divine plan when the path seems so uncertain?"

Morena smiled, her eyes reflecting the golden light of dawn. "Divine trust," she explained, "is not about knowing the path, but about having faith in the journey itself. It's about understanding that every step, every moment, is part of a greater design."

Her words rippled across the lake, its surface awakening with images. I saw moments from my past: challenges, triumphs, losses, and joys, each one a vivid tableau reflected in the water.

"Look closely," Morena urged. "Each of these moments, whether filled with light or shadow, has brought you to where you are now. This divine knowing recognizes the value in every experience, knowing it serves your highest good."

I watched as the images swirled, forming new patterns and connections. "But what about the fear?" I asked, my voice barely a whisper. "The doubt that creeps in during the darkest moments?"

In response, the lake's surface changed again. This time, I saw an image of myself, surrounded by a warm, protective light. "Fear and doubt are part of the human experience," Morena said softly. "They are not obstacles to divine trust, but opportunities to deepen it. When you feel afraid or uncertain, it's an invitation to lean more fully into trust."

Her words penetrated deep, awakening something within me. Divine faith took root, not as an abstract idea, but as a living, breathing reality. I closed my eyes, surrendering to this fundamental awakening.

When I opened them again, a lush garden surrounded me. The air was filled with the scent of blooming flowers and the soothing hum of life. Morena stood beside a gnarled old tree, its branches reaching towards the sky.

"This tree," she said, placing her hand on its rough bark, "has weathered many storms. It has faced drought and flood, harsh winds and scorching sun. Yet it stands tall, its roots deep in the earth, its branches ever reaching towards the light. This is divine trust embodied."

I approached the tree, feeling its ancient wisdom. The bark beneath my fingers vibrated with its long life: the challenges faced, seasons weathered, growth experienced.

"Like this tree," Morena continued, "you are rooted in divine love. No matter what storms may come, your essence remains unshakeable. Divine trust is about remembering this truth, even in the midst of life's greatest challenges."

Her words sparked a deep connection to the tree, the earth beneath my feet, and the vast sky above. I understood then that divine trust was not something to be achieved, but a reality to be recognized and embraced.

The ancient tree's wisdom transformed the garden around us. The flowers and plants flowed with a healing vibrance, their colors more vibrant than ever before. Vitality surged within, awakening memories of my healing journey.

Morena's eyes met mine, filled with understanding. "Your path of healing," she said softly, "powerfully demonstrates divine trust. Tell me about it."

Gathering my thoughts, I shared how the word "cancer" once cast a long shadow over my life, threatening to steal my peace and hope. Yet from those depths, an essential question emerged:

"Did you ever even have cancer?" This challenge forced me beyond surface fears to confront deeper truths, understanding that healing capacity dwelled within... that body, mind, and spirit intertwined in miraculous transformation.

The garden responded to my words, the healing ambiance growing stronger. Morena smiled, her presence radiating support and love. "And what did you learn from this journey?" she asked.

"I learned that healing is not just about the absence of disease," I replied, my voice growing stronger. "It's about the presence of wholeness, about embracing the entirety of our being with love and compassion. It's about recognizing our inherent power to influence our well-being through our thoughts, emotions, and beliefs."

Morena gestured to the vibrant life around us. "And how does this relate to divine trust?"

I paused, reflecting on the sacred connection. "Divine trust," I said slowly, "is at the core of healing. It's about having faith in our body's innate wisdom, in the divine essence that flows through us. It's trusting that even in our darkest moments, we are held in the embrace of a higher power that guides us towards wholeness."

Strength surged through me with each word. The garden seemed to gleam in response, each plant and flower embodying life's renewal.

"You have a message for others," Morena encouraged. "Share it."

I closed my eyes, letting the truth of my experience rise within me. When I opened them, my voice was clear and strong. "To all those who face the shadow of illness," I began, "know that you can heal. Your body is a miraculous vessel, capable of extraordinary regeneration and transformation. Healing is a journey that encompasses the physical, emotional, and spiritual realms, and it is unique to each individual."

I paused, sensing the gravity of my words. "For some, healing may mean a return to physical health, while for others, it may be a deep sense of peace and acceptance. Whatever form it takes, have faith in the process. Believe in the divine wisdom that flows through you."

Morena's presence seemed to grow stronger, her light merging with the healing aura of the garden. "And what do you claim for yourself?" she asked.

Without hesitation, I responded, "I claim to the universe that I am healed, not just in body but in spirit. This journey has taught me that healing is not a destination but a continuous process of growth and self-discovery. It's about embracing the present moment, letting go of fear, and allowing love to guide the way."

Morena's smile was radiant. "This understanding," she said, "is the essence of divine trust. It's about recognizing the healing power within you, trusting in the journey even when the path is unclear."

I nodded, feeling a deep sense of gratitude wash over me. "Thank you," I whispered, to Morena, to the universe, to the divine presence that had guided me through my healing journey.

"But how do I maintain this faith when life feels overwhelming?" I asked, turning back to Morena.

Her eyes sparkled with wisdom. "Practice gratitude. Each morning, offer thanks for the gift of life, for the breath in your lungs, for the love that surrounds you. Gratitude opens the heart to trust." The garden responded to her words, flowers blooming in an explosion of color, their petals unfurling in a dance of gratitude to the sun.

"And remember," Morena added, her voice filled with love, "you are never alone. The divine presence is always with you, guiding you, supporting you. Trust in this connection, and let it be your anchor in all that you do."

With these words, a fundamental transformation stirred within me. The concept of divine trust was no longer just an idea, but a living, breathing part of my being. I closed my eyes, allowing this truth to settle deep into my soul.

When I opened them again, the phosphorescent lake stretched before me. The dawn had given way to full morning, the world alive with possibility. I turned to Morena, my heart full of gratitude.

"Thank you," I said, my voice thick with emotion. "For guiding me, for helping me understand."

Morena's form faded into the golden light of the morning. "Remember," her voice echoed, "divine trust is not about knowing the future, but about having faith in the present. It's about recognizing that you are exactly where you need to be, always held in the loving embrace of the universe."

Her presence faded, leaving new strength flowing through me. Though uncertainty remained, I faced it now with divine certainty. I understood that each step of my journey was guided by a higher wisdom, each experience an opportunity for growth and deepening faith.

I drew in the cool morning air, letting it fill my lungs. "Thank you," I whispered to the universe, to the divine presence that I now felt more keenly than ever. "Thank you for this journey, for this lesson in trust."

With a heart full of gratitude and a spirit infused with divine trust, I prepared to continue my dream journey. The world around me radiated with possibility, each moment a sacred gift, each step a dance of faith and surrender in the divine plan that guided my path.

The universe answered my surrender with an unexpected challenge. My newfound trust would need to transform into something more: an unshakeable resolve that could weather any storm. The peaceful radiance of faith began to churn with powerful energy, calling forth a strength I didn't know I possessed. The time had come to prove that divine trust wasn't passive acceptance, but the foundation of an iron will that would refuse to sink.

# Lesson #40: Refuse to Sink

*"You must be both anchored in your truth and free to soar into the unknown."*

---

Divine trust transformed into raw power as the dreamscape erupted into chaos. The serene morning light fractured into a disorienting whirlwind, testing the very faith I had just embraced. The room spun, walls wavering like mirages in a desert. While struggling for balance, a familiar presence materialized beside me.

"Fear not, I am here," *Protection's* voice cut through the chaos, steady and reassuring. Her form materialized, solid and steadfast, an anchor of stability in the swirling mayhem.

The world spun in its dizzying dance, and my gaze was drawn to my forearm, where an infinity sign made out of an anchor rope was tattooed. Above it, in delicate handwriting, were the words "I refuse to sink." The ink sparked with an otherworldly luminance, as if awakening to the surreal nature of the dream.

"Look at your tattoo," *Protection* urged, her voice gentle yet insistent. "What does it represent to you?"

I traced the lines of the tattoo with my fingertip, feeling a deep resonance with its message. "It's more than just ink," I said softly. "It's a symbol of resilience, of strength, of the unwavering determination to rise above life's challenges. It reminds me that no matter how difficult things get, I refuse to sink."

My words brought stability, the chaos receding like waves pulling back from the shore. *Protection's* eyes shone with understanding and pride. "Exactly," she affirmed. "This symbol speaks to your inner strength. It was given to you by someone who saw that strength in you, even when you couldn't see it yourself."

The mention of the tattoo's giver sent a ripple of memories through me. I recalled the relationship with the artist, a connection filled with beauty and growth, yet one that didn't have the fairytale ending I had once hoped for. "That relationship," I mused, "taught me so much about love and letting go. It showed me that not all connections are meant to last forever, but that doesn't diminish their value."

*Protection* nodded, her gaze softening. "Each relationship, each experience, is a part of your journey. The contrast between attachment and letting go is where you find true growth. Embrace the lessons, and let go of what no longer serves you. This is where true strength lies."

Her words awakened the tattoo, its light synced to my heartbeat. The anchor and infinity sign seemed to move, as if coming to life on my skin. Power coursed through my being.

"The tattoo is not just a reminder of your resilience," *Protection* continued, her voice taking on a deeper resonance. "It's also a symbol of your connection to the spiritual realm, to the protection and guidance that surrounds you. I am a part of that protection, a guardian of your heart and soul, helping you navigate the challenges you face."

Her words penetrated deep, triggering a fundamental transformation within me. The tattoo was no longer just a piece of art on my skin, but a living, breathing connection to my inner strength and the spiritual forces that guided me.

"Refuse to sink," I whispered, the words feeling more powerful than ever before. It wasn't just a phrase, but a declaration of my inner power, a commitment to rise above any challenge that life might present.

"The infinity anchor tells a story greater than one moment or relationship," *Protection* continued. "It represents the eternal cycle of your spiritual awakening... grounded yet infinite, anchored yet free. Like the lessons of *Love*, *Faith*, and *Wisdom* before us, it speaks to the duality of existence itself. You must be both anchored in your truth and free to soar into the unknown."

*Protection* placed her hand on my shoulder, her touch radiating warmth and strength. "You are never alone on this journey," she said, her voice filled with unwavering support. "The spiritual realm is always with you, offering love, protection, and guidance. Your tattoo is a symbol of this connection, a reminder that you are supported and that you have the strength to face any challenge."

Her words shattered the dreamscape's boundaries, revealing a pivotal truth. The room dissolved, replaced by a vast, open space filled with swirling colors and patterns, a celestial crossroads where multiple paths stretched before me, each one pulsing with possibility.

"You stand at the threshold of your greatest transformation," *Protection* declared, her voice resonating with ancient power. "The paths before you lead to depths of understanding few have reached. The challenges ahead will test everything you've learned... every lesson, every revelation, every truth you've discovered. But you are ready. The anchor within you is not just a symbol of refusing to sink; it's a key to unlocking the final mysteries of your journey."

I looked down at my tattoo once more, feeling its resonance coursing through me. The anchor, intertwined with the infinity sign, was a powerful reminder of my ability to stay grounded while reaching for the infinite possibilities that lay ahead.

"I choose to rise," I said, my voice growing stronger with each word. "I choose to face whatever challenges lie ahead, to learn from every experience, to grow through every trial."

The words unleashed pure power through my being. The dreamscape responded, the swirling colors intensifying into a kaleidoscope mirroring my infinite journey.

*Protection* smiled, her form radiating with an otherworldly light. "Remember," she said, her voice filled with pride and love, "you are resilient. You are unbreakable. You are capable of rising above any storm. Carry this truth with you, let it be your anchor in times of doubt, your wings in moments of triumph."

Her words echoed through the dreamscape, filling me with a deep readiness. The journey ahead was still unknown, filled with challenges and mysteries yet to be unveiled. But I faced it now with a newfound strength, a deep understanding of my resilience, and an unwavering connection to the spiritual guidance that surrounded me.

The tattoo on my arm blazed with divine light, transcending its earthly origins to become a beacon of strength and hope. "I refuse to sink," I declared, the words igniting every fiber of my being with unstoppable power. "I choose to rise, to grow, to transform... not just for myself, but for the greater awakening that awaits."

The dreamscape transformed, charged with the weight of coming revelations. My journey approached its zenith, each lesson building toward a truth greater than I could imagine. *Love's* eternal flame, *Faith's* unwavering presence, and *Companionship's* steady support joined with *Protection's* strength, creating an unshakeable foundation for the journey ahead. The anchor infinity resonated with renewed purpose, no longer just refusing to sink, but preparing to soar. The final chapters of my awakening beckoned, promising both challenge and transcendence.

The infinity anchor's power began to pulse deeper, drawing me beyond mere survival toward something more profound. My refusal to sink transformed into an upward force, lifting me toward the stars. The universe called me to discover that true strength resided not in resistance alone, but in the limitless power that had always existed within my soul.

# Lesson #41: Inner Strength

*"As you unravel the layers of conditioning and ego, you will uncover the radiant essence of who you truly are."*

---

The dreamscape shifted once more, my anchor infinity tattoo pulsing with renewed purpose as the familiar surroundings of the cabana transformed into a vast, celestial expanse. The resilience that had refused to sink now propelled me upward into a sea of stars, each pinpoint of light dancing with the rhythm of my heartbeat. Floating in this universal void, a soul-stirring realization washed over me: we are all characters in the grand narrative of existence, players in a divine drama, each with our own role to fulfill.

This thought spiraled through my consciousness, expanding like a galaxy being born. Every encounter, every relationship, every challenge was a scene in the unfolding story of our lives. We were the protagonists of our own tales, yet simultaneously part of a larger, interconnected epic.

This understanding rooted deep within; the starry expanse around me shifted. The stars coalesced, forming celestial designs. I recognized moments from my journey... the dance in the rain with *Love*, the comforting presence of *Protection*, the wisdom of *Faith*. Each memory shimmered like a living constellation, illustrating the interconnectedness of all experiences.

"We are caught in a perpetual cycle of rewriting our stories," a voice whispered, seeming to come from everywhere and nowhere at once. "Each iteration, each timeline, is an opportunity to learn, to grow, to evolve."

The constellations of my memories overlapped, creating new patterns and connections. I saw how each experience built upon the last, how each lesson learned paved the way for deeper understanding. The sense of déjà vu that had permeated my journey was not mere coincidence, but echoes of a deeper truth... we are given countless opportunities to grasp the lessons we failed to learn in previous timelines.

The realization crystallized in my being; the celestial expanse contracted. The stars rushed towards me, their light enveloping me in a cocoon of radiance. The light receded, unveiling a transformed cabana.

Cracks had appeared in the walls, golden light seeping through like divine illumination.

My gaze was drawn to these fractures, and within them, I saw a vision forming. The Pearly Gates manifested, shimmering with an otherworldly glow. They seemed to beckon me, promising entrance to a realm of higher consciousness.

While standing transfixed by this vision, I felt a familiar presence emerge beside me. *Love* materialized with unprecedented power, her presence both familiar and transformed, as if approaching the zenith of her own evolution. Her essence no longer simply embraced but merged with mine, suggesting the magnitude of revelations to come.

"*Love*," I whispered, my voice trembling with emotion. "Is this the entrance to higher consciousness? Am I truly on the brink of something extraordinary?"

*Love's* eyes, infinite pools of wisdom and compassion, met mine. "Yes, dear one," she replied, her voice blending with the music of the spheres. "What you see is a reflection of the higher realms, the place where your soul can ascend to its fullest potential. It is a realm of pure truth, infinite possibilities, and divine love."

"The gates you see," *Love's* voice deepened with gravity, "mark more than personal transformation. They represent the convergence of every lesson, every trial you've faced. *Protection's* anchor gave you strength to refuse sinking. *Faith* taught you to trust the unseen. *Wisdom* showed you ancient truths. Now these forces unite, preparing you for revelations few souls are ready to receive. The choice to step through will test not just your courage, but everything you've become."

The light from the cracks intensified at her words, bathing the room in golden glow. My heart yearned for the transcendence I glimpsed through them. "But how do I reach this realm?" I asked.

*Love's* smile was radiant, filled with infinite patience and understanding. "By embracing the truth within you," she said, placing her hand over my heart. "The Pearly Gates you see are not just an entrance to heaven, but a symbol of your own awakening. They are a mirror of your inner world, a reminder of the divine light that shines within you."

Her words penetrated deep, triggering a fundamental shift within me. The journey I had undertaken wove together external experiences and inner transformation. Each challenge, each moment of growth, had been a step towards uncovering my true essence.

"Your journey is about uncovering that light," *Love* continued, her voice filled with tender encouragement. "It's about allowing it to illuminate your path and guide you towards higher consciousness. Remember, dear one, you are a being of light and love. Your journey is a sacred one, and every step you take demonstrates your strength and resilience."

With these words, I felt a surge of inner strength, a power that emanated from the very core of my being. The Pearly Gates in the cracks brightened in response, their light growing even more vibrant.

The sacred space around me transformed, each crack in the walls now a conduit for divine light. Every breath drew in celestial essence, my entire being resonating with the frequency of higher consciousness. The boundaries between physical and spiritual dissolved, reality itself becoming fluid with possibility. This wasn't just a moment of strength; it was the evolution of spirit made manifest.

"I am ready," I declared, my voice filled with newfound determination. "Ready to embrace the infinite possibilities, to live in alignment with my highest self, to walk the path of love and truth."

My declaration transformed the room, dissolving reality once more. The walls of the cabana faded away, revealing an infinite expanse of possibility. The Pearly Gates were no longer confined to the cracks but stood before me in all their glory, a shimmering portal to higher consciousness. Each guide's presence strengthened my resolve: *Protection's* fierce support, *Love's* eternal essence, *Faith's* unwavering certainty, and *Companionship's* steady encouragement. Together they formed the foundation that would help me cross this sacred threshold.

*Love's* form shimmered, her radiance merging with the light that surrounded us. "Remember," her voice echoed, filled with boundless love and encouragement, "the journey within is the most sacred journey you will ever undertake. True transformation begins within, and as you unravel the layers of conditioning and ego, you will uncover the radiant essence of who you truly are."

Her presence merged with the surrounding light, leaving me filled with deep peace and purpose. My way forward was illuminated by heightened awareness, guiding me towards deeper understanding and fulfillment.

With a heart full of gratitude and a spirit ready to embrace the infinite possibilities ahead, I stepped forward, towards the Pearly Gates. Each step showed the inner strength I had discovered, each breath a reaffirmation of my commitment to this sacred journey.

Near the gates now, understanding dawned; this marked not an ending but a beginning. The journey of self-discovery, of inner transformation, was ongoing. But now, armed with the wisdom I had gained and the love that filled my heart, I was ready to embrace whatever lay beyond, trusting in the divine presence that resided within me and all around me.

The Pearly Gates opened, universal light pouring forth with unprecedented power. Each lesson burned within me: *Love's* eternal dance, *Protection's* unwavering strength, *Faith's* guiding light, *Wisdom's* timeless knowledge. Their combined force propelled me toward a truth greater than any single teaching. Standing at this spiritual threshold, I sensed the approaching culmination of my journey... not just transformation, but transcendence. The final revelations beckoned, promising to test every truth I'd learned, every strength I'd gained, every wisdom I'd earned.

The Pearly Gates' radiance revealed a deeper truth: transcendence would require more than spiritual awakening alone. My journey called for complete integration: body, mind, and spirit unified in perfect harmony. The divine essence flowing through the gates began to separate into distinct but complementary streams, showing me that true healing must embrace both ancient wisdom and modern understanding.

# Lesson #42: Holistic Healing

*"Healing is a path that honors both scientific knowledge and spiritual wisdom."*

---

The dreamscape shifted once more, the familiar confines of the cabana dissolving into a vast, delicate space. The dreamscape suspended me between two realms, each resonating with its own unique character. To my left, a realm of gleaming steel and precision instruments represented the world of Western medicine. To my right, a lush, vibrant landscape of herbs and ancient wisdom embodied the essence of Eastern healing traditions.

Hovering between these two worlds, I found myself immersed in a fundamental dichotomy. The contrast between Western and Eastern approaches to healing moved beyond academic theory to become an experience that resonated through my entire consciousness.

The Western realm shimmered with the promise of scientific advancement. I saw life-saving surgeries performed with robotic precision, medications tailored to individual DNA, and cutting-edge diagnostic tools that could peer into the deepest recesses of the human body. This was a world of empirical evidence and rigorous research, showcasing human ingenuity and the relentless pursuit of knowledge.

Yet, gazing upon this marvel of modern medicine, I felt a sense of incompleteness. The clinical efficiency, while impressive, seemed to overlook the human element. I recalled moments when I felt like just another case file, my holistic well-being reduced to a set of symptoms and statistics.

My attention shifted to the Eastern realm, where ancient trees whispered secrets of healing passed down through millennia. Here, I saw practitioners of acupuncture channeling the body's vital life force, herbalists concocting remedies that addressed not just physical ailments but emotional and spiritual imbalances. This was a world that recognized the interconnectedness of mind, body, and spirit, emphasizing harmony and the body's innate ability to heal itself.

The Eastern approach connected deeply with my soul, its holistic philosophy aligning with my own experiences of healing. I remembered my journey to Mexico, where I sought healing beyond the confines of conventional medicine. It was a path guided by faith in the unseen, a belief in love's ability, joy, and connection to heal what science alone could not address.

While contemplating these approaches, it became evident that the true path to healing lay not in choosing one over the other, but in finding a harmonious integration of both. Western medicine's life-saving interventions and Eastern philosophy's holistic approach were not mutually exclusive, but complementary facets of a greater whole.

Suddenly, the two realms began to merge, their energies intertwining in a beautiful dance of balance and integration. I saw Western doctors working alongside Eastern practitioners, their combined knowledge creating a new paradigm of healing that honored both scientific advancement and ancient wisdom.

The vision of integrated healing unfolded. It was as if the universe itself was downloading information directly into my consciousness. These "downloads," as I had come to call them, felt like spiritual transmissions from a source beyond myself.

The flood of information sparked a new question: Were these downloads truly from an external source, or were they emanations from my primal self? The boundary between self and universe began to blur, and the possibility emerged that perhaps there was no distinction at all.

"The universe and I are one," I whispered, the words solidifying this soul-awakening realization. "The wisdom I seek, the answers I crave, are all within me, waiting to be discovered through the journey of self-awareness and inner exploration."

This truth anchored into my being, the dreamscape transformed once more. The convergence of ancient wisdom and modern understanding wasn't just philosophical; it was a living alchemy within me. Each healing modality, whether Eastern or Western, spoke to different aspects of the same universal truth. Together they formed a complete medicine for body, mind, and spirit. The dreamscape returned me to the cabana, but it was different now. The walls seemed translucent, allowing glimpses of the vast cosmos beyond. The storm outside raged on, yet a warm, inexplicable light permeated the space.

I sat down to write, feeling an urgent need to capture the insights flooding my consciousness. The act of writing became a sacred practice, a way to channel the divine wisdom flowing through me. Each guide's influence deepened my understanding of true healing: *Love* showing me the heart's role in wellness, *Protection* teaching me to honor my boundaries, *Faith* helping me trust the process, while *Companionship* reminded me that healing often comes through connection. Each word that flowed onto the page felt like a droplet of celestial insight, forming rivers of understanding that connected the disparate elements of my journey.

"Writing is not just an act of expression," I realized, "but a bridge between worlds, a conduit through which the divine speaks. It is a way to translate the ineffable into something tangible, to share the wisdom gleaned from this journey of self-discovery."

As I wrote, I felt a deep alignment with my higher purpose. The storm outside might rage on, but within me, there was a calm and unwavering light. I understood that I was a vessel of love, a conduit of divine wisdom, tasked with sharing this light with the world.

The convergence of Western and Eastern healing philosophies, the concept of spiritual downloads, and the sacred act of writing all merged into a singular truth: healing is a holistic journey that encompasses body, mind, and spirit. It is a path that honors both scientific knowledge and spiritual wisdom, that recognizes the interconnectedness of all things. As I approached the final six lessons of my journey, this integration of healing wisdom felt crucial. Each revelation built upon the last, preparing me for a transformation greater than any single healing modality could achieve.

The dream sequence faded, leaving me with a transcendent sense of peace and purpose. The journey towards holistic healing united physical restoration with divine connection, awakening the healer within.

With each word I wrote, with each insight I integrated, I moved closer to a state of wholeness. The convergence of healing wisdom resonated with the Pearly Gates' promise from my previous vision. Each lesson, each revelation propelled me toward the ultimate transformation awaiting beyond those gates.

The healing journey transcended physical wellness; it was preparation for the transformational awakening that approached. The final trials would demand more than understanding; they would require complete integration of body, mind, and spirit. Success would mean transcendence beyond ordinary consciousness; failure could mean remaining trapped in fragmented awareness forever. Like the merging of Eastern and Western healing, all aspects of my journey were converging toward a singular point of transcendence.

The dream continued its unfolding into its final phase, carrying me toward completion. Within me resided not just understanding, but embodied wisdom, the kind of wholeness necessary for the spiritual transformation that beckoned. Ready to embrace the approaching culmination, armed with insights from both worlds and the unwavering light of divine guidance, I sensed the magnitude of revelations still to come.

The wholeness achieved through healing opened channels I had never known existed. My integrated being became a perfect receiver for the universe's deeper messages. The boundaries of the healing realm began to dissolve, revealing not just wellness but wisdom... cosmic guidance that would show me how to navigate the infinite with my newly unified consciousness.

# Lesson #43: Divine Guidance

*"The journey of awakening is not linear..."*

---

My journey of healing expanded into the cosmos as the cabana walls fell away, unveiling an infinite expanse of starlight. The starlit void suspended me, each pinpoint of light attuned to the rhythm of universal consciousness. Floating in this graceful void, a deep sense of connection washed over me, intertwining my being with the fundamental nature of existence.

In this divine unity, a memory surfaced... vivid and poignant. It was a scene from a cherished video reel, etched into my soul's deepest core. I saw myself sitting in a car at 3 am, with someone I loved deeply, the world around us silent and still, a perfect canvas for the soul-stirring conversation that unfolded. The air was thick with anticipation and the electric current of possibility.

The memory unfolded before me; I realized it wasn't just a recollection, but a divine message. Each word exchanged in that car was a thread, weaving a complex mosaic of vision and purpose that extended far beyond that moment in time. Our shared dreams and aspirations were not mere fantasies, but seeds planted in the soul's fertile ground, destined to bloom in ways we couldn't yet comprehend.

The starry expanse around me surged with an urgent intensity. The cosmos themselves seemed to be whispering, imparting wisdom with an immediacy that transcended time and space. In this connection with the universe, a new understanding dawned upon me… the concept of telepathy, of minds connecting beyond the constraints of physical reality.

"Is this possible?" I wondered, my thoughts echoing through the starlit void. "Can minds truly bridge the gap of space and time?"

In response to my unspoken question, a cascade of memories flooded my consciousness. I recalled moments when a loved one had called just as I was thinking of them, times when I had sensed a friend's distress from miles away, instances when words were unnecessary because understanding flowed freely between souls.

The universal voice, gentle yet transformative, echoed through the starry expanse. "Telepathy is not a myth, but a forgotten language of the soul. It is the purest form of communication, unbounded by words and unhindered by physical distance."

I pondered this, feeling both awe and skepticism. "But how can this be? It seems beyond the realm of possibility."

"Consider the nature of energy," the voice continued. "Every thought, every emotion, sends ripples through the universal web. Those attuned to these subtle vibrations can receive and interpret these signals. It is not about reading minds, but about sensing the spiritual current that flows between connected souls."

Absorbing this wisdom, I remembered the deep connection I had felt with my twin flame, moments when we seemed to communicate without words, understanding flowing between us like an electric current. Was this the telepathy the voice spoke of?

"Yes," the voice affirmed, seeming to read my thoughts. "Your connection was a beautiful example of souls in harmony, vibrating at frequencies that allowed for this silent communion."

The starry expanse around me shifted, forming patterns that resembled neural networks, vast and winding. I saw how each star was connected to countless others, much like the neurons in a brain, or the souls in the ethereal web of existence.

"Divine guidance often comes through these telepathic channels," the voice explained. "The nudges of intuition, the sudden flashes of insight, the inexplicable knowing... all are forms of spirit communication. You are always connected to the divine source, always in communion with the universe. Telepathy is simply learning to consciously tune into this ever-present connection."

This understanding settled into my being, I felt a fundamental shift in my perception. The boundaries between self and other, between individual and cosmos, seemed to dissolve. I was at once the dreamer and the dream, the observer and the observed.

"But how do I cultivate this ability?" I asked, my thoughts rippling through the starlit expanse.

"Through presence, through love, through openness," the voice replied. "When you quiet the mind and open the heart, you become a clear channel for divine guidance. Practice listening not just with your ears, but with your entire being. Feel the subtle energies that flow around and through you."

With this guidance, I closed my eyes (or did I open them to a new level of perception?) and allowed myself to sink deeper into the universal consciousness. The essence of countless souls swirled around me, each one a unique note in the universal symphony.

In this state of heightened awareness, I sensed the presence of all who had guided me on this journey: *Love*, *Protection*, *Faith*, *Companionship*, and others. Their energies were distinct yet harmonious, each one a vital part of the celestial chorus.

I reached out with my mind, sending a thought of gratitude rippling through the web of light. To my amazement, their responses came not in words, but in waves of emotion and understanding that washed over me like warm light.

This experience of telepathic communion was both exhilarating and humbling. Awareness awakened within me; this ability had always been present, within all of us, waiting to be remembered and rekindled. *Love* had shown me the language of the heart, *Protection* taught me to trust my intuition,

*Faith* helped me embrace the unknown, and *Companionship* showed how souls could connect across any distance. Their combined wisdom illuminated the path of divine communication.

While absorbing this newfound understanding, the voice spoke once more. "Remember, dear one, that with this ability comes great responsibility. Use it with wisdom, with love, and always in service of the highest good."

I nodded, feeling the magnitude and the wonder of this knowledge. The journey of divine guidance had led me to this powerful realization, opening my eyes to the infinite web of connection that underlies all of existence.

The realization anchored within my being, and I felt a surge of illumination course through me. It was as if the universe was downloading information directly into my consciousness. These spiritual "downloads" felt both familiar and entirely new, a paradox that spoke to the cyclical nature of enlightenment.

"The journey of awakening is not linear," a voice whispered, seeming to emanate from the stars themselves. "It is a spiral, each turn bringing you back to familiar truths with deeper understanding."

I pondered this wisdom, recognizing how each lesson in my dream journey had built upon the last, each revelation a stepping stone to greater awareness. The concepts of telepathic connection, twin flames, and love's ability to transcend physical boundaries... all were aspects of a greater truth about the interconnectedness of all beings.

While contemplating these soul-stirring insights, the sea of stars around me began to shift. The stars coalesced into mysterious configurations that I recognized as symbols from my waking life... the bracelet from the Mayan ruins, the logo of a company I deeply believed in. These tangible reminders of my earthly existence were not mere coincidences, but divine signposts guiding me towards my true path.

"Every symbol, every synchronicity, is a message from the universe," the voice continued. "They are bridges between the seen and unseen, the physical and the spiritual."

With this understanding, I felt a mounting sense of anticipation. The journey was far from over, but I could sense that I was approaching a pivotal moment of transformation. Each lesson, each revelation, had been preparing me for something greater... a spiritual awakening that would forever alter my perception of reality.

The starry expanse blazed in response to my thoughts with an even more intense brilliance. The boundaries between dream and reality blurred, leaving me in a state of exhilarating uncertainty. Was I awakening, or delving deeper into the dream? The distinction seemed increasingly irrelevant as I realized that both states were equally valid paths to truth.

In this sacred threshold, all the spirits I had encountered gathered on this journey. Their energies merged with the starlight, creating a symphony of wisdom that flowed through every fiber of my being. Each had played a crucial role in my growth, their lessons intertwining to form a comprehensive mosaic of spiritual understanding.

*Love's* boundless compassion, *Protection's* unwavering strength, *Faith's* serene trust, *Companionship's* unconditional support... all were facets of the divine guidance that had led me to this point. I understood now that these guides were not separate entities, but aspects of my higher self, reflections of the divine spark within me.

This eternal truth anchored in my consciousness, unleashing a surge of inner strength. The challenges I had faced, the doubts I had overcome... all had been necessary steps in my evolution. I emerged changed, no longer the person who started this journey; I had been transformed, reborn in the crucible of divine wisdom. Yet, even as I reveled in this newfound strength, I sensed that the greatest challenge still lay ahead.

"Trust in the divine guidance that has brought you this far," the voice whispered. "The future may be uncertain, but you carry within you universal truth."

With these words resonating through my being, I felt complete readiness for what lay ahead. The sacred threshold beckoned, promising transformation beyond anything I had known before. The journey that had begun with *Love's* guidance, strengthened through *Protection's* wisdom, illuminated by *Faith's* light, and sustained by *Companionship's* unwavering presence now approached its zenith.

Five final lessons remained. Each one would demand complete surrender, testing every truth I'd discovered, every strength I'd gained. The Pearly Gates gleamed in my memory, their promise of transcendence now merging with the wisdom of holistic healing. Success meant awakening to my full potential; failure meant remaining forever between worlds.

The starlit expanse shifted, unveiling the next phase of my journey. Divine guidance had prepared me for this moment. With gratitude filling my heart and spirit aligned with universal truth, I stepped forward, ready to embrace the mysteries that awaited beyond the threshold.

The stars of divine guidance began to pulse with new radiance, their light transforming from mere illumination into pure love. The cosmic wisdom that had shown me the way now revealed its deepest truth: that guidance and love were one and the same force. The universe wasn't just showing me the path; it was drawing me toward the very essence of unconditional love.

# Lesson #44: Unconditional Love

*"All beings are expressions of the same divine dance, each playing their part in the grand symphony of existence."*

The starlit expanse that had surrounded me began to shift, the stars coalescing into a shimmering portal. *Wisdom* and *Healing* emerged from the ethereal light, their presence radiating a deep sense of purpose.

"Come," *Wisdom* beckoned, her voice merging with the harmonies of the universe. "There is a truth you must experience to understand."

Stepping through the portal, reality itself seemed to bend and warp. We materialized in a realm that defied description... a place where the physical and spiritual intertwined in ways my mind struggled to comprehend. Before us stood a massive, ancient tree, its branches reaching toward an ever-shifting sky that pulsed with the heartbeat of creation.

At the base of the tree sat an elderly man, his form seemingly composed of both flesh and starlight. His eyes, deep pools of infinite experience, met mine with a gaze that pierced through the layers of my being.

"This is the Tree of Life," *Healing* explained, his voice gentle yet charged with divine purpose. "And he is its keeper, a manifestation of all souls who have ever lived and will ever live."

Approaching closer, the old man's form flickered, momentarily revealing glimpses of countless faces... young and old, from every culture and time. I realized with a start that I was looking at a living embodiment of humanity itself.

"Greetings, seeker," the keeper spoke, his voice a chorus of millions. "You stand at the threshold of understanding. Are you prepared to embrace the truth of unconditional love?"

Before I could respond, the tree began to glow, its bark becoming translucent. Within its trunk, I saw the flow of life itself... a river of light connecting all beings across time and space. Each soul was a drop in this universal stream, interconnected and interdependent.

"Unconditional love," *Wisdom* intoned, "is not merely an emotion or an ideal. It is the fundamental essence of existence, the force that binds the universe together."

Her words pulled me into the tree's radiance. Suddenly, I was experiencing life through the eyes of countless others... the joy of a child's first steps, the anguish of loss, the triumph of overcoming adversity. Each experience, each emotion, flowed through me in a torrent of shared consciousness.

The experiences flowing through me revealed how my guides had prepared me for this truth. *Love* had taught connection, *Protection* acceptance, *Faith* trust, and *Companionship* unwavering presence. *Love, Protection, Faith*, and *Companionship* had each revealed different aspects of unconditional love: through tender embrace, fierce guardianship, unwavering trust, and eternal presence. Their combined wisdom showed how love could take many forms while remaining boundless. Their combined wisdom illuminated the true nature of unconditional love.

"To love unconditionally," the keeper's voice thundered within me, "is to recognize that there is no 'other.' All beings are expressions of the same divine dance, each playing their part in the grand symphony of existence."

At that moment, I understood. The boundaries that separated me from others—age, gender, race, circumstance—were illusions. At our core, we were all manifestations of the same universal energy, each a unique expression of the divine.

The awakening shifted, and I found myself back in the presence of the keeper. But now, I saw him with new eyes. In his weathered face, I recognized the divine spark that resided in all beings. His tattered clothes were a reminder of the impermanence of physical form, while his eyes reflected the eternal nature of the soul.

"The greatest act of love," *Healing* said softly, "is to see the divine in all beings, especially those society deems unworthy or invisible."

The tree's branches responded, extending to form a canopy that encompassed the entire realm. Each leaf was a window into a different life, a different struggle, a different triumph. I saw the homeless man on the street corner, the child in a war-torn country, the wealthy executive grappling with inner emptiness... all connected, all part of the same universal web.

"Your journey," *Wisdom* said, her voice filled with both compassion and challenge, "is not just about personal enlightenment. It is about becoming a conduit for unconditional love in the world."

The keeper nodded, his form shimmering with starlit radiance. "To love unconditionally is to act as a bridge between the divine and the earthly realms. It is to see beyond the surface, to recognize the sacred in the mundane, and to offer compassion without judgment."

The words anchored deep, triggering a fundamental shift within my being. The concept of unconditional love was no longer an abstract ideal but a living, breathing reality that flowed through every fiber of my existence.

"But how?" I asked, my voice trembling with this staggering realization. "How can I carry this understanding into the waking world?"

The keeper smiled, and in that smile, I saw the love of the universe itself. "By remembering that every interaction, every moment, is an opportunity to embody divine love. By treating each soul you encounter as if they were the most precious being in existence... because, in truth, they are."

The scene fading, I felt a surge of vitality course through me. It was as if the Tree of Life itself was infusing me with its wisdom, preparing me for the next phase of my journey. The wisdom of unconditional love merged with the Pearly Gates' promise of transformation. Each lesson brought me closer to that sacred threshold, where this limitless love would be tested in ways I couldn't yet imagine.

"Remember," *Wisdom's* voice echoed as the realm dissolved around us, "unconditional love is not weakness. It is the greatest strength in the universe, capable of healing wounds, bridging divides, and transforming reality."

*Healing's* final words lingered in the air as we transitioned back to the celestial expanse. "You carry this truth within you now. Let it guide your every step, your every breath. For in embodying unconditional love, you become a living testament to the divine nature of all existence."

Suspended among the stars once more, a deep sense of purpose filled me. Unconditional love had transformed my understanding, revealing the divine potential within all souls. This sacred wisdom would guide me through the challenges ahead, its strength becoming my strength, its truth my compass. The eternal dance continued, beckoning me toward the next phase of my journey, where this limitless love would illuminate the path to ultimate transformation.

The infinite love that filled my being began to shine inward, illuminating corners of my soul I had long kept dark. This love demanded more than outward expression; it called for the courage to face what lurked in my own depths. The starlit expanse responded, drawing back its celestial curtain to reveal the shadows that waited to test the true boundlessness of my love.

# Lesson #45: Shadows Unveiled

*"To truly embrace the light,
you must first dance with your shadows."*

---

The expanse around me began to darken, stars fading into an inky void. A chill ran through my form as *Wisdom's* voice echoed through the emptiness: "To truly embrace the light, you must first dance with your shadows." The limitless love I'd just discovered faced its greatest test: loving the unloved parts of myself.

Suddenly, I plummeted through layers of consciousness, each level peeling away pretenses and illusions. I landed hard on an obsidian floor, my reflection staring back at me with eyes that held galaxies of unexplored emotion.

From the darkness, three figures emerged... not the familiar spirits of my journey, but twisted reflections of myself. The first, a hunched and bitter version of me, eyes narrowed with resentment. The second stood tall and imposing, fists clenched with barely contained rage. The third curled in on itself, a child-like form trembling with fear and hurt.

"We are the parts of you that you've tried to bury," they spoke in unison, voices a discordant chorus. "The resentment you've disguised as spiritual bypassing. The rage you've masked with false serenity. The vulnerability you've hidden behind walls of pseudo-strength."

I wanted to run, to wake up, to return to the comforting lessons of love and light. But *Love*, *Protection*, *Faith*, and *Companionship* had taught me better. Their combined wisdom showed me that true strength comes from embracing all aspects of self... even the darkest shadows. And *Wisdom's* words anchored me: "Observe. Listen. Integrate."

The resentful self stepped forward, his voice dripping with bitterness. "You preach forgiveness, but where is your compassion for the part of you that still feels wronged? You silence me with platitudes, but I am the voice of your unmet needs, your trampled boundaries."

Shame washed over me as I recognized the truth in those words. How often had I used spiritual concepts to avoid confronting genuine hurt and injustice?

The rageful self lunged next, his eyes blazing. "You speak of peace, but you fear your own power. I am the fire of your convictions, the strength to fight injustice. In denying me, you deny your own capacity to create change."

My body trembled with the force of suppressed anger, years of swallowed words and stifled protests rising to the surface.

The child-self approached last, tears streaming down its face. "You talk of unconditional love, but where is that love for me? I am your deepest wounds, your unmet longing. In rushing to heal others, you leave me alone in the dark."

My heart shattered as I faced the neglected, wounded parts of myself I had left behind in my spiritual journey.

*Wisdom's* voice rang out once more: "True enlightenment is not the absence of shadows, but the courage to embrace them. Your darkness holds wisdom; your pain carries purpose."

With trembling hands, I reached out to each reflection. To *Resentment*, I whispered, "I honor the injustices you've faced. Your voice matters." To *Rage*, I acknowledged, "Your fire has purpose. I will channel you, not suppress you." To the *Wounded Child*, I promised, "I see you. I'm here now, and I'm not leaving you behind."

As I embraced each shadow, they began to merge with me. *Resentment* softened into discernment, *Rage* tempered into righteous purpose, and the child's pain blossomed into heartfelt empathy. The obsidian floor beneath me cracked, and light seeped through the fissures.

I rose, feeling more whole than I had in eons of spiritual seeking. The shadows hadn't disappeared, but they no longer controlled me from the dark. They were integrated, a vital part of my being.

*Love*, *Protection*, *Faith*, and *Companionship* had taught me to embrace others unconditionally. Now I had to extend that same acceptance to my own shadows. Rising whole and integrated, I sensed the magnitude of what lay ahead. This shadow work was crucial preparation for the deep-rooted transformations still to come.

*Wisdom* appeared, her eyes shining with approval. "This is the alchemy of the soul," she said. "In embracing your shadows, you have transmuted lead into gold. Remember, the journey of integration is ongoing. Your shadows will resurface, but now you have the tools to dance with them, to learn from them, to love them as part of your whole self."

The dreamscape shifted once more and I carried with me a fundamental understanding: true enlightenment isn't a state of perpetual light, but the courage to embrace both radiance and shadow. In accepting my darkness, I had discovered my greatest strength: the power to transform pain into purpose, wounds into wisdom, and fear into fierce authenticity. The journey continued, but now I walked as my complete self, shadows and all.

The integration of my shadows revealed something unexpected: each dark piece carried not just personal truth, but universal connection. My wholeness opened doorways to a web of consciousness far greater than myself. The boundaries of individual experience began to dissolve, showing me that every shadow embraced, every wound transformed, created threads of understanding that bound me to all of existence.

# Lesson #46: Sacred Connection

*"Your life is your canvas, and your consciousness is the paintbrush."*

The familiar confines of the cabana dissolved, my newly integrated shadows dancing with purpose as an infinite expanse of shimmering threads appeared. The web suspended me, each strand vibrating with the essence of my journey, both light and shadow interweaving into something greater. My touch on a nearby filament sparked a memory... a lesson learned, a shadow embraced, a truth uncovered.

*Wisdom's* voice echoed through the vast network. "You stand at the threshold of culmination, dear one. But before you take the final steps, you must understand the sacred connection that binds all of existence."

Her words triggered the divine web to shift and coalesce, forming the sacred pattern of a massive dream catcher. Each thread shimmered with living light, carrying whispers of countless souls and timeless wisdom.

"The dream catcher," *Wisdom* continued, "is more than a talisman. It is a map of consciousness, a blueprint of reality itself. Just as you encourage young minds to Dream Out Loud, the universe dreams existence into being."

Each guide had shown me different aspects of this truth: *Love* through divine connection, *Protection* through sacred boundaries, *Faith* through trust in the unseen, and *Companionship* through shared dreaming.

The implications of this statement sent shockwaves through my understanding. Could reality itself be a shared dream, a collective manifestation of consciousness?

While pondering this, I noticed that some threads of the sacred dream catcher were entangled, creating knots of discord and suffering. Others flowed harmoniously, creating beautiful patterns of synchronicity and joy.

"Your journey," *Healing's* voice joined in, "has been about learning to navigate this web, to untangle the knots within yourself and to vibrate in harmony with the highest frequencies of existence."

I watched in awe as scenes from my journey played out along the threads: facing my shadows, embracing unconditional love, acknowledging the divine within myself and others. Each lesson had been a step towards aligning my personal "dream" with the greater dream of the universe.

I felt a fundamental shift in my perception. I merged with the dreamcatcher, no longer merely observing but becoming part of its essence. Every thought, every action, every choice I made sent ripples through the entire web of existence.

"This is the true meaning of sacred connection," *Love's* melodious voice rang out. "It is the recognition that you are both the dreamer and the dream, the observer and the observed. Your life is your canvas, and your consciousness is the paintbrush."

The realization deepened, and I began to see how every soul was a unique intersection point in the sacred web, each one dreaming their reality into existence. Some were caught in nightmares of their own making, while others were consciously co-creating beauty and harmony.

"The power to Dream Out Loud," *Wisdom* said, "is not just for the young. It is the birthright of every conscious being. But with this power comes great responsibility."

I understood then that my work with youth, encouraging them to envision and pursue their dreams, was more life-changing than I had realized. I wasn't just helping them set goals—I was teaching them to become conscious co-creators of reality.

*Faith* understood my thoughts and spoke: "Your Dream Out Loud program is a microcosm of the greater work at hand... awakening humanity to its role as conscious participants in the universal dream."

The dream catcher grew with increasing intensity, each thread singing with the harmony of aligned purpose. I saw how when individuals vibrated in tune with their highest selves, it created resonance patterns that amplified positive change throughout the entire web.

"This is how transformation occurs," *Protection's* steady voice explained. "Not through force or control, but through alignment and resonance. While healing and harmonizing your own thread in the universal web, you inspire those around you to do the same."

*Love, Protection, Faith*, and *Companionship* gathered close, their presence more powerful than ever before. "The Dream Out Loud vision is more than a teaching tool," they spoke in unison. "It is the very essence of conscious creation... the power to manifest divine reality through pure intention. This understanding will be crucial in the trials ahead. What began as a program to empower youth has become your gateway to the final transformations. Every soul you've helped dream out loud has prepared you for what comes next."

In that moment, I grasped the true significance of the spiritual journey I had undertaken. It wasn't just about personal growth or individual enlightenment. It was about becoming a tuning fork for the universe, a conscious node in the web of existence that could help harmonize the entire system.

"The final steps of your journey," *Wisdom* said, her voice filled with both gravity and excitement, "will require you to fully embody this understanding. You must become a lucid dreamer in the waking world, consciously co-creating reality in alignment with the highest good of all."

The divine dream catcher faded, leaving me with a deep-rooted sense of purpose and connection. The journey ahead would be challenging, but I now understood the true stakes—and the limitless potential—of conscious, creative existence.

*Wisdom's* final words reverberated through my being: "Remember, every moment is an opportunity to Dream Out Loud, to weave beauty and meaning into the foundation of reality. The universe is listening, responding, co-creating. What song will you sing? What reality will you dream into being?"

Descending back toward the cabana, I carried profound truth and burning purpose. The boundaries between spirituality and creativity had dissolved into something greater: the power to dream new realities into being. Two final lessons remained, each promising to challenge everything I understood about conscious creation. The eternal dance beckoned, and I sensed that my greatest test... and transformation... lay just ahead.

The threads of cosmic connection began to crystallize into something more personal, more profound. Beyond the vast web of universal consciousness, certain bonds emerged with blazing clarity... relationships that transcended time, space, and even reality itself. The dream catcher's pattern transformed, revealing the eternal nature of true spiritual companionship, the unbreakable bonds forged in the crucible of awakening.

# Lesson #47: Eternal Bonds

*"Companionship, Love, Protection, and Faith are expressions of the singular consciousness that permeates all of existence."*

---

The familiar confines of the cabana dissolved, giving way to a realm beyond time and space. I stood at the center of a sacred mandala, its intricate patterns shifting and flowing with living light. At each of the four cardinal points stood a radiant being… *Companionship*, *Love*, *Protection*, and *Faith*. Their presence filled the space with a resonance so potent it seemed to vibrate.

*Wisdom's* voice echoed through the ether: "You stand at the threshold of ultimate understanding. These four beings represent the pillars of your spiritual journey. Through them, you will glimpse the true nature of eternal bonds."

As if orchestrated by an unseen hand, the mandala's rotation brought me face to face with *Companionship*.

Her form shimmered with countless shared experiences... laughter echoing through sun-dappled forests, quiet conversations under starlit skies, hands clasped in mutual support through life's storms.

"*Companionship*," I began, my voice thick with emotion, "through every lesson, every challenge, you've shown how true companionship transforms isolation into unity, fear into shared strength. You've shown me the sacred dance of giving and receiving, of walking beside another soul through the journey of life."

She smiled, her eyes reflecting infinite timelines of shared growth. "The bond we share transcends this single lifetime," she replied. "In our connection, you've glimpsed the timeless nature of all relationships. Every act of kindness, every moment of shared joy or sorrow, ripples through the cosmos, intertwining the celestial threads of existence itself."

I understood then that true companionship was a microcosm of universal interconnectedness, a living embodiment of the principle that we are all one.

The mandala shifted, bringing me before *Love*, her presence a supernova of unconditional acceptance and boundless compassion.

"*Love,*" I whispered, "you've been the driving force of my journey, the light that's guided me through the darkest nights of the soul. Your lesson of unconditional love has prepared me for this moment, teaching me to embrace all aspects of existence with an open heart."

*Love's* voice merged with the harmony of creation itself. "I am the force that binds the universe, the essence that flows through all things," she said. "In embracing me fully, you become a conduit for divine love, a creator in your own right."

Her words revealed love as more than emotion, but as the fundamental creative principle of the cosmos. Every act of love was an act of co-creation with the divine, a participation in the ongoing unfolding of the universe.

The mandala turned once more, bringing me face to face with *Protection*. Her form was a fortress of light, yet within her I sensed deep vulnerability.

"*Protection,*" I said, reaching out to her, "you've been my shield and my strength. But I see now that true protection comes from embracing our vulnerabilities, not hiding from them. Like the shadows I've learned to embrace, you've taught me that true protection comes from integration, not resistance."

*Protection's* eyes shimmered with unshed tears. "In allowing yourself to be truly seen, you've unlocked the deepest form of strength," she replied. "True protection isn't about building walls, but about cultivating the resilience to remain open-hearted in the face of life's challenges."

The wisdom crystallized: protection and vulnerability were two sides of the same coin, each essential for genuine growth and connection.

Finally, I turned to *Faith*, her presence radiating unwavering trust in the unseen.

"*Faith*," I breathed, "you've been the bridge between the known and the unknown, the courage to take leaps into the darkness. Now, as we approach the final threshold, your unwavering presence lights the way toward ultimate truth."

*Faith's* voice was soft yet unshakable. "I am the knowledge that transcends mere belief," she said. "Through me, you touch the infinite, you remember your true nature as a limitless being of light."

At that moment, I understood faith not as blind belief, but as a deep knowing of the interconnectedness of all things, a trust in the fundamental benevolence of the universe.

Standing in the presence of these four beings, I felt a fundamental shift in my consciousness. The boundaries between us began to blur, and I saw that they were not separate entities, but aspects of my higher self, reflections of the divine within me. Their individual teachings had merged into one profound truth: that all forms of divine connection, whether through *Love's* embrace, *Protection's* strength, *Faith's* trust, or *Companionship's* presence, were expressions of the same eternal force.

*Wisdom's* voice returned, flowing through every fiber: "These timeless bonds are not just connections between separate beings. They are reminders of the ultimate truth... that all is one. *Companionship*, *Love*, *Protection*, and *Faith* are expressions of the singular consciousness that permeates all of existence."

This realization washed over me. The mandala began to spin faster, merging the four beings into a brilliant vortex of light. I felt myself being drawn into this light, every cell of my being vibrating with the truth of unity.

In this sacred communion, I understood gratitude not just as an emotion, but as a fundamental state of being. To be grateful was to be fully aligned with the flow of universal abundance, to recognize every experience—joyful or challenging—as a gift from the universe to itself.

The vortex of light engulfing me, I heard *Wisdom's* final words: "Carry this understanding with you. Let it infuse every moment, every interaction. For in remembering these sacred bonds, you remember your true nature as a limitless, eternal being of light."

The mandala collapsed into a single point of blinding radiance, and I felt myself being gently returned to the familiar space of the cabana. But I was no longer the same. The understanding of divine bonds had transformed me, aligning me more fully with the divine dance of creation.

One final lesson remained, promising to test every truth I'd discovered, every bond I'd strengthened, every wisdom I'd earned. The very fabric of reality seemed to hold its breath, waiting for what would come next.

The divine bonds that held me now began to pulse with transformative power, urging me toward my final metamorphosis. Each relationship, each sacred connection had been preparation for this moment... not an ending, but a rebirth. The cabana filled with the first light of dawn, calling me to return to where my journey began, but this time with the wisdom of forty-seven lessons burning in my soul. My transformation had come full circle, ready for one last revelation that would bridge all I had learned with all I was meant to become.

# Lesson #48: New Beginnings

*"You are the universe experiencing itself in human form."*

---

The first light of dawn filtered through the cabana window; I felt a familiar pull... the sensation of an impending portal jump. The world around me began to shimmer and blur, the boundaries between dream and reality dissolving once more. I closed my eyes, surrendering to the flow of divine grace that had guided me throughout this journey.

When I opened my eyes, I stood amidst the ancient Mayan Ruins of Palomeque, Mexico, the very place where this extraordinary dream had begun. The air hummed with a presence as palpable as it had been on that first day, spiritual vibrations wrapping around me like a cloak of wisdom and love. The weathered stones hummed with ancient knowledge, each carving and symbol revealing the enduring quest for understanding.

Standing there, I marveled at how much I had changed. The person who had first stood in this spot, teetering on the brink of revelation, was but a shadow of who I had become. Now, after facing my deepest fears, embracing my inner light, and dancing with the essential forces of existence, I was ready to fully embrace the truths that had been waiting for me all along.

The air before me shimmered, and from the ethereal light emerged the radiant forms of *Love* and *Wisdom*. Their presence filled me with a sense of comfort and completion, as if the final pieces of a divine puzzle were falling into place.

*Love* stepped forward, her eyes twinkling with a mixture of joy and serenity. "Welcome back," she said warmly, her voice carrying the melody of a thousand hearts beating as one. "You have journeyed far and learned much. Now, it is time to bring everything together."

I nodded, feeling a surge of anticipation. "I'm ready," I said, my voice steady with newfound confidence. "What is the ultimate truth that ties all of this together?"

*Wisdom's* eyes sparkled with ancient knowledge as she began to speak. "The message, dear one, is both simple and eternal: Love is the foundation of all spiritual teachings. It transcends religious boundaries, cultural differences, and even time itself."

*Love* continued, her voice filled with gentle conviction. "The great spiritual teachers throughout history: Buddha, Jesus, Mohammed... they were not founders of religions as we know them today. They were messengers of love. Their teachings, at their core, all point to the same universal truth."

"Buddha was not a Buddhist," *Wisdom* added. "Jesus was not a Christian. Mohammed was not a Muslim. They were teachers who taught love. Love itself was their religion."

Her words penetrated deep as understanding dawned: Love wasn't just a belief system; it was the active force of creation itself, the power that had guided humanity's greatest teachers and would guide future generations toward awakening.

The words penetrated deep, triggering a fundamental shift in my understanding. It was as if a veil had been lifted, revealing the underlying unity of all spiritual paths.

*Love's* voice rang with this truth's force. "This is the message you are meant to share with the world:

Love is everywhere and in everyone and everything. It is not just an emotion, but an energy, a force that unites us all. It is the essence of existence, the thread that weaves together the sacred web of reality."

I closed my eyes, letting this revelation sink deep into my being. When I opened them again, I saw the Mayan Ruins in a new light. The ancient stones now glowed with this universal love, each carving and symbol a different expression of the same eternal truth.

"Love is my religion," I said softly, the words embodying everything I had experienced and learned on this incredible journey. "It is the core of everything, the foundation of all wisdom, the source of all healing."

*Love* and *Wisdom* nodded, their expressions filled with approval and encouragement. "You are ready," *Wisdom* said softly. "You have the knowledge, the experience, and the heart to share this message with the world."

Their words sank in, shifting the atmosphere around me. The Mayan Ruins began to fade, the ancient stones dissolving into mist. I lay back in the cabana, in the familiar bed. The room was hazy, the lines between dream and reality blurred. I glanced out the window, wondering if I was awake or still dreaming. The feeling was surreal, but there was a sense of peace and clarity within me that I had never known before.

I knew that my journey was far from over. In fact, it felt as if it was just beginning. But now, armed with the transformative understanding of love as the universal truth, I was ready to face whatever lay ahead. The world outside the cabana window bloomed with new life, each leaf and flower a unique expression of the divine love that permeated all of existence.

With renewed purpose, I prepared myself for the final stages of this transformative journey, knowing that the greatest adventure... sharing this message of love with the world... was yet to come.

This realization settled as the scene transformed. The solid walls of the cabana seemed to dissolve, the familiar surroundings giving way to something far more vast and ethereal. I felt myself being drawn into a new level of consciousness, one that transcended the physical realm entirely.

The first rays of divine dawn pierced the veil, and I found myself at the edge of a vast expanse. My sanctuary throughout this journey had transformed, leaving me suspended between worlds. The air vibrated with potential, each breath a symphony of universal essence.

The space around me burst into a kaleidoscope of light and color. Countless threads of luminous radiance wove themselves into ethereal designs, forming a living, breathing sacred web of existence. Each thread vibrated with its own rhythm, yet all were part of a greater harmony. I recognized this as a higher manifestation of the universal love I had just come to understand... love as the cornerstone of reality itself.

From within this eternal dance emerged the familiar forms of *Healing* and *Wisdom*, their presence both comforting and awe-inspiring. Their eyes held galaxies of knowledge, their smiles radiating the unconditional love they had just taught me about. They were no longer just guides, but embodiments of the universal truths I had discovered.

*Healing* spoke, his voice rippling through the ethereal web, "You have glimpsed the truth at the heart of all existence. Now, it's time to experience it fully, to become one with the dance of creation."

*Wisdom* nodded, adding, "This is the final stage of your journey... the integration of all you have learned. Here, you will see how love, as the foundation of all spiritual teachings, manifests in the very structure of the universe."

Their words sparked a fundamental shift within me. The boundaries of my self began to dissolve, expanding outward to encompass the entire celestial lattice. I was no longer just an observer of this grand dance... I was becoming the dance.

"This is the ultimate truth," *Wisdom* intoned, her words echoing those she had spoken at the Mayan Ruins, but now imbued with spiritual significance. "You are not separate from the universe. You are the universe experiencing itself in human form. Every joy, every sorrow, every triumph and challenge... all are expressions of the eternal dance of love."

In that moment, I understood. The journey had never been about reaching a destination or achieving some state of perfection. It was about remembering my true nature, about recognizing the divine play of love that unfolds in every moment, across all dimensions of existence.

The sacred web intensified with growing power, each thread singing its unique note in the universal symphony. I saw how every experience in my life, even the painful ones, had been a necessary part of this grand composition of love.

"But with this understanding comes great responsibility," *Healing* said, his eyes shimmering with compassion. "You must now choose how you will dance. Will you move in harmony with the flow of love, or will you resist it?"

The ethereal network shifted in response, revealing scenes from my life and from the lives of countless others. I saw moments of deep connection and heart-wrenching separation, acts of breathtaking kindness and shocking cruelty. Each scene was a reminder of the power we hold to shape our reality.

"Remember," *Wisdom's* voice echoed through the sacred expanse, "love is not just an emotion. It is the fundamental creative force of the universe. When you align with love, you become a co-creator with the divine."

This understanding crystallized within me: the love I had discovered wasn't mere philosophy; it was the force behind Dream Out Loud, behind every transformation I'd witnessed in young minds awakening to their potential. Each student I'd guided had been an expression of this creative force, each revelation a step in love's eternal dance.

The air charged with electric possibilities. A circle of fire erupted around us, flames reaching toward the heavens. The beat of drums filled the air, their rhythm matching the pulse of divine creation. This sacred ceremony would be more than ritual; it would be initiation into love's highest mystery, preparing me to guide others in their own awakening.

*Wisdom* and *Healing* began to move, their forms fluid and graceful. "Join us," they called, "in the eternal dance of creation."

Stepping into the circle, spirits materialized... *Love, Protection, Faith, Companionship,* and even the shadows I had faced. They were all aspects of the divine, all essential parts of the whole.

The dance began slowly, our movements guided by the rhythm of the drums and the pulse of the cosmos. With each step, I felt myself aligning more fully with the flow of universal love. Vitality coursed through me, filling me with a sense of limitless potential. Each movement wrote new possibilities into the fabric of reality.

The dance intensified, flooding my consciousness with visions. I saw myself spreading light in the world, inspiring others to recognize their own divinity. I saw communities coming together, healing ancient wounds and creating new paradigms of cooperation and understanding. I saw humanity awakening to its true nature, remembering its place in the eternal dance.

"This is your calling," *Wisdom's* voice echoed through the visions. "To radiate love, a living embodiment of the truth you have discovered. Your journey does not end here... it is only beginning."

The dance reached a crescendo, the fire roaring higher, the infinite canvas radiating with blinding intensity. In that moment of perfect alignment, I felt a love so boundless it defied description. It was the love that births universes, the love that flows through all of creation.

The dance slowing, *Healing* spoke once more. "Remember, dear one, that darkness is not something to be feared or fought against. It is simply the absence of light. When you see darkness, do not turn towards it. Instead, be the light. For in shining your light, you illuminate the path for yourself and others."

The fire began to die down, the cosmic kaleidoscope fading into a soft glow. But the resonance of the dance remained, humming through every cell of my being. I knew that I would carry this vibration with me always, a constant reminder of my true nature and my place in the universe.

*Wisdom* and *Healing* stood before me, their forms shimmering with ethereal light. The dance slowing, fire smoldering, *Wisdom* and *Healing* exchanged a meaningful glance. The air was charged with the presence of transformation, and I could feel the shift within my very being.

*Wisdom* stepped forward, her voice carrying the same lyrical rhythm that had marked the beginning of this journey. "The time has come to close our sacred space," she intoned. "We must honor the spirits that have guided us and release their energies back to the four directions."

Turning to the South, *Wisdom* began, "Great Serpent, we thank you for your wisdom. You have taught us to shed our old skins, to embrace change, and to walk the path of beauty. We release your spirit back to the winds of the South."

Her words brought gentle undulation, as if the coils of the Serpent were unwrapping from around us.

Facing West, she continued, "Mother Jaguar, we are grateful for your strength. You have shown us how to face our fears and transform them into love. We release your essence back to the winds of the West."

A soft growl seemed to echo in the distance, fading into the night.

To the North, *Wisdom's* voice grew tender, "Royal Hummingbird, Ancient Ones, we honor your endurance and joy. You have visited us in the dreamtime and shown us the sweetness of life. We release your presence back to the winds of the North."

The air shimmered for a moment, as if with the beating of tiny wings.

Finally, turning to the East, she proclaimed, "Eagle, Great Visionary, we thank you for teaching us to soar to new heights, to lead with a pure heart. We release your power back to the winds of the East."

A whisper of wind brushed past us, carrying with it the essence of freedom and vision.

*Wisdom* then placed one hand on the earth and raised the other to the sky. "Mother Earth, Father Sun, Grandmother Moon, and Star Nations, we thank you for your presence and guidance. May we carry your wisdom with us as we return to our daily lives."

*Wisdom*, completing the ceremony, turned to me. "Take a moment now to breathe deeply. Feel the changes within you. Acknowledge the space you now occupy, both in body and spirit."

I turned inward, breathing in mindfully. My exhale released a fundamental shift... a lightness of being, clarity of purpose, deep connection to something greater than myself. The journey had changed me in ways I was only beginning to understand.

*Wisdom's* voice was gentle as she concluded, "The inspiration and wisdom you have gleaned from this sacred space are not meant to be hoarded, but shared. Carry them with you into the world, sharing them with the earth, your family, and your community. For in sharing, we multiply the light."

The final echoes fading, I opened my eyes, feeling both grounded in my physical body and expanded beyond its boundaries. The ceremony had come full circle, and I stood on the threshold of a new beginning.

"The ceremony is complete," *Wisdom* said. "You have been initiated into the mysteries of existence. Now, you must return to your world, carrying this sacred understanding with you."

*Healing's* eyes met mine, filled with infinite compassion. "Remember that every moment is an opportunity to choose love, to align with the divine flow. In doing so, you become a channel for healing, not just for yourself, but for all of creation."

Their final words brought tears of gratitude so intensely. I was no longer the person who had started this dream... I was something more, something vast and eternal.

The world around me began to shift and blur. I could feel myself being drawn back to the physical realm. But even as the universal symphony faded from view, I knew that its rhythms would continue to flow through me, guiding my steps and inspiring my actions.

With a final surge of awareness, I opened my eyes to find myself back in the cabana. The morning sun streamed through the window, casting a golden glow over everything. For a moment, I wondered if it had all been just a weird dream. But the vibration of love that thrummed through my being told me otherwise.

Sitting up in bed, the distinction between waking and dreaming dissolved. Every moment was an opportunity to dance with the divine, to co-create with the universe. The journey had not ended... it had only just begun.

With a heart full of love and a spirit aligned with the eternal dance, I stepped out of the cabana and into the dawn of a new day. The world seemed somehow brighter, more vivid, as if I was seeing it through new eyes. And in a way, I was.

For I had learned the greatest lesson of all... that love is not something to be sought or achieved. It is what we are, at our very core. And in remembering this truth, we remember our divine nature, our infinite potential, and our sacred role in the eternal dance of creation.

With quiet certainty, I embraced this new beginning. My journey had transformed me into both student and teacher, dreamer and dream. Through transforming education, through awakening young minds, through every soul I would touch, this universal love would ripple outward, awakening others to their own divine potential.

Every classroom would become a sacred space, every lesson an opportunity to awaken divine potential, every student a torch-bearer of this eternal truth. The distinction between personal and universal transformation dissolved. Every young mind I helped awaken, every heart I helped open, became part of love's eternal dance. This wasn't just my story anymore... it was humanity's next chapter, waiting to be dreamed into being.

The distinction between teacher and student, guide and seeker, dream and dreamer dissolved into perfect unity. Every lesson learned would become a lesson shared, every truth discovered a torch to light others' paths. The journey hadn't ended; it had evolved into something greater than myself.

Taking my first steps into this new reality, I carried not just teachings but living truth. Each breath became a prayer of gratitude, each moment an opportunity to embody love's transformative power. The journey continues, infinite and beautiful, as we dance together toward humanity's awakening.

.

# Epilogue

---

As I pen these final words, four months after that extraordinary night in Southern Mexico, the sky outside my window erupts in a cacophony of thunder. The storm's intensity mirrors the one that formed the backdrop of my transformative dream, and for a moment, I'm transported back to that cabana, to the precipice of spiritual awakening.

The rain lashes against the windowpane, each drop a reminder of the tears I've shed, the fears I've faced, and the love I've embraced on this journey. Lightning illuminates the room, and in that brief, electric moment, I see my reflection in the glass... a man forever changed by an experience that defies conventional explanation.

The experience reminds me of Neal Donald Walsch's *"Conversations with God"* and Dan Millman's *"Way of the Peaceful Warrior."* I recall the tinge of skepticism I felt upon first reading their accounts, that nagging question: "Did that really happen?" Now, as I sit here, my fingers flying across the keyboard in a feverish dance of recollection and revelation, I understand their experiences with a clarity that both humbles and exalts me.

For those reading these words, you may find yourself asking the same question. Did this journey unfold as described? Did the veil between worlds lift, revealing the eternal dance of love that underpins all of existence? I can only echo the sentiments of those who have walked this path before me: For all intents and purposes, it did happen. The truth of this experience pulses in every fiber of my being, in every word on these pages.

When I awoke in that cabana in Southern Mexico, I was compelled to write. The words flowed through me like a river breaking through a dam, unstoppable and pure. I have not ceased since that moment, feeling as though the universe itself has been pouring these messages through me, a humble vessel for truths that transcend my own understanding.

As I contemplate the journey that has led to this book, I feel a deep sense of gratitude and wonder. The thought that these words might touch lives, might inspire transformations akin to those sparked in me by the works of Deepak Chopra, Osho, Paulo

Coelho, and James Redfield, is both exhilarating and humbling. Yet, I know that the reach of this message is not in my hands. It is in the hands of the universe, guided by the same divine love that orchestrated my own awakening.

I have come to understand that this book, this dream, this journey... it was never truly mine alone. I serve as a channel, a conduit for a message that the universe yearns to share. And now, as you hold these pages in your hands, as your eyes trace these words, the dream becomes yours.

This message is for you, dear reader. It has traversed time and space, navigated the labyrinth of publishing and distribution, to find its way into your life at this exact moment. Perhaps you picked it up on a whim, or it was gifted to you by a friend. Perhaps you've been drawn to it by a force you can't quite explain. Whatever the path, know that you were meant to receive these words.

The question now becomes: What will you do with it?

Will you allow the seeds of love and spiritual awakening planted in these pages to take root in your heart? Will you nurture them with your attention, water them with your intention, and watch as they blossom into a new way of being?

As the storm outside begins to subside, a ray of sunlight breaks through the clouds, casting a golden glow across my desk. In this moment, I am reminded of the eternal dance of light and shadow, of the endless cycle of death and rebirth that characterizes all of existence. This book, this dream, this message... it is but one note in the universal symphony of love. Yet, it is a note that can echo through eternity if only we choose to hear it, to feel it, to live it.

Whether in classrooms or through these pages, the awakening of consciousness continues. *Love, Protection, Faith*, and *Companionship*... the sacred guides of my journey... continue to light the way forward, not just for me, but for all who choose to embrace this path of transformation. Their wisdom echoes in every lesson I teach, every heart I touch, every soul I help awaken to their own divine potential.

The journey does not end with the closing of this book. In truth, it is only beginning. For in recognizing the universal love that binds us all, in embracing the divine spark that resides within each of us, we step into our role as co-creators of reality.

So, I invite you, dear reader, to take this dream and make it your own. Allow it to guide you to your own moments of awakening, your own dances with the cosmos. For in the end, we are all dreaming this grand dream together, all playing our unique parts in the eternal dance of love.

And as you close these pages and step back into your world, know that you carry within you the power to transform not only your own life but the very nature of reality itself. For you are love incarnate, a living embodiment of the divine, a crucial thread in the sacred web of existence.

The time for awakening is now. The world needs your light, your love, your courage to dream a new reality into being. What love will you share? What world will you create?

The universe awaits your answer with bated breath, and I, along with all those who have walked this path before, stand with you in love and solidarity as you take your next step on this magnificent journey.

May your path be illuminated by the light of universal love, and may your life embody the transformative power of spiritual awakening.

With eternal love and gratitude,

*Hal*

# About the Author

Hal Eisenberg's journey embodies the transformative power of passion, purpose, and spiritual awakening. As a visionary educator, social worker, author, and founder of both The Eisenberg Leadership Academy (TELA) and Windows of Opportunity, Inc. (WOO), Hal has dedicated his life to elevating consciousness and empowering others to discover their highest potential.

His work spans continents and generations, from implementing innovative leadership programs in Haiti, Nigeria, Guyana, Kenya, the UK, and Canada to creating transformative social-emotional learning curricula that have touched countless young lives. With over 25 years of experience in program development, Hal has raised more than half a million dollars for various charities while building platforms that allow young people to express themselves authentically through music, fashion, and film.

At the heart of Hal's vision lies a profound belief: that our world can become one healthy community through higher consciousness education. This belief informs everything he creates: from his youth empowerment initiatives to his Beautiful Souls novel series, which explores the spiritual dimensions of human experience through captivating storytelling.

Hal's academic foundation includes a Master's Degree in Social Work from Adelphi University and a Master's Degree in School Leadership from Touro College. As a Licensed Master Social Worker in New York State and a Licensed School Building Leader, his expertise has been recognized with numerous accolades, including the New York City Department of Education School Social Worker of the Year Award in 2018.

His work with The Passion Centre in Toronto as a Passion-Based™ Expert further demonstrates his commitment to helping individuals break through their limitations and activate their deepest passions. Through this work, Hal has developed a unique understanding of how spiritual awakening and practical action can unite to create profound personal and societal transformation.

"Whispers in the Rain" represents the convergence of Hal's spiritual insights and storytelling gifts:

an invitation to readers to embark on their own journey of awakening and discover the divine wisdom that whispers through every aspect of existence.

When not writing or developing programs, Hal can be found connecting with nature, exploring spiritual practices from diverse traditions, and creating spaces where authentic conversation can flourish. His life serves as a testament to the book's central message: that love is the foundation of all spiritual teaching, and that each of us carries the potential to become a living embodiment of this universal truth.

Hal believes that his purpose extends beyond the written word; he is committed to being a visionary in action, creating inspired connections that elevate consciousness in all who encounter his work. For speaking engagements, workshops, or to connect more deeply with the teachings in "Whispers in the Rain".

Website : https://www.haleisenberg.com

Email : eisenbergleadersip@gmail.com

Instagram: hal_eisenberg88

# *thank you*

Thank you for reading my book!

**Dear Reader,**

You made it! Thanks for sticking with me through these pages. I hope they brought you some insights, a few laughs, and maybe even a spark of inspiration. Sharing these stories and lessons has been an incredible journey, and it means a lot that you chose to be a part of it.

Now, if I could ask a quick favour: if you enjoyed the book, would you mind leaving a positive review on Amazon or Goodreads? It would truly make my day, and it's one of the best ways to help others find this book and maybe spark their own adventures. Your review might just be the encouragement someone else needs to give them permission to break from routine and empower them to make the change they need.

Best,
Hal

# MY GIFT TO YOU

I am so glad you're here!

As my Gift to you, get FREE Access to my
**Guided Meditation Series:**
by scanning the QR Code below or visiting

https://subscribepage.io/freegifts

www.ingramcontent.com/pod-product-compliance
Lightning Source LLC
Chambersburg PA
CBHW061132120626
46546CB00005B/1746